# More Than I Could Have Imagined

## Ponderings of my Past

Lorraine Ann
Hagen Meland

ISBN: 978-1-57579-426-6


Library of Congress Control Number: 2010908321

For more copies, contact either Karen or Norris:

| | |
|---|---|
| Karen Asfeldt | Norris Meland |
| 2124 E. Tamarac Dr. | 43809 156th St. |
| Sioux Falls, SD 57103 | Wallace, SD 57272 |
| 605-929-9182 | 605-520-6448 |

*Printed in the United States of America*

PINE HILL PRESS
4000 West 57th Street
Sioux Falls, SD 57106

To Mom,
who saved our letters,
and for my seven grandchildren
who sang along with me.

 # Acknowledgements

I am grateful for:
- God's Spirit who allows us from time-to-time to fulfill our dreams.
- Norris, who was beside me in this project in scores of cherished practical ways. Words cannot be found to adequately express thanks to a loving husband for encouraging this project. He is "The Wind Beneath My Wings."
- The kids and their families, who lend credibility to my belief in the worthiness of writing about one's family.
- Cheryl Larson Huntington for skillfully taking my notes to manuscript form. You poured yourself into this book, and were the needed link to making this life account a reality.

*My heart runneth over with satisfaction and love*
*for each of you and all who may read this.*

# Contents

Preface
Introduction

 # Preface

It was a powerful journey of self-renewal that ironically, and ultimately, led my mother to her last days. Lorraine Ann Hagen Meland passed away on January 12, 2009, having spent the last several months working to complete a manuscript filled with ponderings on her life of 72 years.

With the writing complete to the words, "the end," and a portion of the editing done, Mom experienced heart failure, hospitalization, a stroke and a steady decline. Despite our difficulties communicating during the last two weeks of her life, she made it clear that she was ready to go and that it would be "really nice" to see Jesus. I suspect that, after 48 years of marriage, Mom had a pretty good idea of how determined Dad would be in seeing her book through to completion.

As Dad and I worked to bring Mom's manuscript from a myriad of unfamiliar files to the treasured life story you hold in your hands, I became increasingly aware of her persistence and creative spark. These attributes were the seeds for this flower she will not see in bloom.

It was Mom's wish that readers would, as they pick up this humble book, look beyond the sweat and tears of life and profit by the experiences and the precepts of those who have gone before. One of the many clippings she saved states her intent: Without a heritage...every generation starts over.

As her daughter and one of the next generations, I am so grateful for the characteristics she has passed on to me and for the heritage that she has preserved in this book for us all.

— Karen Lorraine Meland Asfeldt

 # Introduction

"How long will you be remembered?" was a headline I once read, and it stuck in my mind. It triggered the poignant realization that my life had been an interesting journey; maybe I should record some of it for future generations.

Until 1993, my years rolled along at an ever increasing clip, being a wife, mother, homemaker and teacher, active in church and community. Since that professional retirement year I've enjoyed time to occasionally reflect upon where I've been and make sense out of the string of years God granted me.

My mind had stored lots of memories of how things were. This book got its start out of a desire that those who are young now, and in the future, deserve to know about their forebearers, how they lived and thought. It has been compiled from memories, personal diaries, family records, letters and memorabilia that had been saved over the years.

History helps us understand and appreciate the present and offers guidance for the future. As far back as 86 AD, Roman poet Martial wrote, "To be able to look back upon one's past life with satisfaction is to live twice." Sifting through my experiences, what I pondered in my heart gave me repeated joys.

Along the way, many people have blessed my life. We take a little bit of each other with us wherever we go. To those who know me, thanks for your touch on my life. I am indebted.

I tried to describe accurately the events and people in the fabric of my story; however, I, like you, am a unique person: no carbon copy. As a disclaimer, I state that my perception may differ from yours, so to my peers, please understand and forgive.

Sophocles said that one must wait until evening to see how splendid the day has been. I disagree. Each year of my life has held some splendor.

*You made all the delicate, inner parts of my body*
*and knit me together in my mother's womb.*
*Thank you for making me so wonderfully complex!*
*Your workmanship is marvelous—how well I know it.*
*You watched me as I was being formed in utter seclusion,*
*as I was woven together in the dark of the womb.*
*You saw me before I was born.*
*Every day of my life was recorded in your book.*
*Every moment was laid out*
*before a single day had passed.*

— Psalm 139:13-16 (NLT)

## Chapter One

# My Beginning
## — 1935 —

I have no diary which refers to my birth on December 1, 1935. I was told only that, for the first three months, I was a very colicky baby. I imagine that newborn Lorraine was a major disruption to the quiet home of my family, consisting of my mother, Anna Dale Hagen, age 33, my father, Lawrence Hagen, age 35, my grandmother, Mary Hagen, age 73, and my grandfather, Lars Hagen, age 77.

With my arrival, we were suddenly three generations under one roof. However, as time passed, I always knew that I was wanted and loved! I always knew that my life had significant value and purpose.

The birth of my one and only sibling, Corinne Mae Hagen, however, was recorded in diaries kept by both my mother and father. She, too, was a winter bundle. My parent's record: "Too much snow. We'll never make it with the car. Good thing we have Prince and Barney." So, they hitched the faithful horses to the front of the car, and thus, got a mile west to the highway, leaving the team in a neighbor's barn near the corner. Mom and Dad proceeded to the Peabody Hospital in Webster, South Dakota, arriving at midnight. Mom was hospitalized, and Dad

*I was photographed in my baby carriage at six months. This same carriage was used by my father when he was a baby. I gave it to the Webster Museum.*

sat in the waiting room. When early morning arrived, but baby still hadn't, my practical Dad decided to take advantage of the opportunity to drive to nearby Bristol, South Dakota, to look at some advertised farm machinery. I don't know if a deal was made, but Dad was back in the waiting room by 9:30 a.m.

At noon, March 8, 1938, my younger sister, Corinne, was born. Dad left for home at 2:00 p.m. He got stuck in the snow on the last mile, but a neighbor and friend, Elmer Sunne, came with horses and sleigh and pulled him through.

Mom had kept a diary that year. For that day, Dad wrote in it, "Anna had a girl today," and he included the details of the travel. He also kept note of the next nine days. On March 12th: "Aunt Clara called. She had been up to see Anna and the baby. They are fine." He also wrote about grinding feed for his brother, Myer Hagen, and neighbors Bennet Haugen, Myron Hjermstad, and Helmer Wibeto. Spring planting was on his mind: seed grain needed to be cleaned, and so did the barn. A bin in the granary needed patching. Buttermilk needed to be hauled from the Wallace Creamery to feed the pigs.

On March 17th, Mom continued the story. "Nice day. Lawrence came to Webster to get baby and me. With side roads impossible for travel, we drove early in the morning when they were frozen, so we made it home alright." Mom did not tell of her days with a newborn. Ten days pass before there is any more mention of "the baby." Neither did she write about her last two weary months of pregnancy, January–February, except for the weather and outside farm work.

Since both parents were of stoic Scandinavian stock, the unspoken rule of not showing emotion probably prevailed at both births. Not much fuss was made over the occasions. Yet, I'm sure they felt a profound sense of gratitude to God for safe delivery and the gift of healthy children.

My getting a name was stalled. Dad made a lot of big decisions in his life, but naming his daughter was an act never-to-be-changed. They called me "Baby." Finally, one day Dad was going to Wallace on farm business. Mom took charge and filled out the legal paper and had him mail it. I would be Lorraine (starting with "L," like my father Lawrence), with the middle name Ann (starting with "A," like my mother Anna). Now, I had a moniker.

The winter passed, and on March 22, 1936, Pastor C.K. Malmin baptized me at St. Pauli Church. This was one of my earliest outings. Mom's brother, Clarence Dale, and sister, Mable Dale, were my godparents. This was the beginning of a meaningful relationship with Aunt Mable. Mom was very good at keeping my baby book current. About my christening, Mom wrote that I wore the same dress that my dad and Uncle Myer had worn at their baptisms. No video cameras recorded the event. Dad had a box camera, but I don't think any picture was taken. Again, there was no fanfare.

Mom listed sixteen people who had called on us at the hospital when I was born. She wrote about the gifts from them, plus many other presents received during the first year. The social visits are recorded. We went to see Aunt Clara and six-month-old Dale Ronning, and also Aunt Thea Hagen and three-year-old Harlan, my two oldest cousins.

I had dark red hair when I was born, but it soon turned blonde. At two, I could say whatever I wanted to, but not always in the same language. My grandparents usually spoke Norwegian to me. I quoted my father: "Papa says, 'Hello, you Little Monkey Tosse nar han komomer in.'" (Dad says, "Hello, you Little Monkeyshine when he comes in.")

I started to walk at about twelve months and kept going. A favorite place to explore was the pantry. On the Christmas page of my baby book, Mom wrote, "We're very thankful for our Christmas gift baby, and I hope we can spend many Christmases together." (We did. It would have been forty-five years, except we were in Papua New Guinea for nine.)

For my second birthday, one of the gifts was $1 from Grandpa Lars. With this, they bought a little red chair. I often tipped it upside down and pushed it around, so I wore much of the paint off and eventually broke the back. I have used it in recent years to hold a plant!

Corinne and I also had a woven rocking chair, which I loved.

*My childhood chairs.*

## 1935 in Review

- Franklin Roosevelt was President.
- Scientists discovered Vitamin E.
- Social Security was signed into law.
- "I'm in the Mood for Love" was a popular song.
- The average income was $1,632.
- A new house cost $3,400.
- The average price for a new car was $625.
- Gasoline was 10¢ per gallon.
- Bread was 8¢ per loaf and milk was 47¢ per gallon.

Chapter Two

# Family Lineage

4

# My Grandfather, Lars Hagen

My Grandpa, Lars Hagen, was born at Telemarken, Norway (southwest of Oslo) on May 24, 1858. It is probable that he was baptized and confirmed in the little village of Ulefoss. As a teenager, he learned carpentry. He lived near water surrounded by forested mountains and worked for a lumber company in Namløshagen. Jobs were so scarce, and the economy was so poor, that people ate bark off the trees to survive. This, plus the hope of a better life and a youthful readiness for adventure, led him to save enough money to buy a ship ticket to America. He left Norway in 1880 at the age of twenty-two.

I don't know where Lars spent his first two years in the United States (maybe in Wisconsin or Minnesota), but in the spring of 1882, Lars moved to Dakota, to the city of Watertown. It was a very small town at that time. Lars spent the first winters working for room and board at Northwestern Hotel in Watertown. Later, he worked at Burlington-Northern Railroad building coal sheds and water tanks. One day, he and two fellow Norwegians hired a man, somewhat acquainted with the county, to take them around to see which land was still open to new settlers. Much of the best land had already been taken. It took a couple days to decide what they would try to get. They spent the night on the floor of Hans Wibeto's house, where Burdette Wibeto's farm is now. They went back to Watertown to apply for 160 acres each. Lars then walked back to what is now great-great-grandson Nathan Meland's place. He had a bag of groceries on his back and $2 in his pocket. He would do his best to fulfill the legal requirements of breaking up a few acres and erecting a small shanty so that he would not lose his claim. (I wonder if this is the building Nathan's family calls the "bunk house"? I'm glad they restored it to preserve history in a practical way.)

Being a carpenter, Lars got involved helping neighbors build their houses. This included homes for the Paulsons, Lovicks, Ekses, Vestols, Hogstads, Dales, and a barn for Halvor Thompson. These houses were lived in until the '50s. As payment for construction of the Hogstad home, Mr. Hogstad broke up the required five acres for Lars. In this way, Lars began carving a farm out of the virgin prairie.

Between 1884 and 1888 Lars established his dream farm. The kitchen of the house in which I grew up was built at this time. By the spring of 1888, Lars started living on his own land and farming it. By now, he had two oxen of his own. Mr. Faehn, a neighbor on what is now known as "the Karpinske place," had two oxen also. With a sixteen-inch breaker plow, progress felt good!

On May 18, 1889, a patent was issued by the President of the United States, Benjamin Harrison, to my grandfather under the name of Lars Johnson. This gave him legal rights to his land. To clarify Lars' last name on this patent, I offer the following: First, I think his parents' family name was Larson, but his father's given name was John. So, in keeping with Norwegian tradition, Lars became "John's son," or "Johnson." Later, realizing how many Johnsons there already were in America, Lars changed his name to "Hagen." Second, knowing that he had worked at Namløshagen, which literally translates to "nameless garden," I think he may have chosen the Hagen name because it reminded him of the mountains, forests, and gardens of Norway.

The land transaction was now officially placed in the *General Land Office Records,* vol. 15, page 147. Monetary cost was $200, but sweat and toil were probably not measurable. A number of times, mortgages were taken. Interest was 10-12 percent. There were no roads or fences yet. Grandpa owned an eight-foot drag and a drill by now, and had built a hog shed.

Meanwhile, the Fjelstad family lived three miles east. The wife, Helena, came from an upper middle class family in Toten, Norway. Her father, Paul, had been a successful businessman. Several of her uncles were notable musicians. Paul overlent, and hard times came upon them. They came to America and spent fourteen years in Wisconsin. Then, they moved to Dakota, seeking land of their own. They came with two box cars of farm animals, machinery, lumber for a house, furniture, and personal effects. Thus, the Fjelstads skipped the sod house stage and had the first wood house in this area. This was 1883. I wonder if Lars had been working on that house. Anyway, on December 19, 1888, Lars married Paul and Helena's daughter, Anna Fjelstad.

Their first son, John, was born October 1, 1890. Their second son, Palmer, was born on October 4, 1892. Times were rough for the pioneer men, but my heart identifies equally with their wives. Birthing and rearing children with no medical services or conveniences brought much hardship and sadness. Anna (Fjelstad) Hagen died on November 12, 1892 at the young age of

*John and Palmer Hagen*

twenty-two. Could it have been from childbirth complications? The two little boys went to live with the Lars Benson family.

On July 5, 1896, Lars married Mary Anderson. I wish I knew more about her. She was born on October 17, 1862, in the same part of Norway as Lars. As a young single woman, she traveled solo from Norway to America, where en route across the Atlantic, she suffered much seasickness during the twelve-day voyage. She was hired to do house work in Chicago, earning $2.50 per week.

Maybe Lars' house got bigger after this marriage. The house was completed between the years of 1897 and 1903. I grew up there and always appreciated it. If only the walls could speak! Grandpa Lars lived there for 69 years; Dad for 75 years; Norris and I and our family for 15 years; and our son Nathan and Kathy and family for 16 years.

Good fortune had arrived! Besides a second marriage, Lars had a good crop. They decided to build a horse barn. He hauled wheat to Bradley, South Dakota and sold it for 30¢ per bushel. He brought back good Minnesota lumber for $16 per thousand linear feet. Pioneering continued to be expensive, energy-wise, but progress was happening. A six-foot grain binder was used to cut the grain now;

*Mary, Lars, Meyer and Lawrence Hagen on their homestead in the early 1900s.*

7

schools and townships were beginning to take shape; and the farm was expanding. On a time basis, Lars and Mary purchased eighty more acres to the south.

On October 26, 1897, their first son (Lars' third) was born. Unfortunately, little Arthur Julian lived only five days. Grandpa must have been deeply affected. He walked a cow to Webster and traded her for a large family Bible. This lay on what was called a library table in the front room throughout my youth, and I always saw Grandpa as a Godly person who read his small Norwegian Bible daily.

On October 22, 1900, their second son (Lars' fourth) was born. This son, Peter Lawrence Hagen, became my father. A final son, Alfred Myer, arrived on August 11, 1902. He would grow up and farm across the road, west from my dad. Myer's three sons, Harlan, Merlin, and Larry Hagen, lived and farmed all their lives within three miles of us.

A rosemaled box, dated 1893, and with my grandmother's initials painted on it, was important to both Grandpa and Grandma. In it, they kept their most treasured memorabilia, such as newspaper clippings, funeral programs, and a few pictures. A Norwegian newspaper clipping from 1921 honors the 95th birthday of a widow, Anne Larson, who could still read without glasses, and who had worked all summer picking and preserving berries. She was the mother of four: two sons, who had gone to America, and two daughters, living in Holla and Graaten. Her husband had died ten years earlier. All this fits the description of Grandpa Lars' mother. A funeral program gives December 11, 1826 and August 11, 1923 as Anne's birth and death dates.

*The rosemaled box that held treasured family history.*

This box also contained two very precious letters: one simply dated November, and one dated August 13, 1908. The translation of the August letter reads:

*Dear Son:*

*We thought that God did not intend to let you be gone so long before we could see you again. The parting was awful. Now, your grandfather is very sick and his life is in the Hand of the Almighty. Now, the question is, 'Will you meet him in Heaven?' You must not forget to thank God that you have it good here on earth. Many things have happened here since you left, but it is too much for me to write about. Oskar met someone on a boat who said he knew you well. We were so glad to hear it.*

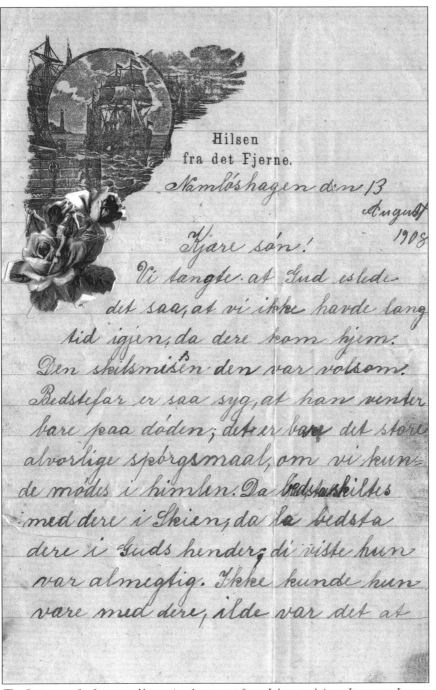

Hilsen
fra det Fjerne.

Namløshagen den 13
August
1908

Kjare søn!

Vi tangte at Gud eslede
det saa, at vi ikke havde lang
tid igjen, da dere kom hjem.
Den skilsmisen den var volsom.
Bedstefar er saa syg, at han venter
bare paa døden; det er bare det store
alvorlige spørgsmaal, om vi kun=
de mødes i himlen. Da bedstskiltes
med dere i Skien, da la bedsta
dere i Guds hender; di viste hun
var almegtig. Ikke kunde hun
vare med dere, ilde var det at

*The first page of a four-page Norwegian letter sent from Johan and Anne Larson to Lars Hagen in 1908.*

9

*However, we must not set our hearts only on things of the earth. I am concerned that you bring up your children in a Christian way. Your own growing up years were so short. I didn't realize they would go so fast. I ask God's forgiveness for my ignorance. I should have taught you more about His paths. Human nature is not to pay attention to God. I urge you to give your heart to Him. I have thought so long about writing this. Seems like we don't hear from each other very often.*

Lars' only brother, Ole, also emigrated from Norway to South Dakota, where he homesteaded three miles southwest of Lars. Ole had seven sons and one daughter at that point, and would have two more sons later. Most of his children lived their lives around Wallace, South Dakota, and the boys were known as the Johnson brothers.

During the winter of 1908, Lars, now 50, and his brother Ole, age 45, traveled to Norway to see their parents and friends. It had been twenty-eight years, so I wonder if the letters moved Lars to go to Norway for a visit. I don't know how long Grandpa and Ole stayed in Norway, but Grandpa's return to the farm left him disappointed and determined to make a change. He decided he'd rather do carpentry than farming. He held an auction and rented out the land for five years to Chris Olson (Dee Nogelmeier's great grandparent). Grandma didn't like the

*The South Dakota homestead, as pictured above, was complete by the late 1940s.*

idea, but she had to adjust. So, Lars and Mary moved. They lived on the Carson Sheep Ranch, southwest of Wallace, on what is now Highway 25. Back at the homestead, the trees kept growing, and by 1912 a nice grove had established itself around the Hagen farm. It provided a warm welcome when they returned.

A major family change took place when sons John and Palmer, at ages 18 and 16, went with their maternal grandfather and several uncles to look for free homestead land in Canada. John settled and farmed in Saskatchewan and never returned for fifty years. Palmer went to British Columbia and became a steam shovel operator.

## My Father, Lawrence Hagen

In 1914 Grandma decided it was her turn for a trip! At age 52, she took my father, Lawrence, now 14, and Myer, age 12, back to Norway, intending to stay a couple of months. I believe their arrival was unannounced, evidenced by another letter in the rosemaled box telling Lars how totally surprised his Norwegian relatives were to see the family. Meanwhile, World War I broke out. Ships back to America were not available for a year, so the boys went to school in Skien, Norway.

My Dad kept a diary while there. Each day he recorded the weather, where they went, and what they did; but he added no personal reactions or connected feelings. They stayed with both sides of the family, but mostly with Grandma's brother, Hans Anderson.

In my precious box is an aged clipping about Hans and his wife, Andrea, who celebrated a diamond anniversary at sixty years of marriage. Translated, it states that he was known as a 'vognmann' (wagon man). He was good and kind to his horses, and they looked so nice. He was also interested in politics and religion. Nothing extra is said about his wife (Women's Lib had not yet begun.)

Dad's notes about school say that, because of the war, all students practiced marching. He had a hard time keeping step, so was sent out for extra practice. All subjects were studied via writing in a small notebook. In keeping with the nature of many Americans from Norway, his notes are written without superlatives. His entry for the day they returned to the Hagen farm reads, "Nothing has changed: only Pa has one new horse."

Dad then rode his bicycle to Wallace and took his 8th Grade exam. That was the end of his formal education, but I always considered him self-educated to high degrees.

## My Mother, Anna Dale

My Mother, Anna Helena Dale, never told us much about her background. I once asked her to write some things, and she did; but after only three sentences, she declared it to be enough.

Through conversation, however, she shared the following facts with me. Her grandfather, David Larson (September 1, 1841–October 12, 1906), and grandmother, Ingeborg Knutson Larson (September 18, 1846–February 5, 1922), were born near Kristiansand in southern Norway. They married and had seven children.

Their two oldest, Anna and Elizabeth left Norway with their father David and traveled to America in 1887. At that time, Anna was seventeen. She later became the mother of a clan of Gulbraa relatives, some of whom continue to live in or near Wallace, South Dakota. Elizabeth was fourteen. She later married Ole Johnson, my Grandpa Lars' brother, and they had ten children, as already explained. Elizabeth was known to be a strong farm woman who walked behind the plow pulled by horses and who could milk the cows, as needed.

David and Ingeborg missed one-another, so David thought to go back to Norway.

*David and Ingeborg Larson, my great-grandparents on my mother's side of the family.*

*David Larson laid claim to a quarter of land. Nathan Meland, his great-great-grandson, now owns and farms it. The original farm buildings, pictured above, were northwest of Wallace, South Dakota, in Clark County.*

Before he communicated this, Ingeborg had sold out and made other plans. She and the younger children joined David in 1889. According to oral tradition, they wore wooden shoes and had to walk from the train depot in Webster out to the farm, a distance of seventeen miles. They had visions of a grand place in America, but such was not the case. It was a big letdown. The pioneer house was small and basic. Legal papers show the actual homestead ownership didn't happen until 1895. Their fourth child, Lars, died at age fifteen.

## My Grandmother, Christine Dale

The fifth child became my maternal grandmother, Christine (July 26, 1877–October 13, 1938). On August 4, 1900, she married my grandfather, John Dale (September 4, 1875–October 31, 1955).

John Dale's father, Hans, died when his children were young. Hans, Jr., also died as a young boy. John's older siblings came on their own to America first. The younger ones came later with their mother, Anna (1830-

*John and Christine Dale, my grandparents on my mother's side of the family.*

*Roy Engstrom and I are standing in front of the house where my mother, Anna (Dale) Hagen was born.*

1916). She and many others of the family have graves at Highland Cemetery near Lily, South Dakota, where they settled.

In the early years, John and Christine Dale lived with John's brother in a very small home, consisting of one room upstairs and one room downstairs. It was located near where Calvin Engstrom lives. It was in this house that my mom and four of her siblings were born. John and Christine had a total of eight children, several of whom were delivered without a midwife.

Other folks told me that the Dale kids were shy in public. Mom didn't want to go to school, so Christine enticed her to do so: if Mom would go to school, she could carry—in her half-gallon lard bucket lunch box—a beautiful cut glass cup with a red edge. Bribery worked! Mom treasured the cup for many years and finally gave it to our daughter Karen on Christmas Day in 1977. Karen kept the cup and the gift tag, which reads, "To our only granddaughter, I hope you will treasure this little gift as much as I have. Love, Grandma."

*The "bribery cup" is more than 100 years old and is now in the home of Karen Asfeldt, Christine's great-great-granddaughter.*

The school mom attended had thirty-five or more children, and sometimes adults came, too, just to learn. Only slates were used for writing. A common school lunch was lard sandwiches and a hunk of bologna made with stuffed intestines when butchering.

It seemed that every direction of life brought hardship and work. Grain, for instance, was hoisted in 1½ bushel sacks into upstairs bins in the granary. Grandma Christine tried to make dolls for her little girls by wrapping cloth around corn cobs. A quarter for Christmas was a huge amount of money. Sometimes an apple or orange came with it.

Lacking toys, the children amused themselves in various creative ways, like swinging on the hay ropes in the barn, playing in the grain loads at harvest, and carrying water in little buckets for the animals. Grandma Christine canned peas in two-quart jars. That's a lot of pea pods to shuck! I'm sure the kids helped with gardening and canning.

The family had moved several times, but the final time was in 1917, when they hired a carpenter named Mr. Ness to build a house on what became known as the John Dale place.

Mom's early life was far from easy. Being second to oldest in a family of eight children, she quit school after the 5th Grade in order to help at home. She also hired-out to help in homes over the years, seven of which had new babies. Thus,

*The John Dale place, where Mike and Linda Dale live today.*

she knew only too well that babies meant work. As a child, I don't ever recall her rejoicing when neighborhood family increases were announced.

Mom's parental home was nine miles northwest of the Hagen place. I was never told anything about Mom and Dad's courtship. Dad's cousin, Sophie Thompson, and family, lived near John Dale's family, so maybe their romance started through that connection. (Sophie was Grandma's niece, whom she had brought here from Norway.) Also, Dad seemed to go to Wallace often, and Mom worked a while in a café there. So, interest may have taken root in Wallace, too.

Their marriage took place on December 27, 1932, at the Lutheran parsonage at Florence, South Dakota. Mom was 29; Dad was 32. He had never lived away from home. They had a brief honeymoon in Minneapolis, staying with John and Gurina DeGroff, family friends of Grandma Hagen. Upon returning, the bride moved in with her new husband and the elderly in-laws. Even though this was in the dry '30s, there was never lack of food and shelter or a problem meeting basic needs. However, I suspect Mom passed some emotional hurdles. I never ever did see my parents hug or kiss.

*Lawrence and Anna Hagen's wedding photo.*

15

## Chapter Three

# My Early Years

From early on, I was bilingual. My grandparents spoke Norwegian, and my parents spoke English to me. My precise memories of pre-school years are minimal, but the environment and philosophy of the family and home were, no doubt, imperceptibly imprinted.

Plumbing in the country was unheard of, so carrying water in and keeping a "slop bucket" for the water to go out was standard. I learned that we don't ever waste water! Rain was captured off the roof and drained into a cistern for a water supply. A wash basin and dish pan was much used.

Cooking was done on a wood-burning stove. We had a warm, cozy kitchen. The stove had four lids, an ash pan, and a warming closet above to keep foods warm. A tea kettle was always on the stove. This pot had no connection with tea, but rather held about a gallon of water, had a pouring spout, and was a constant source for hot water.

In winter, the fire was "banked" (stoked, but no draft) to somehow hold the heat until morning. Coal and wood were the fuel. Grandpa provided the wood supply by sawing dry tree trunks and splitting the pieces with an ax. The suspenders across his back left a sweaty track. In the summer, a kerosene burner was used for cooking so that the house would not get so hot.

At butchering, some of the animal fat was used for lard, and some of it was used to make soap. It was mixed with lye and water and then boiled. When cooled, it was cut into bars. Pieces were shaved off and put into the wash machine on laundry days. It was a good cleaner.

Grandma Hagen had a room upstairs. I can remember Corinne and I going to Grandma's room and getting a lemon peel, onto which she had sprinkled a bit of sugar. We must have been short of citrus. It tasted so good! Also, she would drop lemon drops down through the floor register to us kids sometimes. I think they served dual purpose—to remind us to be quiet and to bribe us to do so.

Grandpa Lars lived to the ripe old age of 95. Sitting on his lap in the twilight of the day is a serene memory of my childhood. While my parents were out doing chores, Grandpa and I would watch the flames of the heater stove flicker through the little windows in the door. This was the closest I got to being babysat, except for Mom and Dad's occasional trips to town when Corinne and I would be home with our grandparents. He taught us one Norwegian folksong. He passed away at home when I was in high school.

Grandma Mary died when I was eight. There was very little rough-housing, and being quiet was the expected behavior. To this day, I value peace and quiet. This anonymous little verse says it all:

> Don't like what's noisy and rude.
> Would rather have solitude.
> But, practically speaking,
> The world is a-needing,
> So I alter my attitude.

Grandma Christine died when I was almost three years old. I've always wished I could have known her. Grandpa John Dale lived until I was twenty. He had diabetes and arthritis. His relationship with his twenty-three grandchildren was distant and respectful.

In cooking and baking, Mom was good, but not confident. However, in seamstress work, she knew what she was doing! Sometime in her growing-up years, Mom took a sewing course. I think it was in Aberdeen. She made use of these skills when Corinne and I were little. We were two years and three months apart in age. Mom used to enjoy uninterrupted evening time making same-pattern dresses in two different colors. Mine was usually blue or purple, and Corinne's was red or pink.

We usually had new dresses to start the school year. One Easter, she made new coats, besides the spring dress! Mine had a little bluebird pin which I wore on the lapel. I always felt well dressed.

Mom kept remnant pieces, bought on sale, in her cedar chest so she could tackle a project without waiting for a town trip. Mom

*My sister Corinne (one year) and me (three years).*

17

took Corinne and me on occasional shopping trips, and we learned to get the best buy possible because "you can't spend the same money twice."

Learning, school, and teachers were held in high regard. Dad had finished 8th Grade with excellent marks. He was a life-time scholar of world affairs, agriculture, economics, marketing, and Christianity. He studied, formed his own opinion, and sometimes wrote for the "Letters to the Editor" column of the *Watertown Public Opinion.* In addition to Watertown's newspaper, publications available in our home were: Webster's *Reporter & Farmer, Barron's* (stock and bonds reports), *Lutheran Herald, Missionary, Dakota Farmer, Farmer, Successful Farmer,* and *Dakota Posten* (in Norwegian). He liked to discuss politics, and he had a keen mind for remembering facts and figures.

For Dad, life was mostly serious. He felt responsible to use the talent God had given him to help others in any way he could. Mom was always more apt to see the funny side of an issue. I think humor helped the large family from which she came to survive. If I should pick one word to describe my parents, it would be "contented." They were always thankful for what they had. "We have it so good," was a common remark. In current times, when many folks are ever grasping for more and more, materially, I cherish Mom and Dad's legacy.

Chapter Four

# Off to School

Our country schoolhouse was a rectangular white building known as Ustrud No. 34, located one mile northwest of the Hagen farm. The school yard was a tiny part of the land Nathan Meland now farms. There was no Kindergarten. Dad said that it wasn't necessary anyway. Corinne and I learned to tie our shoes, cut with a scissor, color, and write numbers and alphabet letters at home. We had a self-standing blackboard on which to practice. Paper and pencil had an almost magical appeal. So it was that I started 1st Grade in September and turned six in December of 1941.

*Back row, left to right: Harlan Hagen, 4th Grade; Harold Wibeto, 8th Grade; our teacher, Irene Ihlen; and Mavis Keller, 8th Grade. Front row: I'm first in 1st Grade; Gerhard Munson, 3rd Grade; and Rosetta Karpinske, 6th Grade.*

A young lady from our church, Irene Ihlen, was my teacher for the first three grades. I liked her a lot; she gave me a solid start. I was one of six students.

We didn't have Kleenex at home. I can still see myself standing by the teacher's desk, luxuriously feeling the softness and smelling the fragrance from the tissue box in the teacher's drawer. I also, sometimes, sat on the teacher's lap since I was the youngest kid in school. My teacher's marriage to Duane Hallstrom was the first church wedding I remember attending. Mom, Corinne, and I also called on Irene socially during summer vacation. Aunt Thea and Mom used to visit school once each year. I think they came unannounced. They observed and enjoyed school for about an hour, and then left.

Since school and church were the basic social outlets, activities there were etched in my mind to stay. One year my school and a neighboring one, a few miles north, joined for a program. Music had been a passion for me from early on, and the teachers must have sensed that, as I became student director of the rhythm band at the evening performance. Mom made me a special dress by sewing ruffles of gathered white crepe paper onto a white cloth petticoat. A tasseled hat completed the outfit. I felt so proud, beating the rhythm with a director's wand in front of my band! (That costume was still on Mom's shelf, thirty-five years later, when Norris and I bought the house.)

Another favorite program was when I was in 6th Grade. I wore a dress with a blue checked top and a solid blue skirt. The belt had three cloth-covered buttons on the front. We had a make-shift platform, and sheets hung on wires for curtains to open and reveal the stage. On that stage, we presented plays with memorized lines, poems, and songs, all the while feeling important and accepted by family and neighbors. Self-esteem seemed to develop naturally, rather than by a planned schedule. Flash, slide, and video cameras were not there to preserve this history. Hence, I write!

Each school organized a Young Citizens League, with monthly meetings

*This is my Young Citizens League group in front of the Capitol building on May 5, 1947. I am the youngest student, holding my new purse.*

20

held within the school day. While in 6th Grade, I was one of the students chosen to represent Codington County at the State Convention in Pierre. Our County Superintendent took us. She was a very large woman, physically. At the hotel, I had to share a bed with her. I did not sleep much because I clung to my edge of the bed, fearing she would roll over on me. Mom had given me a purse for the trip. This was special! I had a hard time focusing on the parade, because I was more concerned with my new purse.

I didn't like to eat breakfast before going to school, but my folks insisted I have a little bowl of oatmeal and a teaspoon of cod liver oil to carry me through the morning. The common meal from my lunch box was a small salami, cold roast beef, or canned salmon sandwich and a half pint of milk. My lunch box was green, flat, and oval. I later contributed it to the Country School Museum in Florence, South Dakota. At the morning recess in winter, we students would put potatoes in the ash pan of the heater stove. By noon, the aroma of baked potatoes filled the classroom. Add a pat of butter, and we had a hot lunch program!

I loved school! All grades were in one room. When we had our own work done, we could always listen to what was going on at the recitation bench, where each of the other grades met for class. Reading, writing, and other subjects were easy for me, and learning about other people and places in geography was intriguing. Science was lower on the list. Since Dad liked math, I could ask him about problems. We would sit together and race to add long columns of numbers. I don't remember having much homework. All subjects, including art and music, were taught by one teacher. By the time I was in upper grades, I could play melodies on the pump organ, so I began early to accompany the songs for music class. Recess provided our physical education. We played Pum-Pum-Pullaway, Anti-I-Over, Hide and Seek, Steal Sticks, Tag, and Fox and Geese. Once, after a snow storm, we rolled repeatedly down a snow drift until one student got an upset stomach and had to go home.

One time, unbeknown to us, a family of skunks decided to take residence under our school house. We tried to start school as usual, but the stink intensified and we had to be dismissed. After we walked home we opened our lunch pail, only to discover that the grease in our homemade donuts had absorbed a full dose of the stench. Several days of "skunk vacation" followed while the school board eradicated the stinkers.

The school had a library—of sorts, but the books were very old and unattractive, compared to today's colorful volumes. At home, I had only three small childhood books of my own. I could hold them in one hand.

At the school, the teacher was also the custodian who would start the fire in the morning and take the ashes out later. Each Friday, near the end of the day, the teacher would spread sweeping compound on the floor. Students would then become helpful cleaning agents by doing high-spirited skidding back and forth between the rows of desks.

All of my eight elementary years were spent in the same building, which was moved to Ortley, South Dakota, to be used as a museum. I had a total of four teachers. After Irene, Myrtle Hjermstad taught 4th and 5th Grades.

During a blizzard, Dad came with a stone boat (two logs with a makeshift platform pulled by one horse) to get Mrs. Hjermstad and us. She waited at our house until the storm passed. Her husband, believing that she was stranded at the school, stopped at our house en route there. He had walked from two miles away (where Dorothy Anderson lives now), carrying a suitcase of clothes and food.

Their son was also a student in our school. In one trying moment, he did something amiss and Mrs. Hjermstad cracked a ruler on him for it. This was the harshest punishment I observed. I guess it put respect in the rest of us. He became an international buyer for a firm in New York, so the one-time incident must not have damaged his ego. I don't remember any badly behaving students.

In 6th Grade, I had a male single teacher, Vernon Benson, who lived near Wallace. Following every afternoon recess, he read from a hard cover book called, *Smiling Jack.*

Agnes Hagen (no relative) was my teacher through 7th and 8th Grade. She lived north of Florence, but didn't drive a car. So, she took room and board at our home. A snow storm came before Christmas, and she could not get to town for shopping. I listened intently while, using the wall mounted party-line phone, she called the Markrud General Store in Wallace to order games and toys for us students.

The highest enrollment at our little school was twelve. The classroom was often quiet enough to hear the tick of the big wall clock as its pendulum swung back and forth. The atmosphere was cozy, like that of a family. I have often felt sorry for modern children in herds of hyper peers.

We were careful to make tablet paper, crayons, paste, and so forth last as long as possible. I had one green-handled scissor all through grade school. We had the kind of desk where the cover lifted up. I tried to keep my stuff neatly arranged underneath. A frame with a swivel seat was attached. I was glad we didn't have the desk style with a storage drawer below the permanent seat.

We walked to and from school. On one spring day, when the snow was thawing, my Hagen cousins offered me 30¢ (three kids promised a dime each) if I would dare to walk through the water as it flowed out of a culvert into my dad's slough. Pebbles shone clearly at the bottom, and the depth seemed only a couple feet. I decided this would be an easy way to earn 30¢, and I accepted the challenge. So it was that I dripped as I walked the rest of the way home and entered the house. There, I was shocked and surprised as I met with immediate reprimand. I don't think I was ever spanked for this mistake—or others—and we had few scoldings; but words about shame, pride, and respect stung and stuck. A few pithy words of wisdom were said and they became signposts on the highway of my life. "Don't let people talk you into doing foolish things," was that particular lesson.

When we were tempted to follow the crowd, we were told about the sheep that fell into a well hole, and the rest of the flock just followed. "Don't be a sheep. Stand alone, if need be," was that teaching. A philosophic message with lifetime imprint was, "Laugh, and the world laughs with you. Cry, and you cry alone." This was to encourage us to look on the sunny side of life. Other quoted aphorisms appeared, like life preservers, at times of stress and indecision.

In spring and fall, we wore dresses to school. When weather got cold, we wore long brown stockings (except on Sunday when we had white ones) hooked up by a garter belt. When the weather got even colder, we tucked long underwear into the hose, making another layer. I had one pair of green corduroy overalls, which also provided warmth, but we had never heard of jeans. Each spring, I thrilled to the ritual of rolling down my long stockings and letting the skirt touch my legs and the breeze gently brush my skin.

Wind-proof winter wear was not invented yet, and people believed we caught colds from being cold. I think I inherited poor circulation from Grandpa Lars and Dad, as I have had cold hands and feet all my life. So did they. One winter morning, I dreaded facing the chilly north wind on my walk to school. I went down the road a ways and then decided to go back home and plead for a ride. No such luck! Dad walked with me out the west driveway, pointed to the school house, and told me I'd better hurry my walk or I would be late. I think I ran backwards to protect my nose from Jack Frost. I also learned perseverance.

The aroma of Mom's freshly baked bread and scalloped potatoes in the oven when we came home from school topped my list of favorite smells.

Somehow, we eventually got a bicycle—but only one—and we were two girls in need of transportation. The solution was to take turns: one of us would ride in the morning; the other in the afternoon. Sometimes, if the road was firm and wind was nil, one could pedal and steer while the other sat on a small carrier seat over the back wheel. We'd had no tricycle or training wheel experience, either, so I remember crashing into the windmill while learning to ride the bike. When our bike was quite new, I left it standing by the back fender of Aunt Thea's car, parked in our yard. When she started to back up, the bike suffered injury. Many years later I learned that, as a youth, my husband Norris had a bike for only one week. It was bought second-hand from a neighbor, and the first-hand owner asked to have it back a week after the sale. He had earlier promised it to a cousin. I guess my half ownership of a bike for some years was luckier. Eventually, Corinne and I got a second bicycle.

Chapter Five

# Childhood Diversions

As a child, my main job was playing. There were regular litters of baby kittens to pet until they purred. When the mama cat hid them in the haymow, we would dig through the alfalfa hay to find them. Our dog was an old male named Pet. I thought a female with pups would have been more interesting.

Mom made a hammock out of heavy white denim. It hung between the two pine trees (now over 100 years old) behind our house. A rope swing was attached to a bough of one of those trees. In the shade of the other, we organized a play-house. It had a discarded cast iron stove, bench, and cupboards made from apple box crates. Vines grew partially around the sides. There, we contentedly made mud pies and cookies, using surplus cutlery, dishes, and various tools and containers from Mom's kitchen. We served many make-believe meals in the summertime.

Dad was quite handy mechanically, and he repaired his own farm machinery. Sometimes, I was his assistant, handing him the right wrench or running errands. I also spent frequent bits of time on my own experimenting with hammer, saw, nails, and scrap wood, trying to make things in the shop.

We converted the old corn crib into a respectable store. Dad nailed empty peach boxes onto the wall for shelves, and he provided a counter by placing a long board across the tops of two barrels. We stocked our store with empty cartons and tin cans. Pretend shoppers could select their groceries and bring them to our red adding machine to figure up total sales. We used homemade coins for cash.

Junk found out in the trees had possibilities. Longing for a boat ride, we dragged an old rectangular gas tank, with top removed, down to the slough in the farm pasture. Corinne and I could both sit in it. If only it would float! It didn't. We sat, wet and disappointed, in a sunken craft. Next, we wished the slough had a sandy bottom rather than soft, squishy, mossy mud. Then, at least, we could have had good wading.

Maybe the watering tank would be a better place to play. The tank had once been a huge steam engine wheel, but now, it lay horizontally on the ground by the windmill. It had a smooth cement bottom, was watertight, and welcomed us to cool off on hot days. We sat on the edge and kicked and splashed in water that was intended for watering the horses and cattle. Sometimes the Hjermstad cousins, who lived a mile east (on what is now the Benthin place), joined the splashing party. Neither of my parents could swim. If we did get to Lake Kampeska on the Fourth of July, they sat with aunts and uncles on the shore to watch that Corinne and I and other non-swimming cousins did not venture out into the deep water.

As a little girl, I had three dolls. My first was a little China doll, which, oddly enough, consisted of just the head! She had black hair on her one-inch-diameter head. This head was attached to a green stuffed sock-type material, with no arms or legs. I'm guessing that, at about age seven, I was given my second doll. She was a full-body rubber doll, about twelve inches long, with a cute, hard-surface face. She wore a red velvet suit with a zipper down the front. I think Mom made that outfit and some others. Having only one sister, and she being not much younger than I, my baby knowledge was quite limited. Dolls didn't seem exciting. Live cats were better! Also, I was more impressed with Dad's wind-up Caterpillar toy tractor. It had tracks and could crawl up over my legs when I sat on the floor. Nevertheless, when we were about twelve and surely would not break them, Corinne and I received large dolls for Christmas. These were close to live-baby size. This third and final doll was named Lily. She had a cloth body and brown hair.

Peeking into the past I see, as plainly as if it were yesterday, Corinne and me as two little girls sitting at a 24x30-inch homemade table. It had geometric patterned linoleum on top, and the frame was painted dark green. On it laid a paper doll book and scissors. Cutting out paper dolls and their clothing brought pleasant satisfaction. Thunder could crash and rain could fall heavily, but this would not interrupt our play. We were secure in that upstairs corner, which later served as Nathan and Kathy's bedroom.

Weaving small yarn or cotton string squares on an adjustable metal frame was another form of entertainment. We also built huge, elaborate Tinker Toy structures.

Some activity was connected with whatever the folks were doing. We ran between machinery in the yard and jumped from the height of platforms or wheels. We did summersault stunts on the front lawn. In hay season, we swung on the slings that lifted loads into the barn. We had an old cart with clumsy steel wheels. With it, we gave each other rides. I'm glad our grandkids have had a chance for some of these simple joys.

One fall, Mom and Dad were shocking grain on the field southwest of our current home. We were very young, and were told to stay in the car. It must have been a warm day. A desperate wish to swim in cool water overcame us. We stripped off all of our clothes and, pretending that we were in a pool, dove back and forth over the car seats. This was met with parental disapproval. What would neighbors think if they saw the nudists?

My interest in horticulture began early, taking root from both sides of my family. Grandpa Lars had a big strawberry patch, which he tended almost to his dying day. When eyesight was failing and the doctor said it would only get worse, he said that it would not be a big problem because he had already seen everything he needed to see. Then, he continued to crawl on his hands and knees to see and pull weeds and pick berries. He was also in charge of apple, chokecherry, and plum trees. We learned to help pull weeds and pick berries.

My Mom kept a sizeable vegetable garden up north where Nathan now has a discarded machinery lot. She also kept a flower spot by a row of lilacs south of the house. She took Corinne and me along as garden companions and gave us little spaces in which to plant seeds. Early on, I respected the wonder of a seed turning into a plant and later bearing a flower. I used to carry five-gallon buckets of water to the lawn and flowers.

Having lived along the fjord in Norway, Grandpa Lars and his brother Ole loved to fish. They would go to Blue Dog Lake near Waubay for overnight two-day trips, and come home with a burlap gunnysack full of fish.

I don't think Grandpa ever drove a car, but Ole was five years younger and was most likely the driver. Ole died in 1942. After that, Mom became the driver. Dad was too busy farming. Grandpa, Mom, Corinne and I would sit for hours in the row boat. The most exciting time was when a fish stole Grandpa's one and only rod. Shore fishing was done with a long bamboo pole. En route to the lake, this was tied on top of the car. Each winter, Grandpa would order a 25-pound box of various kinds of frozen fish, most likely from the Great Lakes up north, so some fish were in our diet during all seasons.

I believe that, sometime in his life, Grandpa had bad luck playing cards. This was alluded to, but never explained. At any rate, we never had regular playing cards in the house. We played checkers, Chinese checkers, Rook, Monopoly, and Pit. Listening to the radio was also off limits for us kids. Hearing world news and certain evening programs like "Fibber McGee and Molly" or Art Linkletter's show was okay.

Mom and Dad were both quite social and placed value on people connections. On the weekend, we always did what was called, "Saturday's work." This meant dusting the furniture, cleaning floors, and a general tidying up of the house in preparation for Sunday. It also included baking a cake, cookies or pie and planning the meat or main meal for Sunday noon. I always helped with the housework part, but was not much involved with the food.

On Saturday afternoon, Mom might take us two girls along to visit one of her aunts. It was not a child-centered world, so we were happy just to go along and sit on the sideline, listening to adult conversation. No regrets. Always, we were included in the coffee time lunch. I can still hear Mom's Aunt Anna Gulbraa asking, "Vil du ha en fricake?" (Do you want a donut?) We learned respect for—and value of—elders. On Sundays we went to church, then had a nice dinner followed by a rest time for reading Sunday School or other religious papers. Then, Dad would go along in the afternoon to visit aunts, uncles and cousins; or maybe they would come to our house. To this day, that seems a good way to spend Sunday.

Chapter Six

# Daily Life

In the kitchen corner where Nathan and Kathy had a refrigerator, we kept a wood box. Here we stored chunks of dry wood for use in the cook stove. Corinne and I would often carry wood in bushel baskets to supply the box. When it was full, we would sit on the lid. It was our favorite place to perch and get ourselves into a giggling frenzy (kind of like my granddaughter Jordan does now most anywhere).

Another source of cooking fuel was corncobs from the pigpen. Dad kept quite a few hogs inside a fenced area. When cobs were dry, we kids picked them into our basket and carried them to the kitchen. One bin in the basement was always reserved for coal, a third source of fuel.

Dad had installed a Delco 32-volt gas-driven generator with battery storage for our electric light system. The engine charged the batteries; big, wet cells in a series of many eighteen-inch tall by ten-inch square glass containers. They filled one shelf in our basement. I had no experience with kerosene or gas lamps until I was twenty-seven years old and in New Guinea. Though Dad's electricity was only for lights, it was quite advanced for the time. I don't recall neighbors having the same. Mixers, refrigerators, toasters, television, microwaves, curling irons, hair dryers, stereos, and any computers or electric appliances were yet to be invented.

Instead of a refrigerator, we would carry to the basement any food that needed to be kept cold. There was a table just for that purpose. Milk was kept in gallon jugs in a special wood tank by the windmill where cold water was daily pumped over it.

A steer and a pig were butchered once a year, in the fall. Meat was frozen in a barrel that stood in the corner of the old machine shed which was in the shade of a big tree. Some chunks of beef and pork were preserved by frying and sealing them into crocks with warm lard. Some meat was canned in quart and pint jars. This required a long cooking time in the boiler. Grandpa's teeth were not good anymore, so pieces for meatballs were ground twice by a hand-powered grinder. After being formed into round balls, they were baked in large black square metal pans. One pan filled the big square oven. The smell of delectable spiced meat permeated the whole house. This process took about a week, and I'm sure Mom was tired and glad when it was done.

Spring house cleaning was a custom most housewives followed. This meant washing walls, windows, curtains, and tidying up shelves, closets, and cupboards. The spic-and-span ritual was often part of community conversations. I've often wished I'd been that disciplined. One season, Mom even washed calcimine—a white coating for plastered surfaces—off the walls upstairs and replaced it with paint.

I never saw my mother or my mother-in-law in a housecoat. Their custom was to rise, dress, and get to work. I've always appreciated the luxury of lounging and just savoring life in short spells when possible. "Sleeping in" was unheard of, and would have been considered shameful.

Dad often referred to his big, thick "doctor book" for diagnosing animal problems. He also had one for human beings. Ailments for both species were researched and treated accordingly. Colds were treated with Vicks rubdowns and Listerine or saltwater gargle. I have few memories of going to the doctor until I became a teenager and was involved in a car accident.

We must have been blessed with good health, as I don't recall being sick at all. My legs ached, "from growing pains," they said, and Mom would massage them. We stayed in the shade-drawn bedroom when we had measles, and refrained from itching when we had chicken pox, the only childhood diseases I recall. Taking care of our teeth was also important. We went to Dr. Berg, a dentist in Watertown, and got many fillings. Mom kept her own teeth for life. (I'm thankful that Norris and I still have ours, too.)

Gas for the tractor and car was purchased and delivered into fifty-gallon barrels. Dad inserted a rubber hose into the barrel and sucked on it to get the upward thrust needed to start the flow of gas into a five-gallon can. This was then poured into the tanks of the tractor and car. Tires were patched at home, and there was a lot of it done, in order to make tires last a long time.

We were not hard up in the Dirty '30s, as were some people. Maybe that was one advantage of our two-generation household. World War II is a clear memory. We listened to the radio every day, and Grandpa and Dad discussed the happenings. Blackouts were practiced in order to darken the country if enemy bombs would come to United States soil. Sugar, gas, and tires were some of the items that were rationed. People were issued stamps allowing limited purchase. School children collected milkweed pods. The silk was used to make life jackets for the military.

The telephone was in a two-foot by nine-inch box, mounted on the north kitchen wall. Our ring was two short and two long sounds. I think Myer and Thea's ring was three shorts. Several other families were connected on the same party line. The coming of small private dial phones didn't happen until 1972 for us, and this brought a thrill to communication. Later, the push button phones became still another luxurious improvement, and now we have all manner of various cell phones and hand-held communication devices. We are in the culture of newer, bigger, better, and more.

How about a little coverage on the outhouses? This may seem crude, but it was a necessary part of life. This is how it was. With no plumbing on the farms, no one had indoor flush toilets. Country people had a small outdoor building which accommodated a two-holer bench over a pit. Ours also had a little hole for kid-sized bottoms. Catalog pages were used for tissue. We crumpled and smoothed them several times to make them soft before using.

Before sanitary pads were available, females used rags for menstruation. Even these were washed and reused. Information on sexual matters was very minimal.

Baths took place in a tub on the kitchen floor, using water that had been heated on the stove. In summertime, the tub was set on the lawn west of the house so that the sun could warm the water. When I became a modest teenager, the closet upstairs became my bath facility. We had a wash basin, towel, and soap. In this limited space was also a shelf which held our games and toys. Two bars supported the clothes on hangers. In the cold of winter, this little closet also housed a white enamel commode. (This area of the house became a modern bathroom in 1983 when Nathan moved home from Louisiana and became a full-fledged farmer.)

Bedding consisted of flat sheets. People hadn't thought of making them fitted. Quilts were homemade and considerably heavier than the factory ones made of modern material.

Mom didn't have a regular wash day. It was usually determined by the weather. Several weeks passed between laundry times. It always seemed like a lot of rigmarole. Water was heated in a big boiler. Butter was smeared on grease spots, and that usually removed the stains. Mom was always thankful for her good Maytag ringer machine. She had two rinse tubs. One of them held bluing—a preparation used to counteract yellowing of the white fabrics. She used a stick for moving the clothes around. Liquid starch was made from raw potato water. Tablecloths, pillow cases, shirts and dresses were dipped in it and wrung out.

During three seasons of the year, the west half of what is now the bunkhouse was the laundry room. We always called it the "wash shanty." The machine was moved to the house in winter, where clothes were then washed in the kitchen. Colored clothes were always hung in the shade north of the shanty, so the sun wouldn't fade them. Mom's clotheslines were way across the yard (where the grandchildren's swing set has recently been), so there was a lot of lugging connected with laundry.

Ironing was accomplished with flat irons heated on the cook stove. The handle clipped on, so when one iron grew cool from use, it was exchanged for a hot one. Later, gas irons came into use. Mom was leery of them, and we used ours sparingly. Also, soot on the edge of the iron easily could spot a garment. I remember doing a whole white shirt and spoiling it with a streak of soot. Most clothing was cotton, not wash-and-wear. So, once clothes were line dried, we dampened them with drops of water from a sprinkler-topped bottle. Then, we rolled each piece of clothing up tightly and placed all the rolls in a bushel-sized basket until the next day. It seemed a disgrace to wear things that were wrinkled. My Mom even ironed the dish towels so they would fit neatly in the drawer. At a young age, I learned to iron by pressing towels, hankies, and pillow cases—flat stuff first. I knew enough about human beings in far away places with lack of clothes and food, so I grew up being thankful for both. Washing and ironing seemed like tasks of the privileged.

In early years, Corinne and I wore straight short hair, with a loop braid on one side. On Sundays, a ribbon bow was added to match our dresses. Mom was always the one who cut our hair. Maybe at around ages 8 to 12, our fine hair had grown enough for full braids. Mom knew how to French braid it for special occasions. Once, I was allowed to stay overnight with Aunt Mable. She curled my hair with little green rubber twist curls. I felt very queenly! Some kids' moms used Shirley Temple metal curlers for Sunday styling, but my hair was always thin and beautiful locks were hard to come by. When Toni Home Permanents came in, I used this aid through high school, college, and through the years in New Guinea. Mom had shop and home perms, but never any regular sets as many older women schedule today.

In a shoe repair box, which was kept by the cellar steps, were small tacks and nails, pieces of leather, waxed string, and an awl. The life of family shoes could often be extended by a fix-it job at home.

In summer, Corinne and I slept upstairs, but when winter came, we moved our bed into our parents' bedroom on the first floor. The room became crowded, but at least we didn't have to trudge upstairs to unheated rooms for sleeping.

Mom and Dad were both stoic and basically healthy. I don't remember either one spending a day totally in bed for flu, cold, sinus, etc. Dad did a lot of hard physical work and had at least one hernia surgery and also wore belts to soothe or prevent more. Once, he somehow got dragged behind runaway horses in a hayrack accident. At another time, he suffered a ruptured appendix. On those two occasions, I remember Mom expressing in prayer to God our need for Dad's healing.

My mother had a weak ankle, and sometimes, a sprain would hurt her for weeks when walking. She usually just wrapped it and kept working. In later life, she battled gall bladder attacks for thirteen years. Finally, while unloading grain, pain became unbearable, and surgery followed.

Meals were cooked and served on a routine schedule. Our family came to the table and ate together almost without exception. Mom liked every vegetable, and so did I. Dad was a meat-and-potatoes only guy, missing out on all the good veggies. The humble potato was daily, cooked in skin or peeled, fried, baked, riced or mashed. Dad's favorite cake was white with chocolate frosting.

Dad always kept his two favorite kinds of sweets, chocolate covered peanuts and orange slice candy, in the "sjenk" (taken from the Norwegian word, "sjenken" which translates to, "the buffet"). This corner cupboard is the only item remaining from Grandpa Lars' homemade furniture. Nathan and Kathy now have it in their office.

Dad and Mom usually milked eight cows. Corinne and I learned to help with chores as needed, starting at about age seven. The feeling of cool breeze was wonderful when opening the barn door to turn out the cattle after milking on a hot summer day. Milk was poured into a separator which, when cranked, seemed to magically cause cream to come out of one spout and skimmed milk out of the other.

The cream was sold at the Wallace Creamery, except for what was saved for household use. We could make a meal on cream-and-bread, which was, simply, cream poured over bread and topped with jam, jelly, or sugar. When cooking vegetables, Mom usually added cream to enhance their flavor. Cream was a staple ingredient in baking homemade cake, cookies, and pie. No one knew of, or worried about, cholesterol. The delicacies of butter and eggs were indulged in without general concern. This was sometimes a problem for Mom. She gained weight easily and tried several diets.

I don't think that casseroles were common in the '30s and '40s, with the exception of goulash. Cooking seemed very basic. I remember when celery and lettuce started being part of the groceries, and I thought they added such a delicious crunch. Prior to that, we ate garden lettuce for only a brief time each spring. Bread was mostly homemade, and even as I write, I'm hungry for the great bread my mom and mother-in-law made, which I could never duplicate. It was critical to keep dough warm while it rose. Flour was bought in fifty-pound cloth bags. Once these sacks were emptied and washed, they were recycled into home-sewn clothing.

Mom canned a few vegetables. I loved the homemade tomato soup made from canned tomatoes. Her vegetable soup was perfect. Sauce was an everyday dessert, so peaches, pears, cherries and plums were bought in lugs (wooden crates) and canned each fall. Mom enjoyed reading recipes in farm journals and would clip them, but used mostly a handful of favorites.

Each fall, we butchered and canned chicken. (One such day in the family assembly line, I cleaned thirty gizzards!) Home-canned chicken was a sure standby for drop-in Sunday guests. Served with Mom's potato salad made with her homemade dressing, it made a yummy meal.

Sleepovers are common now, but were not for me as I grew up. When in high school, I stayed one overnight with a school mate, Joanne Lovick, because I rode with her family to a basketball tourney at Bristol. On another wintry storm night, because roads were blocked to my home, I stayed with Erlis Gulbraa on the farm where Larry Hagen now lives. Both overnights were fun, but that was the extent of my sleepovers. After one all-roads-blocked blizzard, I stayed a whole week in Wallace with Louise Hogstad. It seemed like pure luxury to live in a house with plumbing and walk just two blocks to school.

I had no really close friends all through grade school, so I had a favorite spot in the haymow where I would either sit and talk to the dog, or just think—and sometimes cry—trying to understand my life. In high school, girls were friends, but not soul mates. But during college, I enjoyed the association of young people who were mature. The intellectual atmosphere on campus was stimulating. New solid friendships developed.

There were rumors that some kids received allowances. I didn't know any who did! The financial planning that I grew up with meant that I was given a quarter or half dollar when we went to town. I explained my need for a purchase and then it could be made. The first paid job of my life was picking weeds out of soybean rows (where Nathan currently has silage and other cattle feed). I earned five cents per row. The weather was hot, and I was not used to long hours, so I don't recall getting very rich. My second paid job was a week of babysitting for a neighbor, Ruby Trygstad. I was also asked to bake a cake. Having no experience in this line of work, the 9x13-inch production had a sunken middle. This dear mother's reaction was, "Oh, well. We'll just fill that up with frosting." I have loved her ever since.

Being squeamish about bugs, snakes, mice, or frogs was not cool for us farm girls. Once, we had a rat problem in the old wash shanty. Dad told me to keep cover on a hole while he sought to end the rodent's life. I didn't enjoy standing guard and being ready to execute, but to refuse wasn't an option, either, so the invader met its fate. Many years later, a screaming college girl was stranded atop a table, held hostage by a mouse. I could calmly take charge, kill the unwanted visitor, and rescue my dorm friend.

We had a big yard and usually kept it quite nice. When there was need of a place to have a Luther League social or a Sunday School picnic, it often took place on our farm. Mom saw this as a good way to use the deadline to get things in order. We all scurried around to get prepared, and then enjoyed hosting the event. Since my Mom was the oldest sister in the Dale family, we also hosted the Christmas dinners at our place. She liked using her pretty dishes, and we would set the table for twelve with her rose patterned china. The menus varied, but riced potatoes seemed to be synonymous with company.

## Chapter Seven

# High School

In the spring of 1949, I sat with all the other Codington County eighth graders for a final exam. No problem! Our study manual had helped prepare us. September came, and it was time for me to start high school. There, I had a problem. During the first eight years of formal schooling, I was the only one in my class. Now, the only other kids ready for 9th Grade at Wallace High were three boys. At age fourteen, I wished desperately for just one bosom girlfriend. Dad said there was still much I could learn at home, so after family discussion, it was decided that I would delay starting secondary school for one year.

In those nine months at home, Mom taught me to crochet. As gift items, I made edging on handkerchiefs and fancy dresses on decorated dolls. Embroidery and quilt making were also on the agenda, plus other home economic projects in the broadest sense of the word. I cut almost 1,000 2x3-inch quilt pieces from various scraps of cloth which were left over from Mom's sewing, and then I stitched them into a quilt top. In 1999, I found this quilt in a trunk. I was amazed! I could vividly recall which prints had been in each garment. Looking back, I should have practiced cooking and baking that year, but I thought that was not important. After I got married, I learned otherwise.

This was also my second year of confirmation instruction. We met at St. Pauli Church. Lessons were taken very seriously. Not having other school work, I could readily memorize the catechism, along with its explanation. One Saturday, on the way home from church, the kids were racing. I was riding with a cousin, and he lost control of the car. We flew across the ditch and bounced over frozen plowing in the field south of Burdette Wibeto's farm. No seat belts or locked car doors! So, I was thrown out hard. We picked ourselves up and started walking home, but I felt that there was something wrong with my right shoulder. Yet, my family did not easily rush off to see the doctor. We ate dinner. Pain persisted. We decided a trip to the Peabody Hospital in Webster would be necessary. Diagnosis was a broken bone just below the shoulder joint. This was the first and last incident of broken bones in my family, even until now. I was anesthetized so that the ball of the upper arm bone could be lined up with the lower part again. Waking up was a deep, spiritual experience for me. I rejoiced that my injury wasn't worse, and that God kept me from hitting my head. I was so grateful to be alive. Through fourteen days of unpleasantness, lying on my back with a forty-pound traction pulling on my cast, I sensed God's gracious call via a spared life to make it a useful life. I felt humbled by the many visitors who came and by the cards which I received.

One day, I heard my Dad talking with the doctor out in the hall: "You have to do something different or we're taking her to another hospital."

Dad was not one to complain easily, and decisions were made with caution, but I've always been glad he made a firm request. I was taken back to the operating room where Dr. Karlins, noted to be a good orthopedic surgeon, pinned my severed bone together properly. It's been good ever since. Unfortunately, the weighted cast had already worn a hole in the skin on my forearm, so I had another week in the hospital then and two scars for the rest of my life.

At least, I didn't miss any school! And yes, I did get confirmed on August 6th. Aunt Judy and Uncle Harold Buer came from Meadow, South Dakota, and they, plus other relatives, helped make it a special day. This was also Judy's birthday, so we've had that in common for many years. Mom and Dad gave me my first wristwatch as a gift.

The fall of 1950 was the right time for me to start high school. Three other girls and six boys were in my class—the biggest one in the history of Wallace High at that time. I was a shy country girl, and fear of the unknown was strong. Two perceptive senior girls, a second cousin, Lorraine Hjermstad, and a friend from church, Dorothy Hogstad, met me at the door and helped orient me. Maybe my Mom had arranged this. Anyhow, I was glad. After getting signed in, probably all of thirty or forty minutes' procedure, I walked a block to the telephone office. (This is now part of the Webster Museum.) I called Mom, "Come and get me. I'm already done."

So began the next stint of my education: four good years, just four miles from home. Up to that time, I think I had seen one basketball game. Fund raisers, girl's sports, football and band were not part of school as they are today. My life was pretty plain and simple. The first big social event was initiation. I had to wear a gunnysack and an onion necklace and lots of curlers in my hair. I also carried a corncob pipe. At the evening program, I was directed to sit on one boy's lap while two other boys sang a lullaby. The next evening, there was an all-school party. Girls wore dresses with full skirts. Boys wore jeans and shirts in the '50s style.

We played round games, like "Skip to My Lou," in the gym. I was immediately accepted socially and went home feeling great.

Student body enrollment at that time was thirty-four, with four basic courses offered for each year: English, algebra, general science (no lab) and history. (I later took biology as a college elective so that I could see what was under the microscope.) I liked and respected my teachers. Neither of my parents had high school experience, so I felt blessed to have that opportunity, and I did well in my subjects.

My first date came about as a sophomore. One afternoon, at the end of the school day, a boy whom I thought was kind of cute asked if I'd like to go to a movie that evening. It had been a cloudy, rainy, wet day. Not knowing what to answer, I joked that it would be okay if the sun came out. Lo and behold, in early evening, a rainbow and sunshine appeared. So did this neat guy! With him also was the second coolest fellow in the class. I asked my parents' permission to go, and I can still hear their consideration, "Well, you know, if she starts going, she'll want to continue."

Being careful was part of their long range plan for me. Down the road was college, and I should not be distracted. I did go to the movie, and that was the start of a just right dating life: casual, but no steadies.

This same male friend promoted my becoming a cheerleader in my junior year. Being part of the cheering squad for boys' basketball definitely provided some status, even back then. Our uniforms consisted of black and gold mid-calf length, full flare skirts with long-sleeved blouses, white socks, and "saddle shoes." We four cheerleaders on the team found our own rides to the other seven towns where our boys competed. One yell, which reflected the ethnic culture of the hometown was:

*Wallace Bulldog Cheerleaders in 1954. Left to right: Joanne Gulbraa, Arvella Lauen, Lorraine Hagen and Ilah Wibeto.*

> *Lutefisk and lefse, Copenhagen snoose;*
> *Come on, boys, we're yelling like the duce!*

Schools in the Little Eight Conference were: Henry, Bradley, Florence, Raymond, Thorpe, Lily, Garden City, and Wallace. The fact that now only two of these schools exist, illustrates the demise of small schools in rural America.

Mechanization in agriculture led to larger farms and less population. School districts consolidated, and the towns declined. Wallace, at that time, had a bank, restaurant, gas station, bar, band shell for Saturday night performances, hardware store, and two grocery stores. Pete Dragsten, who was also my Dad's godparent, ran a blacksmith/mechanic shop east of what is now a park. Dad made many trips to Wallace to get something welded at Pete's place.

A favorite occasional after-school snack was a small bag of Planters peanuts and a bottle of Coke, a 15¢ total purchase at the local café. There were no school buses. Cousin Merlin Hagen drove a car, and Corinne and I rode with him. I suppose Dad helped buy the gas. The main entrance to Wallace was via a high bridge over the railroad track. Sometimes, that was slippery and almost dangerous.

We had no special Awards Night at the end of the school year. The giving of awards was incorporated into graduation ceremonies. Receivers were selected by the teachers. I remember getting a medal each year and feeling very proud of my accomplishment, as follows: Freshman - All-Around Student; Sophomore – Music; Junior – Citizenship; Senior – Salutatorian.

At the end of each year, we had an all-school picnic at Stony Point by Lake Kampeska. Entertainment was roller skating at the wonderful round Spider Web Roller Skating Rink. Cool breezes blew from the lake through the large open wall spaces. Some kids were going steady and had boy/girlfriend security and obligations. I always felt free and did not envy them.

Senior Skip Day allowed a class trip to Minneapolis. We girls rode with Joanne's older brother. For a country girl in the '50s, staying in a hotel and just sitting in a bathtub was big-deal fun. Attending the evening Ice Follies was the highlight. The only trouble was that, with the excitement of new places and things, we had not slept much. One of the girls fell asleep. An ice skating teddy bear glided right up to us. She awoke with a shout when his paw touched her. I was happy that I was awake.

*Later in my school life, I wore a fancier net-covered dress with rhinestones across the top of the bodice when I was the accompanist.*

I liked to sing, but was also the only one who knew how to play the piano, so I ended up accompanying the Girls' Glee Club each year. (It was a thrill when I got to college to find out that boys could also sing, even in bass and tenor harmony!) This led to my playing the piano for vocal performances, commencement marches, and so forth. For these, I wore a blue taffeta formal as a freshman. I knew I was really important.

We did not have proms, but a very low-key Junior/Senior Banquet was held in the back room of a Watertown restaurant. There was no dance. Three of us couples went in one car. On the way home, the driver kicked the speedometer up to ninety miles per hour. I had been in one accident and considered that enough. Being my own self, I was not bound by peer pressure. I politely asked to be let out, saying I would walk home. I don't remember walking, but I think they slowed down and took me home first. Rumors were that the girls were going to smoke a cigar that night, and I didn't want to be in on that either, so my own bedroom was a safe refuge.

Graduation night was a profound milestone for me. The gym was packed with people. Most of my aunts and uncles and cousins were there. "Onward and upward, God willing" was our theme. There were no computer banners, so each letter was cut from construction paper and strung across the stage background. I delivered the Salutatorian speech with all the idealism and confidence my youthful heart could muster. I had worked hard, done well, and was pleased with my four-year investment. I wore a blue linen dress with white embroidered flowers on it, and high heels, which were called "baby doll pumps." Not having worn high heels before, walking the stairs to the stage was most precarious.

The emotional depth of all the excitement hit me when I got home. I went behind the house and had a good cry by myself. I just felt overwhelmingly thankful, happy, and tired—all at the same time. When I recovered my composure, I went inside to meet the relatives and receive their congratulations. I was the second oldest of twenty-three cousins in Mom's family, and the fourth in eight on Dad's side. Only three of all the parents had gone to high school. I knew I was setting a new trend for my generation. Later, all the cousins graduated from high school, and nine finished college.

Chapter Eight

# Off to College
## — 1954 —

Having a car of my own and wheels for independence never entered my mind. Most of that summer and the next three were spent helping Mom and Dad on the farm. I had learned to drive the 1938 Allis Chalmers WC tractor, and so I was able to plow, disc, dig, help swath, haul grain, and combine. The crops were wheat, oats, flax, barley, and millet. I could rake and haul alfalfa and other hay, depending on the season.

Besides the cattle chores, there were also pigs, sheep, and chickens to feed. It was called "mixed farming." Without government programs, supply and demand ruled the market. If one kind of crop failed, maybe another was good, so that was a form of insurance for financial security. We all worked together. There was little talk about money, and no mention of being poor. As a farmhand, I got my suntanned skin and bleached blonde hair in the fields. In my mind, I wondered and dreamed about what college would be like.

The fall of 1954 came. I was the only one from my family and from my graduating class to go on to college; so again, this was like plowing new ground. My clues for preparation were meager, mainly what Augustana College in Sioux Falls, South Dakota, and their official enrollment process offered.

I knew I wanted further studies, and I knew why I wanted them. I couldn't remember not having a personal relationship with Jesus. I was blessed with more than just a go-to-church-Sundays faith. I wanted to acquire tools so I could be of more use in spreading the Kingdom of God on earth. I would aim for a minor in Christianity. Most of my activities were driven by a desire to be a good influence with others.

I had seen the struggles of farm life. I would go get a profession and be independent. Mom had always said her girls should have an education so that they wouldn't have to wash baby diapers for a living, as she had done when she was very young. Further motivation was that Dad wanted us to have a vocation, so that we could and would help others.

Into the family car I packed some carefully selected skirts, blouses, dresses and a new blue wool jacket, a plaque that read "What a Friend We Have in Jesus," a few school supplies (no stereo or computer) and other miscellaneous items. Mom, Dad and Corinne took me to Sioux Falls. I moved into the far north room on the second floor, north wing, of Tuve Hall.

The folks went home. I remember feeling like a single lost fish in a big sea, but strangely confident that, together with God's help, I could handle this. I wept softly on my pillow the first night. An Iowa girl was my assigned roommate. She and her friends went down to a bar the first evening.

Everyone wore dresses in those times. I wore a pretty homemade one with flowered print and lace collar the next morning as I walked to Old Main to register for my first semester. I had a $25 scholarship from Luther League. Not counting book expense, I paid $213. I bought second-hand textbooks as much as possible. I took Introduction to Education, Children's Literature, Christianity, Phys Ed, English, World Geography, and Music. My love affair with music only increased in college and has enhanced my life ever since.

## Chapter Nine

# Music, Music, Music

I have had a life-long passion for music. I drummed with spoons on a green metal kitchen stool until most of the paint chipped off. My cousins had an old phonograph with a hand crank and vinyl records that played ancient songs, and I loved listening to that.

I couldn't wait for my fingers to grow long enough so that I could take real piano lessons. I had been a "pretend pianist," moving fingers on most anything, until I turned eight. This was the age our neighbor had said I could start music lessons with her.

We didn't own a piano, but we had a big house. A neighboring family who had a tiny house needed somewhere to store their piano. Their pianist daughter had grown up and left home. We stored their piano, and the owner, Edwin Johnson, was glad that a little girl could use it. Nobody in my immediate family played, but both Mom and Dad were in high hopes that I could learn. Myrtle Keller, Vernon's mom, and her family lived where Orville and Janice Johnson live now. The day came when I could ride the bicycle there and pay her 50¢ per lesson. I would go straight home from a lesson and practice my assignment, lest I should forget how to do it.

The Kellers later moved to the current Larry Hagen place. As I rode my bike to my lesson, Ed was pulling their brooder house behind his tractor. He offered me and my bike a ride in his brooder house. I enjoyed this unique mode of transportation to that weekly lesson!

As soon as leaders of our church discovered that Corinne and I could sing, we started performing special musical numbers for programs. Two little Gulbraa girls, Erlis and Janice, did the same, as did many of the Lutheran Daughters of the Reformation (LDR) girls. Parents and older members were always encouraging us, even if our worship leadership was not perfect. We had no show-and-tell in school, so this was one way we learned confidence before people in public.

As a child, I often heard Dad tell about his love for accordion music. When he was in Norway, his cousin had played one while they were out in a boat. The beautiful melodies reverberated across the water between the fjord walls. With the promise that he would pay half the cost if I'd earn the other half, we would buy an accordion. That motivated me to start a chicken enterprise, wherein I raised chicks to frying size. Over several summers I accumulated $75, so we went to Minneapolis. A pretty pearl gray instrument caught my eye, and we purchased it. A *Teach Yourself* book came with it. I sat in the back seat of the car and played most of the way home. The treble clef keys, played by the right hand, were the same as the keys of a piano, with which I was already familiar. I just had to learn the chords, played by the left hand. Mom and Dad must have had good nerves and lots of patience.

By that time, my folks knew that I was genuinely interested in music. I had finished three books of piano instruction with Mrs. Keller, but she said she could not teach me more. I had been given no real theory, nor had I performed recitals, so my parents paid for twenty professional lessons with a dear elderly lady in Watertown. Mrs. McIntosh was classy! She had a grand piano in a fine home. This fed my enthusiasm in good style.

At my first lesson, she told me that I had to cut my fingernails, but that I need not feel sad about that. "Anybody can grow fingernails; not many can make beautiful music," she said. Mrs. McIntosh made me also promise to practice an hour a day. Chickadee feeders outside her window attracted interesting birds. Sometimes, we would take a brief lesson break and watch them. I truly enjoyed my sessions with her in the fourth level book. Under her tutelage, I learned two solos, "Caprice" and "Romance," which I retained in memory and recorded later on a CD.

From early on, I'd had many people connections and much joy through music. I found myself including music for gatherings whenever and wherever possible. One neighbor, Alice Ristvedt, told me, "Keep it up! Music will always wash the dust off your life." Another neighbor many years later remarked, "Wherever Lorraine is, there will be music."

While registering for college classes, I paid for private voice lessons one semester and piano lessons the next. An old army barracks on campus had many rooms with a piano in each. Students would go there and practice. I spent many hours in that hall. Hearing people rehearsing music in other rooms made the world seem like a grand place. I met many students more talented than I, but I determined to hone what I had.

This all fit in well in college. During my first two years, I was in one of the Lutheran Student Association outreach groups. We sang in churches, nursing homes, the penitentiary, and pretty much wherever we were invited. I sang in the Chapel Choir. I enjoyed our annual concert series tours as we performed in Lutheran churches throughout the Midwest each spring.

Through it all I was growing, maturing and dealing with the great and small questions of faith and life.

## Chapter Ten

# College Continued

I lived very frugally at Augustana, more often eating in my room than at the cafeteria. I received a check for limited dollars from Mom and Dad to cover expenses as needed. Only once was I totally penniless, for two days.

I would travel by bus to Watertown. Aunt Clara Ronning lived there, and her home was often a waiting place for my coming or going. Sometimes, I caught a ride with other students from Clark or Watertown.

I did babysitting for spending money at 50¢ per hour. Three families would call me for evenings, as needed. I could usually play with the children a couple of hours and still have study time after putting them in bed. The wives learned that I could iron, so I earned extra money that way.

During the second semester, I took Christianity, Teaching of Reading, Teaching of Math, English, Natural Science, and History. This small town country girl was very impressed with the lectures, concerts, school parties and festivals at Augustana. I wanted to take advantage of every opportunity. This gave me lots of relationships for social life, but also took a lot of time.

There were thirty-nine girls and one young man training to be elementary teachers. This male was good-looking, and nice besides, and didn't lack for attention. I noticed there were many other really fine guys besides the teacher trainee. I appreciated being asked out, so I adjusted my full schedule. That means I should have slept more, but walking to 7:30 a.m. class in winter definitely woke me up and got me in gear for the studies of the day!

The last test of my freshman year was on Friday, June 3, 1955. My family came to get me. Again, we packed everything in the car and then had a picnic dinner in the park. We drove to Beresford to look at St. Peter Church. I had answered their bulletin ad regarding their need for a summer Bible School teacher. I got the job. We picked up the materials which I would be using for the rest of June. We got back to the farm by midnight. I thanked the Lord for safe travels and helping me to complete my first year at Augustana.

## Chapter Eleven

# Summer
## — 1955 —

On the next day, I was immediately transported back into the world of farming at home. I helped mow the lawn and clean the house. We cleaned the St. Pauli Church. I did some lesson planning.

On Sunday, after worship, Mom and Dad took me to Watertown. We had pie à la mode in the park, the pie being brought from home, and ice cream purchased in town.

I left on the 5:15 a.m. bus for Sioux Falls. Morris Ellison met me at the depot. (Forty-four years later, I served on the Women of the Evangelical Lutheran Church of America State Board with Morris Ellison's wife, Edith. Their son, David, had been one of my students that summer of '56. He now had a family with a wonderful music ministry of his own. Christ was the focus of that family, and faithfulness was rewarded.) I would stay at their home the first three nights and shift to six other homes during my month-long teaching stint in the Beresford area. My desire to share Christ and see the world was now growing beyond its embryonic stage.

Fifteen children of all ages came to my classes. I had all eight grades. They came from good families. Discipline was not a problem. It was a hot month, so I was glad we met in the basement. Supplies were minimal.

I relied heavily on my own background. Irene Hallstrom, Stella Ihlen, Helene Kinstad, Helen Jesme, and Jean Ustrud had been my Sunday School teachers. Pastors Engh and Stangeland had also been a good influence. The National Pocket Testament League challenged members to commit to reading three chapters a day from the Bible and five chapters on Sundays. Thereby, I had read The Good Book through several times by now, so I could aptly handle the lessons. In the lonely times of growing up, playing and singing hymns had always been my therapy, so I knew lots of songs and could accompany or lead with ease.

From the start of my teaching, I planned a program for the end of the month. That would be the grand conclusion of this experience. The day after the final program, the Olson family took me to my parental home. This time, and many others it seems, a car would have made life simpler.

The Fourth of July was next on the calendar. Between teaching Bible School and the Fourth of July at home, I cut my own hair and put in a Toni so I would be ready for summer activity. Corinne and I went with Uncle Delmer's family to the Dale family picnic at Kampeska Lake and then to the fireworks at the Watertown Stadium.

My teeth needed repair so, on the 5th, I went to see Dr. Berg. This resulted in 3½ hours in the chair, costing $40 for eight fillings. Shopping that day included the purchase of two song books and two desired books just for reading, and a gold necklace which cost $9.75. This was a productive day in Watertown.

Diary entries for the rest of the summer show that I participated in:

- Helping with corn and bean cultivation.
- Pruning the pine trees.
- Selling lambs at 18¢ a pound with Dad.
- Canning apricots, peaches, and pickles.
- Scything burning weeds in the hog pasture.
- Buying and painting a new mailbox post from Uncle Myer for 60¢.
- Selling small pigs for 13¢ a pound.
- Cutting and sewing a pair of pajamas.

I didn't seem to have time for merely "hanging out." That summer, and the next three, all included some work on the home farm. A pheasant was caught under the swather canvas one day. Another day, while coming down the driveway hill, I ran the truck into the tractor. This was pretty exciting! Also scary.

For a week at the end of July, I served as Bible Camp Counselor at Ne-So-Dak. I was responsible for five girls in the cabin where I slept and fifteen others in three nearby cabins. A pastor from the Lutheran Bible Institute at Minneapolis taught lessons from the book of Mark, and counselors led the follow-up discussions. Some of those girls wrote to me for several years afterwards.

Uncle Ludvig, Mom's oldest brother, who was unmarried and boarding with us, had a drinking problem. He would disappear for several days of spreeing. On the last Saturday before leaving back to college, Uncle Ludvig was drunk and in a car in a ditch. Dad went to rescue him. That same afternoon, Corinne and I sang for an LDR meeting. On September 11, 1955, summer vacation was over, and I was totally in the mood for returning to Augie as a sophomore.

## Chapter Twelve

# Sophomore Year

My visit with the Dean of Women the year before was fruitful: she had moved my original roommate out and matched me with a rural girl from Bristol, Marilyn Thorson. As freshmen, Marilyn and I had made plans to live in The Cottage, a home that had been converted into a dorm for twelve girls.

I had washed and packed my school clothes and hemmed the top and bottom of a piece of drapery to cover our one north window. Mom had covered two wooden apple boxes with brown adhesive shelf paper, which I took along as a bookshelf.

Dad always wanted to learn as much as he could about everything, so en route to Sioux Falls for the new school year, we drove to Garden City to see the new 630-foot television tower. This later extended to 900 feet. A few hours later, I moved into The Cottage, and a banner year began.

I registered for Music Theory, Health, Christianity, Art and Psychology. The whirl of social involvement got underway again. I belonged to the Lutheran Student Association, a Bible study group, and attended other campus activities. I was again in Chapel Choir, which practiced three hours a week. I went home only three weekends that semester.

A professor who taught several of my Christianity classes that year and others made a forever impact on me. Rev. Emil Erpestad seemed to be the embodiment of peace, love, wisdom and many other virtues and graces. (Later, when he died, someone called to let me know about the funeral. I had a difficult time tending to the duties of the day. I had so enjoyed sitting under his instruction and wished that in some way I could pay tribute.)

My sophomore year was interrupted by the death of my maternal grandfather, John Dale, about whom I provide this background information:

Mom's youngest brother, Clarence Dale, married Mariam Baukol in 1941. She moved to the farm where Clarence lived with his father, John Dale. (Mike and Linda Dale live there now.) Grandpa John Dale had diabetes; and Mariam, who was a nurse, gave him insulin shots and controlled his diet for the next 16 years, during which time she also birthed and cared for five children. Grandpa became seriously ill in 1955. Mom, who saw that Mariam had her hands full, empathized with the situation. She, too, had lived with in-laws for twenty-one years, caring for Grandma Mary Hagen until her dying day in 1943 at 81 years of age. (I was eight years old then.)

Now, I was nearly twenty, and Grandpa Dale was living in our house. But he was in and out of the hospital a couple of times. He had a heart attack in the fall, which ended his earthly journey at age 80. I took the morning bus home from Sioux Falls for the November 4th funeral at Highland Church, and I returned by bus to school the next day.

My maternal grandma and John's wife, Christine, had already passed away. Grandma Hagen was not outwardly warm and loving, like the grandmas of today, so I hadn't felt really close to her even though we lived in the same house.

I had always felt more of a bond with Grandpa Lars, who lived with us from the time Dad and Mom married until the last weeks of his healthy and active life. Mom and Dad cared for him. He died at our home on June 16, 1953, two months short of the age of 95. I was eighteen. His coffin was brought into our living room for the viewing and prayer service. He was buried in the St. Pauli Cemetery, near the rural Wallace church he had helped build in 1900.

In our family, we truly loved each other and were loyal to each other, but shows of affection were restrained. I wish now that I'd made more effort to talk to, and learn from, my grandparents, but that is not the way of youth. After Grandpa John's funeral, as I was riding the bus back to Sioux Falls, I reflected on this thought and upon the fact that I had just lost my last grandparent. But, sadness could not linger. I had to get on with school.

On Veteran's Day, I was invited to go with Gladys Dahl, one of the nursing students, and three other classmates for a day at her home in Clear Lake. We had a wonderful time, and it was the beginning of an association that led to a Christmas vacation trip to Athens, Ohio.

My parents had always been interested in world missions, so when I asked permission to go to an international student conference on this theme, they agreed. I was glad. Mom bought me a new blue sweater and a pleated plaid skirt to match. One carload was going from our college. I traveled with Gladys, a male student from Korea, and Danny, the son of a missionary in Africa.

We left on December 25th and drove a day, a night, and half a day, stopping only three times for gas and eating. I spent a total of 50¢ on food! I must have survived on 15¢ hotdogs! Sessions were led by noted speakers and authors from many places in the world. Meetings were enhanced by music, and I was like a sponge, soaking up all this new exposure. The trip home gave me my first look at Chicago, with its skyscrapers, underground streets, slums, and museums. It was also the beginning of a special friendship with Danny. He was a humble, intellectual, not-very-husky young man. I was attracted to him, but I guarded my heart.

After experiencing all of this, my return to normal school routine left me feeling as though I'd been kicked off a cloud. Having missed some classes, I suffered a poor grade in my music theory test, and this zapped my confidence for a while. However, when I went to the mailroom, cookies and donuts from Mom got me recharged to hit the books and not give up.

During the second semester, I began observing classes at different elementary schools, and I later became a student teacher. I practiced under Mrs. Barber at Franklin School on Cliff Avenue north in Sioux Falls. I recorded these comments in my diary from those months: "This is not a lazy girl's job. I feel too little for such a huge task. I must keep on. All went well today. Things are nerve-wracking sometimes. Kids are mostly interesting and nice. Mrs. Barber smells like bacon each morning, but I like her motherly ways. She lives in my part of town, so I even can ride to school with her."

April was decision-making time. I would soon have a teaching certificate. I checked with Watertown and Wallace schools, and I even went to the Twin Cities for a job interview with the Bloomington School System. I settled on the hometown offer in Wallace: 4th, 5th, and 6th Grades for $2,600 per year, or $265 per month. By accepting Wallace's offer, I could live at home and save money towards getting my Bachelor of Arts degree later. Mom and Dad had basically paid for my first two years, but if I wanted more, it was up to me.

Spring was a mixture of more excitements. Our choir made a concert tour throughout South Dakota. I began a waitress job at Rushmore Café in downtown Sioux Falls for 75¢ an hour. I came home many nights smelling like a hamburger. My favorite customer called me "Sunshine." On May 1st, I added a retail sales job at the Montgomery Ward store, earning 85¢ an hour. Now, I would really make and save money! The ladies' wear department was on the second floor, and the weather was hot. I thought that I would suffocate while selling dresses in ninety-seven degree weather with no air conditioning. A high sale day for me was $133. Meeting customers from other states and even other countries was fun.

One weekend, Larry and Thea Hagen picked me up and we went to Parkston, South Dakota, where I sang a solo at Orville and Dorothy Anderson's wedding. (Orville was a life-long neighbor, and Dorothy became a close friend, and has remained so to this day.) I caught the bouquet.

A visit to the optometrist showed I needed glasses, as my eyes tested 20/40 and 20/50 vision. When I walked out of the office, I was surprised to be able to see individual leaves on the trees. I then went home for Corinne's high school graduation. She was one of three classmates. This time, she gave the Valedictory address.

On Memorial Day, I joined a carload of Augie students to enjoy a day at the lake cabin of fellow classmate, Denny Knight. Even though it was early spring and the water would be cold, we were eager to have fun at Lake Cochrane. I had gained confidence as a swimmer during my final elective course at Augustana via swimming lessons at the YWCA. Now, that experience paid off: I was not afraid in deep water. Each of us was given three tries to get up on water skis that day. It was a big WOW when I made it on the third try. Such a free-flying feeling! This was high adventure for me.

During the six weeks of summer school, I moved out of The Cottage and over to Mrs. Rudd's house. I thought summer school and city jobs were much easier than farm life, and it was my hope to stay and work in Sioux Falls. But, by mid-July, I was needed at home. Dad had been to Missouri for hernia treatment. I always felt sorry that he didn't have any sons to help him on the farm. Mom had some ear troubles that summer. I needed to be flexible.

So, I moved home and began helping with the farm work. This included such duties as pulling wild oats and other weeds, hauling bales, plowing down dried-out corn, and grading the road. Rain had been very scarce for a long time. Then, suddenly, we got seven inches of rain in five days! Now, we had the opposite kind of troubles. In one day, we got the digger, combine, swather and truck stuck! Pulling them out was not my favorite pastime. Besides this, while Mom and I were unloading oats, we had elevator problems, too.

I was lonesome for my Augustana friends and life in the city. However, I found an interest in one country recreation—horseback riding; and I would ride up to six miles at a time on a borrowed pony named Queen. She belonged to Myer's family. Two cousins, Don Dale's sister, Carol, and Myrene Hjermstad, each had a pony, so I would ride with them. None of us had saddles.

That August, a new interest came into my life. The Art Meland family lived three miles away, just south of the Goodhue Church. Mrs. Agnes Meland was known for being a very good teacher. Gerald, their youngest son, was two years ahead of me in high school. A middle son, Norris, had just returned home from four years in the U.S. Air Force and was about to begin college at South Dakota State University (SDSU) in Brookings.

Norris came over to invite me to a banquet in our parish. I was not home, so he visited with my Dad. Since Mom and Dad believed that marriages were more stable between people of similar backgrounds, I think Dad saw from the start that this could be a good thing. He told Norris that he was sure I would want to go.

I don't think Norris and I ever got to that banquet, but we had our first date on August 18, 1956. We went to a movie, *The Court-Martial of Billy Mitchell.* This friendship grew slowly throughout the year as we shared time on picnics, roller skating, movies, church activities, and just driving out for a malt.

## Chapter Thirteen

# Hometown Teacher

On August 27th I began my professional career as a teacher in the Wallace Public School. I taught eleven girls and seven boys. On the first day, I wore a straight black skirt and a plaid blouse with a black tie. A fourth grader with hearing impairment sat right in front. He looked up at me and said, "You look just like Dale Evans!" Since she was a famous Christian actress and singer, that was compliment enough to start my year right.

I had visited with Esther Tofte, the teacher in 1st, 2nd, and 3rd Grades; prepared my room and lessons, and attended teachers' meetings ahead of time. The children came from good homes. The Superintendent, Mr. Roach, had been my algebra teacher six years earlier, and I liked him. This would be a good year.

Switching from campus life back to home territory included many adjustments. Prompted by Corinne's leaving for Augustana, I often thought about college social life, but instead, took responsibility in the church and community, which offered many opportunities for service and growth.

For instance, I gave six children weekly piano lessons. I accompanied the Glee Club and several vocal soloists in the high school. I was called on to sing or accompany various other musical performances. I organized a junior choir with sixteen children from our church, and we sang regularly for worship. (One of those boys, thirty years later, played his guitar and sang at the St. Pauli reunion service and publicly thanked me for getting him started. Also, many decades later, a Wallace piano student sent me a warm thank-you letter. I mention this to show how God adds His blessing to our efforts.)

Both Goodhue and St. Pauli held annual lutefisk suppers, so I attended and helped serve that year. Our parish pastor, Kenneth Stangeland, asked Norris and me to help with the high school youth group. This led to many outings with youth just younger than us. I also belonged to the LDR organization, during which time I used my Bible study and musical leadership experience in leading twelve or more girls. (One of those LDR girls, Vikki Kingslien, after a successful career in Washington, D.C., has returned to our neighborhood and has become another special friend.)

This was an election year. On November 7th, Dad spent all day at the town hall as an election officer, and we rejoiced together in Dwight Eisenhower's victory.

In the year 1935, the Social Security system was enacted. In 1956, when I received my first paycheck, Dad lamented that I would be paying social security fees all my working days, and he was right. I was just thrilled to have earned independent income! My first much-appreciated acquisition was an LP record player with a turntable which spun both 33 and 45 rpm records. It had a pink and white case. The next day, as I did Saturday's work, I listened to George Beverly Shea sing "Tenderly He Watches Over Me." I played it over and over, listening as the verse continued with, "every step, every mile of the way." I saved most of my salary, however. After all, that was my focus for this whole year.

During Christmas vacation, our family took a train trip to Vancouver, British Columbia, Canada, to see Dad's half-brother Palmer Hagen and his family. We all enjoyed seeing planes, rivers, and Rocky Mountains from the vista-domed car. We mingled with farmers, sailors, and a general mix of travelers. Palmer had left home early as a teenager. He lived his life in Vancouver as a crane operator. He had married Beth, of Finnish descent, and they also ran a sauna business. Their only son, Paul, Jr., was fifteen years old. They showered us with warm hospitality. Their lack of church connection saddened us, but we created good memories while being together. When we returned, Dad traded cars in Aberdeen, and we drove home in a 1953 Chevy.

School days got easier as the year went along. I liked the students and worked hard to keep lessons interesting. The annual carnival, Christmas program, basketball tourneys, spring testing—besides regular classes—brought my first year to a close.

Within that year, I had come to realize that this Norris Meland was a very fine young man. I pondered over his good qualities, such as a strong work ethic, staying constantly positive, and entertaining with humor. He seemed healthy and caring. Yet, I wished desperately that he could sing with me. Would other traits compensate? What was meant to be? It was a frustrating time for us.

## Chapter Fourteen

# Summer
## — 1957 —

On June 13th, I was off on another mission challenge and adventure. Norris took me to Summit, South Dakota, to catch a bus in the wee hours of the morning. At Minneapolis, I transferred to a train. I was quite enthralled with the views in Wisconsin, with its hills and curves. Farther east, I saw many new kinds of vegetation in the Adirondack Mountains.

I would spend two months as a counselor at Jolly Acres Camp for underprivileged children from Baltimore, Maryland. Seventy college students from many parts of the United States gathered for a week of orientation, which was held at Gettysburg, Pennsylvania. There were lectures and discussions preparing us for leadership at various camps. A sideline bonus was a visit to the spot where Abraham Lincoln delivered the Gettysburg Address. What an awesome feeling to stand there and think about the worth of his words! Twelve of us were assigned to Jolly Acres.

During the first two weeks, eighty 6 to 7-year-old girls arrived. Some were black, and some were white. Most came from insecure, dysfunctional homes. Six would live in my cabin. We were together night and day. We filled the twenty-four hours with Bible study, chapel worship, swimming, walks in the woods, skits, games, campfires—and short nights. By parting time we knew each other well, and the goodbyes brought tears.

The East is laden with historical places and all were new to me. That weekend, five of us staff members visited Fort McHenry at Chesapeake Bay. This was where Francis Scott Key wrote "The Star-Spangled Banner" after seeing the American flag still flying when the battle with the British subsided. In addition, we appreciated an overnight at a deaconess mother house. Delicious sweet rolls along with peace and rest were so welcome.

Session II brought six 8 to 10-year-old boys to my cabin. Typically, they were less emotional and moody; and we did more physical stuff, like hiking, fishing, and independent cook-outs. Again, our twenty-four-hour daily schedule gave us plenty of time to build rapport. They loved me, and I loved them.

During the middle of the second week, I developed mumps on one side of my neck. Some of us staff members had planned a weekend to New York, so I really prayed for a quick recovery. After two days of healing, I held my head at a tilt and went with the gang to see "The Big Apple." The Empire State Building, United Nations Building and many other city sites were new to us. In the evening, we attended a Billy Graham Rally at Yankee Stadium, along with 100,000 people. We held very tightly to each other so that we would not be lost in the biggest crowd any of us had thus far experienced. I was awed by the message and singing.

The nine and ten-year-old girls were the next group. Girls, by nature, are more cliquey and gossipy, so problems happened easily. Doing our best to help them have a happy, uplifting week made our days worthwhile. Pastor Moreland was the camp director. Throughout the eight-week summer, the staff prayed that the children would grow in their faith and love for God.

Our final staff weekend fling was to Washington, D.C., for a peek at the Capitol, Washington Monument and Lincoln Memorial. It was good to be refreshed, because twelve-year-old boys were coming next. They would demand a lot of energy, physically and psychologically. That week started with an eight-mile hike. My most troubled boy was Joe, who stole a baseball glove and kicked a boot through our cabin window. He talked about running away. I relied heavily on daily divine wisdom.

We Counselors had grown pretty close during these weeks, and parting was not fun. My favorite new friend was Effie. Baltimore was her home, but she had worked with horses and liked them a lot. I was intrigued by how her common sense, yet innocent naïve nature, could have been formed in the metropolitan setting. She, in turn, liked my Midwest accent and immediately decided she wanted to come and study on the Plains. We were soul mates.

Paul was a fun-loving pre-seminary student from West Virginia. When facing any temptation, he would utter, "Get you away from me, Satan!" This was a phrase that stuck with me. He was small in stature. By contrast, lifeguard Ed was a tall, husky, handsome black man with a personality comfortable in any situation. Another black friend was Yvonne. Her talent was humor, and she often entertained us with regaling laughter. My frequent sharing of accordion music attracted our custodian, Harry, who was an uncle to John Philip Sousa. I really enjoyed visiting with him.

Home was westward for several of us, so together we took a train to Pittsburgh and then continued via a 1940 Chevy on the Pennsylvania Turnpike to Chicago, driving almost straight through.

Back from the East, I attended the Lutheran World Federation Meeting in Minneapolis and rode from there back to South Dakota with my Aunt Thea and Merlin Hagen. We got home at 3:00 a.m. That concluded the summer.

Recalling all of this, I'm completely amazed at how I managed to always get around. I had big plans, was ready to go, and needed a ride. My folks didn't buy me a car, nor did I think of buying one myself. Arranging transportation took some miracles. Never turning away from opportunity, I even begged rides a time or two!

On this catching-a-ride theme, I'm sure I rode back and forth to Sioux Falls for college with several dozen different people. I must have had a radar system on the lookout at all times for transportation possibilities.

Chapter Fifteen

# Second Half of College

In the fall of 1957, Augustana welcomed me back. Since my freshman year in 1954, I never looked back. I knew from the word "go" that I wanted a degree. There had been wonderful friends, male and female, but none would keep me from the finish line. I registered for Psychology, Crime and Delinquency, History of Music, Church History, Speech, German, and American Literature—19 hours. An extremely heavy load!

Marilyn Thorson was again my roommate, and Pat Eggee from Humboldt, South Dakota, joined us. We three rented a basement apartment a block from campus. We took weekly turns doing basic chores, such as buying groceries, baking, cooking, and cleaning.

We dubbed ourselves "THE" Girls, forming an acronym by taking the first letter from each of our last names. We looked forward to good times! We were older, compatible, jolly, and we had marvelous sharing times. Nobody had a steady boyfriend, so we enjoyed a variety of interesting guys and gals. Healthy laughter happened often, and philosophical issues were discussed in-depth. We kept some rather erratic study hours because social life was also important. Looking back, I'm glad it was so.

During the year at home, I had disciplined myself to practice sight reading and other forms of vocal exercise using *Handel's Messiah* for my personal course. Corinne had taken a job at the bank and lived in Watertown. In the morning, when Mom and Dad would do chores, the house was quiet, so I practiced music. Thus it came to pass that God honored a desire of my heart. After I tried out for Augustana College's prestigious A Choir, I was on the call-back list for a second audition. Two weeks later, I was accepted. My September 24th diary entry reads: "Answer to prayers. I'd feared to even hope this could come true. I'm so happy and grateful." Many friends rejoiced with me. My suitor at the time even gave me a dozen roses. Participation in this choir meant an hour of practice every day, plus parts practice on my own. Singing under Dr. Arnold Ronning was sheer joy. Newfound respect on the campus wasn't hard to take either.

My lifetime connection with the Larson family of Garretson, South Dakota, was one of the by-products of this era. Ruby Larson was a classmate. I was invited for a weekend trip to her home. I was hooked! We would jam together for hours, and it was all so spontaneous and beautiful. Her brother Ray was part comedian, and her father Eddie was a jolly good fellow. The mother, Margaret, provided refreshments. This completed the perfect musical conviviality.

Other Larson farm fun included the fact that Ray had a horse named Nude, which we all rode. During a certain softball game, Ray split the back of his jeans, but kept running the bases, holding the back side together while the rest of us doubled with laughter.

*Ruby Larson played the piano. I played the accordion and my sister Corinne played the guitar. Ruby's sister, Rosella, played the saxophone, and her dad, Eddie, played the violin. Not pictured is Ruby's brother, Ray, who played banjo.*

A community rodeo was held just east of Sioux Falls. Ray and I dressed in western gear and sang "The Star-Spangled Banner" to open it.

Another special aspect of the friendship of this time was that it was shared with our parents. Larsons, Thorsons and Hagens all gathered at the Eggee's home for several Christmas or New Year's celebrations, as well as other back-and-forth good times.

In the spring of that year, Norris and I had serious discussions. We were still two cautious people. We experienced a sad parting of the ways for a while. I think we both cried separately and found it hard to concentrate on tasks at hand. However, he was at SDSU; I was back at Augustana, and we were testing our separate lives.

On January 1, 1958, I was back at college where our choir practiced six hours a day, having intermittent breaks. We did this for a week before the regular classes resumed. Difficult classical compositions, anthems, and chorales had to be mastered before going on tour. We left on January 25th for two weeks, singing fifteen concerts in Nebraska, Iowa, Minnesota, and Illinois. We wore velvet gowns and marched swiftly, in flashy style, to the risers. It was a new thrill every time. Being part of the beautiful harmonies and words praising God gave a tingle to my whole being. Standing in perfect concentration on heeled black shoes for an hour plus brought complaints from some choir members, but not from Yours Truly. She was just thankful to be there.

The trip highlight was a rehearsal in Chicago at the Hilton Hotel's Grand Ballroom, followed by performance in a concert at Orchestra Hall. That evening, we dined at Little Heidelberg, a German restaurant, where a roving violinist serenaded beside my table. This was the ultimate! A final very meaningful note to this tour was the concert back home at Grace Lutheran Church in Watertown, which my parents and Norris attended.

The rest of the semester, I continued my over-achiever frenzy. Besides class work, I continued my membership in the organizations of my first two years. I should have budgeted more time for sleep.

In June and July, I took Psych and German in summer school. A new friendship with a farm girl who lived just east of Sioux Falls was the start of an unchartered horse-lover's club. The borrowed-pony rides from when I was young, my connection with Effie, and now with Dorothy Eide, made me one of ten other girls doing horse camping.

A bachelor-type man had a horse ranch nearby, and we could rent ponies by the hour. He was flattered by having groups of college girls patronizing his horse business, and gave us good rates. What could be finer than moonlit trail rides, sleeping under the stars, and talking way into the night about girl stuff? We had devotions together. Psalm 8 became our signature. In the morning, we fried bacon and eggs for breakfast, took another ride, and then went back to the city. We all swore that this was the best weekend free time we could have. Maybe there would be sun tanning, tennis, and swimming to follow, but ponies and camping started the weekend right.

On August 13th I was back on farm duty. Norris came over one evening, and it was so good to see him. Months had gone by in our separate ways. He and Gene Erickson had been in summer school together at SDSU and were planning to go to the National Lutheran Student Association Convention in the state of Washington. I could invite a friend and go along. There would be room for four in Gene's 1955 Plymouth. WOW! What an opportunity this could be! I called Effie immediately. Four days later, she had convinced her parents and called me back. She would take the train from Maryland to South Dakota and go with us. Our parents really must have trusted the integrity of the four of us to consent to our 1,500-mile camping trip! Our culture then was not obsessed with sex, as it is today, and we all came from homes where Christian character and reputation was an honored value.

I met Effie at the train station in Watertown at 5:45 a.m. on the 21st of August. We had a picnic breakfast for two in the park and reveled in the joy of being together again. Norris had borrowed a tent from a neighbor, Vern Bergan. Norris' mother, Agnes, must have been promoting this situation as she bought a Coleman camp stove, donated some dishes, a skillet, etc., for the trip. After careful packing, we were all on our way by 5:00 p.m.

For three days we drove through South Dakota, North Dakota, Montana, Idaho, Oregon and Washington, spending nights at a roadside park, by a cemetery, and by an abandoned house lot. (To say the United States was safer then than now would be an understatement.) Norris' culinary skills were immediately impressive! We feasted on complete meals, including boiled potatoes, hamburger, and salad.

The first day, before the meetings began, we climbed 7,000 feet up Mt. Rainier and had a picnic by the snow line. Norris still regrets his carrying my jeans, which I never used anyway, in his back pack. We were all wearing shorts. I had never been on a snow-capped mountain before, and besides, I never liked being cold. That was also a harbinger of my tendency to take along more than his minimalist nature requires.

That evening, we attended the keynote address opening the convention. Follow-up sessions were based on Genesis. By the close of the second day, I really sensed spiritual growth.

I also knew that there was a flame of life—or in other words, chemistry—toward Norris. After three days, we drove home almost non-stop. We enjoyed lots of healthy discussion on the way toward the farm. Norris' ability to turn everything into a joke was a quality I enjoyed, but it didn't always fit with my naturally serious side. Effie and I each paid $25 gas money to the guys when we got home, and we parted, hating to see the end of our lark.

Chapter Sixteen

# Last Lap

During the last college semester I had room for one elective. I chose Theater. I liked the drama teacher and braved an audition for a campus play. A Watertown male student and I ended up with the leading roles.

The play was a human interest family comedy; and the work of learning the lines was overshadowed by the fun in practice and production. My Mom caught a ride to Sioux Falls to see me on the stage and gave me a big kiss of pride at the end of the show. The newspapers covered the performance. A suitor sent me roses after the play. The cast clique had follow-up get-togethers, like pheasant suppers and roller skating evenings.

Another highlight that fall was being asked to give the student message at a chapel service. The professors selected student speakers for the daily worship. Certain seniors were invited to have a turn. I saw this as an honor. John 1:12 was my chosen text, and I felt much moved by

*I played Mother Heller, a scheming mom who, along with their pop (Allen Vik from Watertown, South Dakota), interrupted our childrens' romances in "The Family Upstairs."*

God's spirit in the delivery. Compliments were many; and one pre-seminary student told me that I should never marry a minister because I would out-shine him. Thus, I wrote in my diary: "A big day in my life." The idea of women becoming ordained wouldn't be accepted until many years later, at least in the Lutheran church. Then, too, I'd seen more evangelical outreach by lay people than amongst the preachers.

On January 21, 1959, I finished my last class and felt jubilant! Mom and Dad came and got me, and I moved home for a week. I slept until ten the next morning and reveled the rest of the day in pure gratitude to God for giving me strength and ability to come that far.

The college had a graduation ceremony for mid-year graduates, but there was no history of such celebrations in my family. In my mind, Dad's knowledge loomed bigger than mine, in spite of my years on campus. In a twisted sort of way, I felt embarrassed to make anything out of my graduation. I didn't want to seem proud. Many years later, Corinne told me that the folks wondered why I skipped the finishing formalities. They would have wanted to honor it. I wish we would have communicated better.

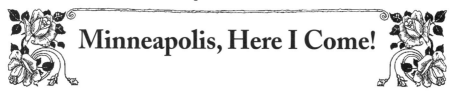

## Chapter Seventeen

# Minneapolis, Here I Come!

I'm always amazed how God goes before me and works out the details to bless my life. Now that I had earned my college diploma, I was eager to start the next chapter of my life. Now, I was an adult!

In the beginning of 1959, Mom and Dad took me to Minneapolis, Minnesota, where we spent the night with the DeGroffs. In the weave of my life, the name DeGroff appears every so often. Mrs. DeGroff, Gurena, had worked for my grandma, Mary Hagen. Her husband was John, a fat, jolly individual. They had one son, Ernie, whose family is still a third-generation connection. There had been childhood trips to this same home, and from there, Dad had taken us through the Ford Factory, to the top of the Foshay Tower, and to other Twin City sites.

My parents had a look at my school and then returned to South Dakota. We met the Principal, Mrs. Flack, and had a look at the 4th Grade class and classroom, which I would take over the following week. The current teacher, Miss Peterson, was retiring. Application, resume, and interviews had taken place prior to this. I settled in to work at Grant School.

Corinne, at this time, had a job in Minneapolis. She lived at the Minnie Woodhouse home. I moved in with her. Minnie worked nights at a factory. Corinne and I worked days. We would share the whole house, but respect each others' boundaries. She was an active widow. She was also frugal, like us. From yards of scrap material she brought home from the Munsingwear factory, we sewed underclothing to last for years.

One of the forty staff members at Grant School was a Kindergarten teacher named Trudy Heinsohn, who was looking for an apartment change. She had grown up in Canada with a family background similar to ours. The house next door to Minnie's had an upstairs apartment for rent. Trudy made her move. She had a car, so the two of us traveled to school together and became close friends for life.

In my desire to help make the world a better place, I had asked for a school in a poor section of the city. Grant more than filled the bill. I had thirty-four fourth graders. Half the class was black. There were a couple of Mexican children, one Italian, and one Jewish student. The rest were Caucasian. Early on, when I attempted to discipline a student, one of the schoolboys advised me, "Get a ruler and use it, as that is what we are used to at home; and make sure it is a strong one!" I never used one.

Fists came up easily, and nosebleeds were not uncommon. One girl's mom was a prostitute. Little Doris knew all about the business. Another student, Craig, tried to commit suicide one day by lying down in the street traffic.

Planning lessons and teaching basic curriculum plus P.E., Music, and Art filled my days. There were also field trips and the PTA. On the last day of school, the children came in Sunday-best clothes. It was a difficult, but successful, half-year.

At the Woodhouse home, I missed having access to a piano. Corinne checked on a piano ad. I walked thirty blocks and bought a piano for $235. We each also purchased a set of pots and pans and Singer sewing machines. We took knitting lessons at Dayton's. It was fun having money to spend. Towards spring, we bought sleeping bags and talked about vacation plans.

By now, some of the Augustana graduates were at the seminary, so I was not short of social visits. I spent one Sunday afternoon with an interesting male friend, but felt a little uneasy because I needed to be back on time for a date with another in the evening. Should they meet, it would not be good! I had also seen Norris briefly at Thanksgiving, Christmas, and Spring Break. The Valentine from him in February was welcome. However, as yet, there was no message from Heaven as to if, when, and with whom I should consider committing for life. I had played music, been a bridesmaid and a candle lighter, and sung for girlfriends' weddings, but remained unaffected. Norris and I saw each other a couple of times that summer. We enjoyed a good old-fashioned marshmallow roast in June and another in July.

Mom, Dad, Corinne, and I took a family trip to Uncle Harold and Aunt Judy's for the Fourth of July. They lived on a ranch by Lemmon, South Dakota. Lots of cousins were there, and we all slept in a tent. We rode horses a lot, and Harold played the guitar and sang for and with us. The door was missing on the outhouse. Harold was always up for a good time. He made a rule that whomever went to his toilet needed to take one other person along to block the doorway. This was part of the weekend entertainment.

During that same summer, some friends and I took a trip to Canada. Corinne, Marilyn, and I went by train from Minneapolis and through Michigan. I had my ukulele along, and we entertained whoever would listen. The locks on Lakes Superior and Huron were new things for us prairie girls.

Sudbury, Ontario, was Trudy's hometown. She and her parents warmly welcomed us. Sunday with them meant church, boating, swimming and canoeing. On Monday, at dawn, Trudy became the driver and tour guide as we proceeded in her car to Niagara Falls. The night light on the tumbling waters made them resplendent. The mist moistened our cheeks. The roar of the falling water made known the power in it. Camping along the way, we went to a Shakespearean play at a Theater in the Round at Stratford. This was our only sophisticated stop. We still wore shorts; however, we sat in the back of the balcony.

On to Chicago! There we visited a museum and a planetarium in one day. An overnight with Pastor and Lois Stangeland was so great.

That July I returned to the teacher mode, serving on staff for two-weeks of outreach home visits in the Plymouth Avenue area of Minneapolis. This was followed by being on staff for two weeks at Camp Knutson. This Camp was for young children who came from troubled homes in the Twin Cities. Immigrant Puerto Rican kids were much more impulsive than reserved Scandinavians.

That August, Norris came over and I was so glad to see him. But after a couple of movie dates, I had to return to Minneapolis Grant School to welcome a new class of twenty-six fourth graders. I set up an aquarium in the classroom, and the kids loved our fish. Memorable students from that year included Kirk, a mulatto child who was cute as could be and Steve, a well-behaved little blonde boy. (Memories of him triggered the naming of our second son, Steven.)

Morgan Avenue Lutheran Church was in walking distance from where we lived. I sang in the choir, worshiped there, and joined in Bible Study and fellowship. With this participation, I gained a Finnish circle of friends. They wanted me to be the organist. I consented, but also signed up for organ lessons with Miss Hutchinson at McPhail School of Music. I practiced hours on end. My instructor told me one day, "You are the most determined student I've had."

The youth leader at Morgan was a tall, healthy Air Force vet with musical talent. We were great companions for canoeing and all sorts of outings. He was a Christian man, meeting all criteria for a good life mate, but there was no chemistry between us.

I thought of all the other super guys I knew. One weekend, I was home with my folks and shared the fact that I did not know what to do about my love life. Mom's counsel was that I would never find anyone nicer than Norris. I knew we had feelings for each other, but could that compensate for the chasm of difference in music? This was a heartbreak factor for both of us. Years of prayer had led up to this point. We certainly had not simply fallen in love. It had been a sacred and nurtured, calculated thing. Maybe skills of practical living were more dependable than my dream of duets.

Our loving God arranged affairs so as to settle my frustration. Mom's brother, Ludvig, died on October 28, 1959. I was asked to sing for the funeral at Highland Church. Norris was a senior at SDSU at the time. I called him and said I was coming home. Two days later, I wrote in my diary: "Date with Norris. Had a wonderful time. I'm sure I love him, and best of all, he still loves me."

We exchanged a couple of letters, and then came Thanksgiving vacation. Scrabble, a shrimp supper at Watertown, rides, and parking ensued. One night, the battery in his 1951 dark green two-door club coupe Chrysler went dead, and we had to walk home. Big problem! I had only a half mile. He had three! (Now, I'm very ashamed that I didn't invite him to spend the night on our sofa.) It was a cold night, too, but he was undaunted; we went out the next evening, too! My best birthday gift that December 1st was the gift of knowing that Norris and I might have a future together.

With the fervor of youth, I had thought I could change my corner of the world. Several experiences with kids who lived out the social, legal and economic pressures of the ghetto convinced me that aiming for a good family of my own might be a better plan. Norris had military security clearance with the Air Force before he met me. That was his excuse for not verbalizing a lot of his intentions or dreams. When very young, I had thought that maybe I'd be a single missionary, perhaps running an orphanage or becoming a nurse. My vision did not include a Prince Charming or a wedding.

I enjoyed my work at school, but I spent every spare minute knitting a sweater for Norris. He came to Minneapolis to get it. Ha! On a lovely December 23rd evening, we went window shopping. I wore a long, tan winter coat with matching high heels and gloves. Feelings of elegance and an earned and settled peace filled my heart. Marriage seemed to be too holy a destiny to specifically discuss. Funny thing was we mostly just looked at diamonds. It must have been foremost on both our minds.

We exchanged gifts by Minnie's Christmas tree in a cozy, private atmosphere. My blue handmade sweater fit him just right! The set of *Handel's Messiah* records which Norris gave me would be listened to over and over. I went home with him to South Dakota, and there was much togetherness throughout that Christmas vacation.

The New Year dawned, and I was back in Grant School, continuing a good year with my fourth graders. This class was more manageable. With two years' experience under my belt, I was assigned a student teacher. There was comfortable camaraderie with the forty fellow teachers on the staff. Many of us had a mixture of dislike and sympathetic feelings for the principal. She was a large, buxom woman with a frail, obedient husband, and no children. She was not a problem solver. We took concerns to each other rather than to the administration.

On one of our to-and-from school rides, Trudy and I confirmed our whim to learn something new. Burying the fact that we were already busy enough, we signed up for a spring semester of Spanish classes at the University of Minnesota. At that stage in life, I could remember new words well, and it was an enjoyable course.

## Chapter Eighteen

# The Engagement

Letters were sent daily from Brookings to Minneapolis, and visa versa. For Valentine's Day weekend in February, I took a bus to SDSU in Brookings. I knew that Norris loved peanut bars, so I had made a batch and tucked them in a pretty box to present to him when we met at the station. After a tour around campus, I was introduced to a girl with whom I would spend the night. At the dorm, I put on a lovely red taffeta dress and combed my hair. I never had spent much time or money on make-up, and I didn't know what "primping" was.

We went out for halibut supper, and it felt like a special night. After lingering over dinner, the faithful Chrysler found its way to a spot behind a country schoolhouse. There, Norris whispered that he had something in the cubby hole to show me. It turned out to be the diamond I have worn ever since. He presented it to me early in the evening so that I could luxuriate in its beauty and meaning the whole night. Valentine's Day has always been special to me since that night.

Back at Grant School on Monday morning, one of the teachers noticed my new ring and declared, "No wonder you seem so magnanimous!" I went back to my room and checked in the dictionary what that exactly meant. The happiness I felt must have shown all over. That evening, I made a batch of peanut bars to share with the school staff the next day. Life seemed all in focus, and it looked pretty rosy.

*This photo was taken on the evening we were engaged, February 12, 1960, at SDSU.*

When we got home from school the next day, Minnie was waiting for us. She had decided to sell her house and move in with her son. We needed to get out within two weeks. Flexibility had been my forte, so the idea of change was not a big problem, but my concern for her was. She treasured her home. Had she been talked into something for financial reasons or convenience? There had been no mention of this heretofore. From this sudden transition, I learned a lesson I've never forgotten: One never knows completely what's under the surface in another person's mind.

A week later, we moved to an apartment a few blocks away. My dear friend, Trudy, helped move Corinne, me and our belongings in five trips with her car. We paid professionals $17 to move the piano. It held its tune, and Mrs. Sherman made room for it and enjoyed the music. So, now, we had a new landlady friend.

## Chapter Nineteen

# Our Wedding
## — 1960 —

Norris and I had started dating in August of 1956. Now it was April of 1960. We had shared over 100 dates! Yes, it took us a long time, but a roast cooked in a crock pot is more tender. Our love was now perfect!

I initiated my new Singer by sewing trousseau items. I went to the library and checked out books on marriage and weddings. The U.S. Postal Service continued to carry our daily letters. I was impressed with Norris' thoughtful writing in neat penmanship.

On the Thursday before Easter, I went to Watertown by bus. Norris met me there. Then, for the first time in our four-year saga, he took me to rural Florence. We had supper at his family home. It, too, was very neat! I was warmly welcomed, yet I decided that the household tone was definitely more hustled than that in the home where I was raised. My parents' home had slightly more cluttered warmth about it. Perfection and time were not as ruling. This was the beginning of a life-time of blending, respecting, gaining from and uniting the background differences of two young people from the same neighborhood.

After Easter, Norris began his student teaching in Webster. We actually started talking about a summer wedding. I wished for a ceremony on the lawn; he didn't object. Pastor Chris Christianson would officiate. Saturday, June 26th was set as the date. This long-term relationship was really making progress!

We went together to Norris' grandfather Karl Wilhelm (Willie) Larson's 90th birthday in Waubay, South Dakota. This was my first exposure to the music and dancing which accompanies Larson family celebrations, and I really liked it. Soon after that, the Hagen family was invited to the Meland's home for supper, and a lasting two-family connection was sealed.

Being mature enough to know we couldn't live on love, we methodically applied and interviewed for teaching jobs for both of us. I resigned from the Minneapolis School System. We looked at Clarkfield, Minnesota, and Doland, South

Dakota, but ended up signing contracts for New Effington, South Dakota. I went from $4,300 salary to $3,300.

School duties continued, but nuptial planning was heavily interspersed. This event would be once-in-a-lifetime. I approached it with fervor. My wedding gown choice was easy. I saw a ballerina length dress in Schaffer's window in Minneapolis. It fit, and I bought it.

Someone who planned a wedding and canceled it advertised two attendant's dresses at a reasonable price. Trudy and Corinne went with me to try them on. They fit. One was blue and one was yellow, so these would be my colors. I sewed a blue lace flower-girl dress to match for Becky Meland, Norris' five-year-old niece.

I sewed aprons for the reception waitresses. A neighbor and friend, Mabelle Nelson, would make the cake. Invitations were ordered. My Mom was very supportive and seemed to vicariously enjoy the fuss she must have missed out on at her own wedding. On weekend trips to the farm, I spruced up the lawn, pruned trees, seeded grass, fought weeds, bought and painted a trellis, and made a yard figurine. My spiritual foundation was built at home, and unless we had a rain storm on June 26th, matrimony would take place on home turf.

Five Augustana classmates who were also working in Minneapolis surprised me one evening with a bridal shower. This was the extent of my showers.

On June 5th, Norris graduated from SDSU with a degree in Vocational Agriculture and Science. I gave him a 35mm slide camera and felt very proud of him.

Six of my 4th Grade girls from Minnesota would come to South Dakota and sing at our wedding, so I practiced with them. I sewed a straight blue linen dress for going away and a set of twin shirts for Norris and me. The shirts had a duck print pattern, and we would wear them on his birthday, the 27th, when he would turn twenty-nine.

Thursday, June 16th, was the last day of my Minneapolis school experience. My tired body attended the end-of-the year duties and parties, but my mind was sometimes elsewhere. Norris and his mom and dad came with a small U-Haul trailer and moved me to South Dakota. En route, a rain shower threatened, and Norris wisely stopped and bought a tarp to cover my worldly goods, especially the piano. We had rented a small three-room house in New Effington for $25 per month, so we unloaded my things there.

On Monday, we went to Watertown and shopped for furniture. The next day, we made the decision and purchased a brown three-piece corner davenport, a kitchen table and chair set, a desk and bedroom set—all new. A day in New Effington got the home and yard all in order, and the rest of the week was spent on wedding preparations at the home farm.

Trudy and I made the corsages on Saturday evening. LeRoy Bergan would take slides, and the Gray Studio from Watertown would take black-and-white pictures. The album would contain eight pages of 4.5x6.5-inch photos. Open-air seating was set up with chairs from St. Pauli and Goodhue churches.

A long race was winding down. Like in a movie, I reflected upon my life thus far. This would be my last night as a single person. I knew that I had prayed much about the coming commitment, and I felt all at peace, so I slept soundly. God's guiding grace would be upon us. Morning brought clear, sunny weather. Three hundred guests assembled to witness our vows.

The ceremony was at two o'clock. Twenty minutes before starting time, someone told me that I'd better get ready. I had no special hair set. I just slipped on my dress, put on my veil and heels, and walked with my Dad down the aisle. The homemade altar had a picture of Christ on it and was decked at the sides with yellow and blue daisy bouquets. My friend, Connie Beck, played the piano from the vine-covered porch. Ray Larson sang the musical version of 1st Corinthians 13.

Former roommate, Pat Eggee, had called me from Colorado that morning and told me not to worry about all the details going wrong or right, but just to concentrate on becoming husband and wife. Good advice. It was an awesome, holy moment—to begin a life together. Like a switch had been flipped, I felt calm and at ease in beginning this new life.

*Our wedding party. Left to right: Friend Trudy Ender, my sister Corinne, Norris' niece Becky Meland, the bride and groom, and Norris' brothers Arvid and Gerald.*

The temperature rose to ninety-five degrees, but neighbors, friends and relatives honored the occasion with their presence. Norris and I received hand shakes, some hugs, and congratulations from all. A big picnic-on-the-lawn reception followed, and we were the excited social butterflies, walking around and chatting with everyone. I seem to remember that we served ham sandwiches, cake, and coffee. My two aunts, Mable Ihlen and Thea Hagen, poured the coffee from Mom's silver service.

## Wedding Costs:

- My wedding dress was $100.
- The attendant dresses were $60 total.
- The going away dress was $17.
- Norris' suit was $50.
- My engagement ring and wedding band was $192.
- Norris' wedding band was $20.
- The marriage license was $2.50.
- The preacher was $10.
- The invitations and wedding book were $20.40.

## Chapter Twenty

# Honeymoon

The custom in that time was to leave for the honeymoon right after the lunch. Norris now had a different car. Our blue and white '57 Ford had been decked with shaving cream and streamers and was blocked up so that we could not move the wheels. We were showered with rice upon entering the car. After moments of merry making and more well wishes, friends freed the car and sent us on our way.

I could hardly believe we had come this far. I think that we felt as if we had been on a long marathon and finally won the Olympic gold. We were eager to begin our first chapter together as husband and wife.

By the time we arrived in Aberdeen, South Dakota, rain was descending, so we swung into Pride Motel and were totally happy just to be alone. Norris' cousin, Delores Gulbraa, and my aunt, Clara Ronning, lived near each other in Watertown. They had engineered the packing of a lunch box. They and other loved ones had included picnic items with funny little notes attached. Our first meal, and many to follow, came from that box. It's still our only picnic box.

Sexual love had not been scattered and wasted along the way, so the gift of virginity was shared the first night. I firmly believe that moral purity is in accordance

*Norris and I as newlyweds in new shirts, looking forward to being together for a lifetime.*

with God's plan for marital happiness. He blesses such a union and makes it strong.

The next morning was Norris' 29th birthday. Norris opened his gift and put on the shirt. I took mine out and put it on as well. We looked sharp!

After we cleaned up the rice from our car, it was noon. We ate, and then headed to Montana. I was impressed with how well Norris knew roads and maps. I could just relax and ride at his side.

We arrived at Norris' Uncle Ed and Aunt Kaia Larson's place in Sunburst, Montana, by the second evening. They were gracious hosts. Seeing oil fields, strip farming, and visiting their daughter, Kathryn and family, filled the day.

During the next six days we totally enjoyed each other amidst the scenery of Glacier, Yellowstone, and Grand Teton National Parks. The tarp Norris had purchased earlier to save my piano from the rain served as a make-shift tent as we camped under the stars most nights. Norris captured the beauty of Old Faithful and Harney Peak with his new camera. He set the timer so that we could both be on the pictures. Later, people asked us which photographer we took along on our honeymoon.

*Norris and I enjoyed the natural beauty and wildlife of Glacier National Park on our honeymoon, early July 1960.*

## Chapter Twenty-One

# Our First Home

Our honeymoon trip ended on July 6th. Upon our return, we picked up our wedding gifts from Mom and Dad's house and traveled to our first home in New Effington, South Dakota.

Designated helpers had opened and displayed gifts at our wedding, but we had taken only a brief peek at them before we left on our honeymoon. Now, we were able to see and touch all of the nice new things for our home, and we felt a sense of gratitude as we found a place for each gift. We also enjoyed reading the cards with loved ones' heartfelt wishes. Norris was handy at setting up book shelves and lamps, hanging pictures, and doing fix-it jobs, so we were soon all organized. (Good thing, as we've repeated the process nine times since!)

Our home was a small wooden house located two blocks from the school. We were content, even though it had just three rooms: a kitchen, a dining room large enough to accommodate my piano, and our tiny bedroom, which had no door. Norris hung a curtain as a substitute. Was there a bathroom? Kind of. Norris hung a rod and a curtain in one corner and, thereby, created a make-shift shower. Rent was $25 a month, and so was our grocery bill at a local store, which we paid at the end of each month.

*Our first house in New Effington, South Dakota, an accommodation of love.*

Since both Norris and I were over-achievers in our own styles, we budgeted little together time. My calendar was booked with requests for solos, accompaniment, piano lessons, and other forms of leadership. Norris was under an eleven-month school contract teaching Agriculture and Science. Despite all this, we managed to maintain our involvement with our two sets of family relatives. Most weekends, we drove the eighty miles home to the Hagens and Melands. Norris helped both his dad and my dad on the farms. I did laundry, using the washing machine at either home. When staying at the Meland's I liked the fresh sheets and starched pillow cases Agnes had on our bed.

How well I recall someone telling us, as they shook our hands after the wedding, that the first ten years would be the hardest. As a new bride, I was appalled at the comment, and thought that they were crazy. In retrospect, I understand. Many adjustments would have to be made.

One autumn Saturday, we did not go to the farm. Norris came home from school and walked through the garden, which had been planted by our predecessors. He commented, as he came in with a couple of ripe tomatoes, "Too bad we couldn't have some like this in winter."

I jumped to the conclusion that he expected me to can tomatoes on Saturday night. I didn't know how to can tomatoes any day! I announced my refusal. Later, we regretted the whole conversation.

On another day, Norris came home for lunch at noon and proceeded to go through the whole of our little house and push absolutely shut every single drawer! I hadn't even realized that my method of shutting drawers was so different from his. I had a habit of just shoving them, not noting if they were closed tight or not. Now, I saw how they were supposed to be shut. Thus began my training to be neat and tidy.

At choir practice one fall evening, I had so much fun singing that I didn't want it to end; so I invited some of the group to our house for more fun. When we got there, we played my piano in our dining room and sang to our hearts' content. Norris was "asleep" in our curtained-off bedroom, and he was psyched up for a 5:00 a.m. rising to go duck hunting. I had no brothers and didn't know anything about the importance of a pre-dawn departure for duck hunting. My Dad never did that. The serendipitous music fest, which had been common in my pre-marital background, was unheard of in his. Consequently, this was an upsetting moment. After some discussion (Norris) and some pouting (me), the need for more controlled planning was accepted. We agreed to be more considerate of each other.

Now, when I sign wedding cards, I always write this counsel: "Be good to each other."

## Chapter Twenty-Two

# New Effington Life

On August 29, 1960, I began my school year with eleven first graders and thirteen second graders. They were all so cute, and I loved them dearly. I planned and did extra things to make it a very good year. Many of the parents were only a few years older than me, so good friendships were formed through school contact.

I'll always remember the first Teacher's Institute for the Roberts County School personnel. A speaker's closing verse was: *I strove to reach the highest peak. I climbed the highest steeple. But Jesus said, 'Go down again; I dwell amongst the people.'* That has been my life's motto: to do my best to God's glory with whatever group of people I dwell.

Norris taught Ag and Science, was Advisor to the Future Farmers of America (FFA) club, conducted adult classes, and seemed ever busy. He joined a weekly bowling team. There were lots of lakes and sloughs nearby, so Norris found fishing and hunting friends immediately.

We were a novel young couple in this friendly little town and, as such, we were invited here and there by young and old.

Corinne was in college in Brookings that year, so we had a couple of college trips back to SDSU and Augustana. St. Pauli still had its annual lutefisk supper. That, and many other special events in the Wallace and Florence communities, kept our lives on a merry-go-round. Since both Norris and I came from small families, a long tradition of being together with family at Christmas started that year.

That winter, before contract time would arrive, we wrote to the Mission Board of our church, asking whether or not our talents could be used somewhere else in the world. Both of us were young and adventurous, and we made a decision that would impact our lives forever. A letter came back, inquiring if we were interested in long or short-term assignment. What was the right thing? I remember crying, praying, rejoicing, and wondering all at the same time. God seemed very near.

Before moving into our first home, we had asked the owner for a rental contract so that we would be assured of at least one school year's stay. He said not to worry about that; he was not planning on selling. However, in mid-January, we were given one week's notice to move! This was a jolt.

How should we handle this, especially since this little town did not have many houses from which to choose? Maybe there was method in this madness. Two blocks away was another small house we could rent for $25 a month. We made the deal.

We spent three hours packing on Friday night after school. On Saturday, at 9:00 a.m., two of the first homeowner's sons came with a truck to help us move. Two other neighbors joined us. This had to be a coordinated house switch. The people moving into our first house were the same couple moving out of the house to which we were going! I guess God provides for His children in different ways. The trucks met each other along the three-block route.

By 11:30 a.m., we were moved. The temperature was negative fifiteen degrees. The old oil burner (which we had inherited from Uncle Albert Meland) had to be installed and lit immediately. We decided we could be love bugs in this house just as well as in the other. Looking at the positive side, we had shelter without too much commotion. In a couple of days, we had everything put away for comfortable living again.

## Chapter Twenty-Three

# Baby on the Way!

In early February 1961, I started feeling generally down. I kept going to school, in spite of nausea. I felt tired, and put in some twelve-hour nights of sleep. I lost my appetite. Norris went to our local grocery store to buy some 7-Up for me. We thought maybe the flu was going around. Clifford Peterson, the store owner, had a little girl named Cleo who was playing in the aisle. Clifford nodded at her and said to Norris, "That's what could be the problem."

My nose was plugged solid for a week. We went to a doctor in Aberdeen, and he drained my sinuses. Norris felt sorry for me. We went shopping and bought a lovely spring suit—blue with a blue fake fur collar. I would proudly wear it for Easter.

We should have suspected pregnancy. Since a family with many children lived by our first house, people had warned us that we were living on "Fertile Street!"

On another Saturday in March, we went to a doctor in Watertown and I took what was called a "frog test." A letter arrived three days later, indicating that we would become parents in the fall, God willing. This was sooner than we had planned, but it would be okay. Our grocer would be proven right.

April, for school personnel, is always decision time regarding next year. Our thoughts of any foreign mission venture would now be put on hold. Single people, or a two-year teacher couple, were needed on an island called Papua New Guinea, but now, we would be a family. Therefore, a six-year commitment would have to be considered. Norris signed the contract for a second year at New Effington. I did not. Rather, by mid-March, I was studying about pregnancy and babies, a totally new subject for both of us.

School and social pace did not lessen. A Rumpelstiltskin operetta was in the making for 1st through 6th Grades. I would accompany it. I worked with the mothers to make costumes, and with the teachers to make the stage sets. Norris had FFA trips, banquets and contests to plan. May 31st was the last day of that school year.

Back on April 1st, when we were home for a weekend, I had told my Mom, Dad and Corinne about the conceived baby. It would be the first grandchild for my folks. Norris had shared the news with his parents, who already had three grandchildren.

In May, I began wearing maternity clothes, some homemade, some purchased. Having done laundry at our parents' for a year, we now bought a used Maytag wringer-style washing machine. This was a necessity with the long range plan for a baby in the house; there were no throw-away diapers. We also purchased our first television that spring.

Chapter Twenty-Four

# Second Honeymoon

June seemed a proper time to take a good vacation. I was feeling fine by then. We drove first to Minneapolis and visited friends there and then drove to Wisconsin. After a stop at Storybook Gardens in the Wisconsin Dells area, I would next meet Norris' Aunt Clara and Uncle Alex, Aunt Bessie and Uncle Albert, as well as several of Norris' cousins and their families. They all lived in Beloit, Wisconsin. Milwaukee was our next stop. Norris' Dad had ten sisters. Some were deceased by now, but the living ones became my friends through a gathering at Clara and Alex's cabin.

In Chicago, we toured the Shedd Aquarium, a planetarium, and the Museum of Science and Industry. Pastor Ken and Lois Stangeland now had a congregation there, and a visit with them was very fun.

It was new for both of us to see southeast states. We passed through Illinois, Indiana, and Kentucky. We stopped at Abe Lincoln's birthplace and marveled again at American democracy by which folks of such humble background could rise to the Presidency. The place where Stephen Foster wrote "My Old Kentucky Home" and many other songs was a delightful stop for me.

In Tennessee, we had a conversation with a Smoky Mountain man. He was sitting in a rocker on his crude cabin porch. There was no more work in the mines for him, but he swore that he would not "go to a city and live on top of all those other people."

We had our camp stove, picnic box, sleeping bags and tarp tent along on this adventure, too, so we found neat spots to camp as we went along. As parents-to-be, we sometimes opted for a motel room, as it seemed a wiser choice.

Along the way in Georgia, we noted the pretty peach orchards. We went to a Southern Baptist church service in the citrus-growing area near Florida. We enjoyed taking a boat ride on Silver Springs Lake, seeing cypress trees, and watching a water-ski show. Next, we swam in the Atlantic Ocean off Florida and, while on the beach, fried some chicken and had a nice supper. It was in Alabama where

I saw my first beautiful magnolia tree. Something not so beautiful and, in fact, very ugly, was the sign that labeled the nearby restroom, "white only." We were in Selma, Alabama, where race riots broke out later. The now-famous Rosa Parks made history in that city by refusing to give up her seat to a white person on the bus.

Our drive through Mississippi, Louisiana, and Arkansas followed the hills and curves, with lots of trees and foliage; again, a contrast to the Dakotas. Finally, we headed northward through the central United States. After two weeks away, we were back at the Meland-Hagen home base, but not for long.

Norris had been asked to represent Zion congregation in New Effington at the annual South Dakota Synod Conference of the American Lutheran Church, to be held in Sioux Falls. He attended meetings; I relaxed by shopping, sunbathing, and reading. I've always enjoyed and appreciated good books as a simple, convenient, and favorite hobby.

Summer came, and we were happy and cozy in our little abode. I bought flannel and sewed layette items, as the baby exercised within. Receiving blankets, kimonos, and bassinet lining were all homemade. I crocheted a baby sweater and booties for "?." Doctor appointments revealed that all was going well, and we thanked God for that.

I wouldn't be teaching, but local people thought I should keep busy anyway, so I became a Campfire Girl leader. The girls were high school age, polite and eager, so I had a pleasant role. Manuals were studied, outings planned, and our meetings were interesting.

At the end of August, Norris began his second year on the school staff. He had now purchased and repaired a used Cushman scooter and loved riding it to and from school. I felt very left out, as kids and buses headed to their classrooms that fall. I used my time to develop culinary skills. I baked all the bread we ate. Norris always loved desserts, so making them took some of my time. Newlyweds, Carol and Kirk Hansen, moved in next door to us in an equally small house. He was a teacher; she a homemaker. I was glad to have her as a young friend.

## Chapter Twenty-Five

# Nathan Arrives
## — 1961 —

On the evening of Sunday, October 1st, we went with friends to a missionary program in Peever, South Dakota. I felt a couple of twinge-like cramps. My due date was already past and, since I had never delivered before, I didn't know what to expect. Our hospital and doctor were in Sisseton, eighteen miles from our home in New Effington.

We went home and went to bed. The start of the new generation within me continued pressing to be born. Shortly after midnight, I woke Norris. When Norris realized that we might have to leave soon, he sprung out of bed, and went out into the night in a shed-cleaning frenzy.

We had stored some of our possessions in a shed by our house. Both the house and the shed were owned by a farmer who had intended—without our realizing it—to store soybeans in this space. He had called earlier that day stating his plans. Norris, whose subconscious motto from childhood on was to never bother anyone, wanted that shed ready before the baby arrived.

Fortunately, my nature was quite unflappable and I trusted that this was a non-urgent time. When Norris finished cleaning out the shed, we drove to the Sisseton Hospital.

Norris would miss school that Monday to stay with me. By noon, pains were more frequent. A pregnant Native American woman, who had already birthed many babies, was waiting nearby. She delivered her twelve-pounder with ease! The Bible often mentions the labor pains of women, so I had opted to experience the natural childbirth process. I had done exercises and read about what to do. I knew there would be no quick fix.

I never had a brother, but had secretly thought that starting our family with a boy would be nice. Hunting season starts in October, so Norris had conjectured how fun it would be to have a son as a hunting companion. Husbands or family were not allowed in the delivery room in those days, and that was just fine with me. Forceps were used to get the infant's head properly aligned. Finally, at 8:30

p.m. on October 2nd, my doctor held our newborn in his hands and gave him a gentle slap, which stimulated a cry. "It's a boy!" he declared.

I was given some injections prior to repair after the birth, but I was totally alert to welcome our child. What an awesome moment! Psalm 103:1 flooded my mind and stayed there for days: *Bless the LORD, O my soul, And all that is within me, bless His holy name.* I had been given the privilege of bearing a new eight pound, fifteen ounce untarnished human being! I prayed that he, too, would always bless the Lord all his life.

Back in the hospital room, Norris and I had devotions together and rejoiced in a healthy gift. Norris went back to New Effington to prepare for school the next day. He would be happy to pass out a few cigars with the blue wrapper marked, "It's a boy!" I'm sure that Norris floated on air through the tasks of the day as he shared the news with everyone. He called our parents, who also offered congratulations and prayers of thanks.

The first name Nathan—beginning with the initial N, like Norris—and the middle name Larry—initial L, like Lawrence—had been selected and agreed upon ahead of time. The dictionary definition of Nathanial was "gift from God." That was too long a name, so we would use Nathan, which still meant the same.

Norris told my Dad that our baby looked just like him—he had no hair! I never saw my Dad with hair, except around the edge of his head. Unfortunately, when in his twenties, Nathan would lose his hair; so the announcement held true. (Fortunately, Nathan overcame the loss. His self-esteem was not dependent upon hair.) Nathan also has hands very much like my Dad's. He has the same gentle and thoughtful nature. In respect for land and the Lord, they are also alike. So Norris' announcement, to some extent, was a prophecy.

After school, my baby's dad came with a half-dozen red roses for me. We both could hold our son. I had been coached on breast feeding, and I nursed him during this first day. My stitches hurt, but life was good.

On the next day, the four grandparents came for a first visit. By day three, lots of New Effington friends joined the welcoming party. Helen Leen, who lived across the street from our home, was a special guest. She became my baby advisor. She had a one-year-old girl and a seventh-grade son. She could see the light, funny side of most anything and I look back on her as my plain-clothes angel for that year of my life.

Friday was homecoming back at our school. We paid the doctor and hospital $200 and Norris and I rode home in our Ford to watch the parade. It felt wonderful to be thin again! I wore a new regular sized red dress for the occasion. By now, we knew all the Kindergarten through 12th Grade students, and our lives were intertwined with their families.

After the parade, we returned to Sisseton and brought our baby home. That night, we faced a challenge. Breast feeding was new, and I was very tired. Norris, being the problem-solver type, was sympathetic, but unable to help. Morning came, and he went goose hunting.

The next day was Sunday. Norris went to church and Sunday School and then went out to look for more geese. Baby and I just solved our own problems and reveled in our private haven.

By Monday, the teachers couldn't wait any longer to see me and our treasure. So, after school, they came to our home with gifts. They were mothers, also, and very nice people who could truly rejoice with me. Norris kept busy with FFA, ballgames, etc. By day nine, I dressed up and walked uptown for groceries, then stopped at Helen's for coffee.

That Thursday and Friday, Norris went to the South Dakota Education Association conference in Huron, so Nathan and I were in charge of the home front. Helen came over several times. We watched television, had coffee, and shared baby talk. Campfire Girls and past students started stopping in with gifts and well wishes. Norris came home with a rattle for Nathan and a little decorative spinning wheel for me. On Saturday morning he washed clothes. In the afternoon he went hunting. That weekend, Nathan was almost two weeks old. The weather was grand. We took him along to church, where he slept peacefully. That afternoon, we went to Sica Hollow State Park near Sisseton for a chicken supper picnic with Helen and her husband, Curtis.

On Monday, we hired a babysitter for the first time. Mildred Fossom was an older neighbor two doors away. She was warm and motherly. Her husband and son were violinists, and we'd had many good times in their home. Mildred would keep Nathan while I went to an American Lutheran Church Women (ALCW) workshop at Milbank. On Tuesday, we went to Forman, North Dakota with Carol and Kirk Hansen to their hometown lutefisk supper. This time we took Nathan along and he was good, even if he didn't get any fish to eat!

Baby cards seemed to come from all directions. I had seventy-five posted around the double doorway arch, which was above Nathan's bassinet. Mothers of my last year's class organized a baby shower and gave me many nice gifts. Now I could make big decisions daily as to what new outfit to put on my baby.

The first trip back to our parental homes turned into a real see-the-baby weekend. Relatives, old and young, showed up. From then on, our routine was no routine. Usual commitments and activities resumed at a before-kid pace. Only the kid was now included. That Halloween brought nearly 100 trick-or-treaters to our door!

Nathan got used to our sharing him with people at organizational meetings or casual get-togethers. While driving back to New Effington from weekends at home, we often stopped in Waubay to visit Norris' grandparents, Willie and Anna Larson. They enjoyed seeing the smiles of their great-grandson.

November 11th became a special day: Nathan's baptism. His Aunt Corinne and Uncle Gerald were sponsors. They and the grandparents came to the worship service at Zion Lutheran Church in New Effington. Pastor Vern Severson officiated and later joined the family for a scalloped potatoes dinner in our little house.

Thanksgiving came, and all the Dales filled Aunt Clara's home. My dear friend, Trudy, joined us. On Christmas day, the same gang, minus Trudy, was at my Mom and Dad's home. Three miles away, we also celebrated with the Melands. There was no time to be pensive. I was maybe lonely, but not often alone.

*Norris and I were proud new parents with baby Nathan Larry Meland at my folk's home for a visit.*

Chapter Twenty-Six

# Off to New Guinea
## — 1962 —

The new year of 1962 arrived, and I wondered just what surprises it held. Based on Biblical verses like James 2:21-26, Matthew 28:18-20, and Genesis 12:2 we had made ourselves available for full time Christian service, if the Lord could use us. It seemed He could. The first surprise seemed momentous! We were invited to interview with the American Lutheran Church Mission Board in Minneapolis on January 22nd. Next, we received a letter stating that we were approved as candidates and that Papua New Guinea could use our talents. Norris' background in agriculture and education would fill a need. After prayerful consideration, we agreed to start making plans to leave.

I'm not sure just when we told our parents about this. Neither set tried to stop us. Dad said that I'd be safe with Norris. Mom would miss Nathan. Norris' Mom said she had always wished to do something similar herself.

On April 13th I went to Milbank for the spring ALCW Convention. I sang Psalm 8 for their special music. On that same afternoon, Norris and I took our first immunizations in a series of shots for going overseas (for small pox, typhus, and typhoid). A week later, we took pictures and got registered at the Clerk of Courts for passports to New Guinea. I shopped for, and sewed, basic clothes for Nathan for the next six years. We started packing personal items into two fifty-gallon jam barrels, bought from Old Home Bakery in Watertown. We also had a trunk and a footlocker.

The High League put on two Easter dramas that spring at the school. Pastor Severson and I directed them. I had also done some substitute teaching that year and was asked to do a three-week Kindergarten course in May, which I did. The mix of these responsibilities, plus regular end-of-the-year school activities and preparing for long-term overseas work, required all the stamina we could muster. The depth and speed of our rooting in New Effington began to show. My guest book shows that we had hosted ninety-two visitors in our little house.

People realized we were leaving. Suppers, parties, and invitations of many sorts started happening. Tearful goodbyes accompanied.

On June 1st, we moved our entire belongings home in a 1937 International truck that Norris had bought for $100, repaired, and painted. While we were unloading boxes, Nathan crawled for the first time. We were at Mom and Dad's house and it was a fun moment.

We sold some furniture. Mom Meland kindly vacated one upstairs room for us to store the rest of our things. We then went on to Decorah, Iowa, for a missionary conference. We heard lots of stories about great stewards, met enthusiastic people who were home on furlough, and learned much from presentations by the Mission Department. Norris and I were much in love with each other, our Lord, and our life. Based on the suggestions of furloughing missionaries we had met, we bought a gas engine Maytag washing machine and had it shipped straight from Decorah to New Guinea.

June 24th was the date of our commissioning service at Goodhue Church of rural Florence. As plans fell into place, I couldn't imagine what it would be like in just six months when we would celebrate our first Christmas in Papua New Guinea. Sixty people gathered afterward for dinner at Agnes and Art Meland's home. Two days later, on June 26th, my aunts, Mable and Irene, hosted a two-year wedding anniversary party in our honor. Corinne bought our blue and white Ford.

On July 2nd, our four parents took us to the Watertown Airport for our 10:15 a.m. departure. No one talked much; all hearts were heavy. Looking back, our parents were wonderfully supportive, even if the pain of separation was poignant. Uncle Ingeman Bergh and his daughter, Delores Gulbraa, my Aunt Clara Ronning, and her daughter Darlene, came to see us off. Ingeman had arranged for newspaper coverage. He also tucked the Bible verse, "Underneath are the everlasting arms," along with some dollars into Norris' hand. That was an especially comforting gesture.

Heretofore, I'd only been in a Cessna one-engine plane for a brief ride over Lake Kampeska in Watertown years before. A small plane took us to Minneapolis and from there we connected to a 707 jet for Salt Lake City, San Francisco, Honolulu, Fiji, and Australia. After nineteen hours in the air, we landed at Sydney.

I had only a small purse and diaper bag with us. At the Sydney Airport, the airlines discovered that Nathan's suitcase had been left in San Francisco! The trip schedule included an overnight in Sydney, thankfully. We went immediately to the hotel. I pinned a small towel around Nathan, and we made ourselves at home while Norris went shopping in the infant department of a large store. His comment upon returning was, "Wow! You should hear how these people talk!" My calm response was, "Surely, they speak English." Neither of us had realized the degree of difference between British English and the English spoken in America. Norris had asked for diapers, and a clerk finally figured out that he wanted "nappies." He also thought that Nathan would need a sweater. One clerk explained to the other, "He's a Yankee. He means a pull-over." So that's how Nathan acquired part of a new wardrobe in Sydney. That evening, his suitcase was delivered.

The next morning, we set out to see a bit of the city in one day. We paid for a guided tour. My most vivid memory is all the red tile roofs. It seemed cold in the southern hemisphere winter. That evening, we were airborne again with Ansett Airlines. This time we had twelve hours to fly to our destination, the Lutheran Mission headquarters in Lae, Papua New Guinea.

Dr. John Kuder, president of the Lutheran Mission New Guinea, and other staff members met and welcomed us. We would stay at the guest house for a week of orientation. Our first breakfast included cereal and paw paw, which is known in the United States as papaya. The climate at the coast of this tropical island is warm and moist: ninety degrees in day hours; skin temperature at night. The sheets smelled and felt damp and clammy. The evening meal was called "tea,"

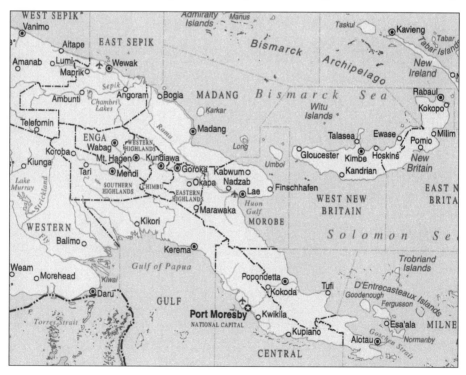

never "supper." Supper was a snack you eat before going to bed. We were invited to various homes to get acquainted with other staff members.

We were shown some local schools. There was paperwork to fill out and there were lectures to attend. Some local girls took care of Nathan. The variety of foliage and vegetation growing everywhere amazed me, especially the lovely flowers. We visited a coconut plantation where boys could learn agriculture.

The next step was going to Madang. We waited from 8:00 a.m. until 4:00 p.m. for the clouds to lift so that we could fly there by Cessna. Instead, we returned to the guest house just in time for tea. We had been assigned to work at a station in the mountains, but it surely was taking a long time to get there! We had to learn a lot about patience. The next day, we got to Madang. We had a look at the Mission Hospital called Yagaum, whose services we would later need, and the Supply House, from which all our groceries would be ordered. We took a boat ride across the bay to Graget Island. I didn't know then that nearby, up the coast, there lived a little girl whom we would bring with us to America ten years later.

Chapter Twenty-Seven

# Kitip School Assignment

On July 18th, we flew to an Australian government station called Banz, landing on a grass airstrip. Australian teacher, Karl Kirsch, whom we would replace, met us there. Shirley Guse, a single Australian teacher, was along with him and would stay on staff and live with us. We proceeded in the station's Land Rover. This was a British-made four wheel drive, two-door vehicle with a canvas canopy over the box.

We drove twenty-six miles on a single-lane gravel road, which swerved between mountains and crossed little rivers via small wooden bridges. Shirley, Karl, Nathan and I sat in the cab. Norris rode in the back. Finally, we were at our assigned destination.

The Evangelical Lutheran Church of New Guinea (ELCONG) had been founded in 1886 at the coast by a German missionary, Johann Flierl. He had to learn the language and the ways of the people before he could share the gospel. After thirteen years, the first baptism took place, and Finschhafen became the first established Lutheran Mission Station.

Later, other missionaries joined him in his efforts. Numerous stations were established, extending across the territory into the Western Highlands. This culture did everything by tribe: communal decision-making. Conversion to Christianity was approved the same way. Since those early days, there had been many joyous occasions of first baptisms and beginning new congregations. We seemed to be part of the harvest as we dealt with individual Christian believers.

Missionaries served in churches, schools, hospitals and support roles. We were assigned to Kotna Station at the Kitip School. Kitip, in the local language, meant "elbow," inferring that students should walk at the side of their teacher.

There were eight young boys enrolled in two classes at this boarding school. They welcomed us with a skit, showing the value of mission schools bringing the light of Jesus' salvation to otherwise dark lives. They were good at drama and played with gusto.

We were then shown to our home. The house was a single-level wood structure with three bedrooms, designed to accommodate whichever family was assigned there. This was a big change from our mini (three rooms—total) house in New Effington! Here, we were at 5,000 feet altitude. The temps were a constant range from forty-five to eighty degrees Fahrenheit. Our house was more like an American lake cabin, in that there was no insulation, only louvers for windows and a galvanized steel roof. Our water supply came from rain collected off the roof into a thousand-gallon tank by the house, using gravity's flow to fill sinks and toilet. Basic furniture, dishes, kitchen ware and bedding were supplied, and used by the family living there.

Heidi was Karl's wife, a sweet twenty-eight-year-old lady of East German background. Her father had been a prisoner of war in Russia. She came to New Guinea as a single. Her first husband had been killed by the Japanese in World War II. She proudly showed us the kitchen. The cupboards had been freshly painted for our coming. Every door was a different color: blue, peach and green with yellow framing. The curtains were a multi-colored print. This was definitely a European décor, meant to be warm and friendly.

After two weeks, Karl and Heidi would leave for another station, and we would be in charge of Kitip. Before his last day, Karl took us to Mt. Hagen, a small business town of 4,000, established by Australian and other ex-patriots (people not native to the country). This was twenty-five miles in the opposite direction from Banz.

In preparing to go, Karl talked fondly about how good it would be to buy and eat a chocolate candy bar and even an ice cream cone. I wondered if we would get to the point where such a small luxury would seem like a big deal.

The school boys had a farewell for Karl the night before his leaving. Everyone wept. We realized what a good impact he had made on their young lives.

Shirley was the first of several "short term" single teachers who would, over the years, live with us. She and Norris would teach 4th and 5th Grades.

## Chapter Twenty-Eight

# New Tasks Begin

The tribal people in the Western Highlands of New Guinea were Stone Age illiterate. Australia was designated by the United Nations to develop New Guinea as a trust territory after World War II.

A Mission, comprised of the Lutheran Church from Germany, the Lutheran Church from Australia, and the American Lutheran Church from the United States developed a plan to build up New Guinea, working with the Australian government.

Native teachers from the coast came to the Highlands and taught 1st, 2nd, and 3rd Grades in the villages. There were eight isolated mission stations in our district. There were two distinct types of schools: 1) the early elementary village schools, and 2) a more advanced District education center, like Kitip Boarding School.

Norris' job was to go to all eight stations to select students who would be allowed to start village school. If a village teacher made the selection, conflict could ensue. Norris was considered an impartial authority. First, since no birth records were available, each child's physical age was estimated. Second, Norris designed and administered a simple non-verbal test to estimate aptitude for learning (matching shapes on blocks within a time limit). Due to shortage of mission and government classrooms and teachers, only the most promising children were selected. Sadly, less than half of the village children would ever enter the door of a school or be enrolled in classes.

At village school, both the boys and girls were taught together because the children came from their own homes at that point. Children who became eligible to progress to District schools were assigned to either a school for boys or a school for girls. The village elders did not think girls' education was as important as that for boys. If girls did go to school, they should be separated from the boys.

Kitip was an all boy school. Kids as young as ten years old who came to our school would leave home, raise their own food, wash their own clothes, and do their studies very conscientiously. Being in school was a privilege. This was their only ray of hope for a better life.

At the end of 3rd Grade, Norris administered a written test to evaluate math, science, and reading skills and selected 40 students out of the 240 children in the village schools. Those with the highest marks progressed to Kitip School for 4th Grade, and possibly 5th and 6th Grades.

At the conclusion of 6th Grade, students had to pass another test to be allowed into what was called Form I and then Form II. Over the years, Kitip School would grow from 80 to 240 students.

The goal of the Mission was to provide as much education to the New Guinea residents as possible. Very few of the natives had been educated. Without schooling, there would be little hope of developing the nation.

*Village children stood in line to be selected for their first year of school. Mothers waited nearby, anxiously hoping their child would be chosen for educational opportunities.*

In the villages, the parents hand constructed the classrooms, using bamboo and other forest material. At Kitip School, however, classrooms were constructed by indigenous coastal-trained carpenters. These classrooms would be wood structures of more permanent nature. Norris would oversee this construction, working towards the goal of building one classroom per year. Funding came from the Mission budget, whatever we personally were given from church offerings back in the United States, and any amount we could save from our personal budget for living expenses.

Norris' background in agriculture was one of the main reasons why we had been assigned this station. In addition to testing and selecting village students, then overseeing the construction of classrooms at Kitip, Norris also taught one class there. He was also responsible for providing a food supply for the students—forty per class each year. Having a hungry student body would not be good.

The land had to be cleared. Garden preparation was begun by hiring workers with eighteen-inch blade machete knives to chop down the nine-foot tall cane-like swamp grass, which was called "pit pit." After drying the pit pit, it was burned. Roots were grubbed out by spade. Then, Norris could plow it with a Massey Ferguson 35 tractor.

For the first pass, he used a two-bladed thirty-inch disc plow. Next, he leveled the ground with a tandem disc. When the soil was sufficiently dry, two ridges were plowed, one into the other, forming a long mound trenched toward the river. With well over 100 inches of rain per year, we constantly had to plan to deal with the water.

Over the years, Norris used various tractors, such as the Massey Ferguson 35, a Ford 3000, and a Ford 4000. In addition, as an ever frugal bargain hunter, he acquired five Ferguson T-20s as government public works bargains at $50 apiece! And as a natural mechanic, he could make anything run. His four years of U.S. Air Force mechanical training and work served him well.

With the preliminary ground work completed, each student was allotted a piece of garden land for their own food production. The staple crop was white sweet potatoes. They were propagated by planting a section of vine from a growing plant. This year's class would get a bearing crop when coming to school. In turn, they were expected to plant a plot for the incoming group next term. Norris was the manager to see that this got done in a timely manner. He knew more

*Norris supervised students as they dug drainage ditches. This was one of the first steps in preparing the swamp land for gardening.*

about small grain farming than growing sweet potatoes, but he would learn fast. The students were also given corn and cabbage seeds to provide more variety in their diet.

For the community as a whole, we had planted over 2,000 gum trees for firewood, 200 guava fruit trees and 11 acres of banana trees. Plans were also made for planting forty acres of coffee the next year.

Our school boys joined in a congregational outreach to teach Sunday School. Thus, almost immediately, we were going full throttle in what we had come to do.

Kitip was only one part of a larger station called Kotna. Norris was headmaster of the school and the station manager; Pastor Bob Jamieson served as the pastor of the congregation; and David Kulow and his wife, Laura, were in charge of the hospital. Both Dave and Laura were registered nurses from Ohio.

When Norris went to the village, I substituted in his classroom. Bob's wife, Marge, would sometimes help care for Nathan while I was teaching. She and Bob were from St. Paul, Minnesota. They worked closely with the native pastors and evangelists. They were our age, and we had a lot in common. Marge and I started sewing, nutrition and literacy sessions with the local women.

Homemaking in New Guinea was different than what it had been in America. I had to make some adjustments. Instead of my familiar gas stove, I now had a wood-burning cook stove. Instead of buying bread at the grocery store, now I would order flour in forty-pound drums and bake all the bread from scratch.

We washed clothes outside in a small, roofed and semi-walled laundry shed. Since we had no clothes dryers, we hung the clothes on wire lines outside by 10:00 a.m. During the rainy season, by 1:00 p.m., showers came over the surrounding mountain. (My clothes didn't need a second rinse.) We would iron the clothes the following day, using a gas iron.

Our only evening light was by kerosene lamps. After two years, Norris, Bob, and Dave developed a generator-based power system for light between 6:00 and 10:00 p.m.

In August, we had a short school break. Taking our children with us, Bob, Marge, Norris and I decided to make a trip to Goroka, eighty miles away. We took turns riding in the back of the truck, because only three could fit in the cab. Whenever and wherever we went, there were two or more indigenous people needing a ride to a hospital or a school, and so on; so our vehicle was always full.

We left at 8:00 a.m.—and after only nine hours en route—we had completed our trip. Again, the roads were narrow, rough, and up and down the mountain. Nathan still liked his milk bottle. The problem was that the bumpy trip had churned the cream in his whole milk into little butter curds, which plugged the nipple. Soon after that, our puppy chewed the nipple up, so Nathan began using a cup from then on.

We spent the night at the Mission's guest house at Goroka and, the next day, attended orientation sessions for newcomers (like us) who would be working in the schools and the church. The following day, we went shopping. Marge and I decided that we each needed to invest in a teapot. It seemed the Australians served tea like we Americans serve coffee. She bought a green one with six cups, and my set was blue. We would serve hundreds of "cuppas" (Australian slang for, "Have a cup of tea with me.") My newly acquired cups would later sit in the cupboards of my home in South Dakota and occasionally be used to serve tea to our American guests there.

When we returned to Kotna, we were met with a sad surprise. In our haste to leave, we had forgotten to close a window. Hundreds of bugs took that as an invitation to come in! Our refrigerator was kept cool by kerosene, but the fuel had run out. Consequently, the fridge got warm, the meat spoiled, and a rotting smell pervaded. The day was spent cleaning.

In addition to starting the work at school, we had to adjust to living in a very different culture:

- Heathen witch doctors could work sorcery on hair, spittle, body excretions, bones, clothing, and anything that belonged to the dead. They could call revenge upon the living. Local Christians appreciated living without this fear, but temptation to old ways was ever present.
- At death, it was customary to return the deceased to their home village. Our tractor boy's baby died one night so we took him, the mother and the dead infant to Ogelbeng at 10:00 p.m., returning at 2:00 a.m.
- The pig was a very important part of the culture. The pig was an indication of wealth: many pigs equaled a rich man. The wives, who usually tended the family pigs, could be seen leading one by rope on the road. Sometimes, the animal's eyes had been poked out to make it weak and obedient. Sometimes, native pigs were savage. Medical support staff would treat patients for pig bites.
- Roasted pig was always the main food at celebrations. During major ceremonial feasts, the heathens killed and roasted as many as 100 pigs to appease bad spirits with the aroma. Meat was given to other tribal members who later reciprocated. It was also a cultural practice to exchange pigs for brides! When a new dorm was completed at our school,

*This photo shows a typical family stroll, the wife always walked behind and led the pig.*

the boys were allowed to have a pig feast. In Pidgin English this is called a "mumu" and the cooking method is similar to what Hawaiians call a luau. Pork and white sweet potatoes were pressure cooked with heated stones in an earth pit lined with banana leaves.

- Banana leaves were much used vegetation. Not only did they serve as a natural "foil" in mumu cookery, but they were also used as umbrellas during the daily rains of wet season. These leaves grew approximately 16x30-inches and could cover the head and upper body. They were readily accessible.

- The natives did not wear glasses. Being illiterate, they didn't need them for reading. With imperfect sight, they could still do gardening, care for pigs, build fences, and chop fire wood. Some pastors and teachers, however, wore reading glasses.

- At one point we had a bedbug problem in the dormitory. One student picked a dozen fat ones out of his bed and brought them in a bottle to show us. So, all bunks were moved out from the wall and beds and walls were treated.

## Chapter Twenty-Nine

# No Dull Days!

By September, we suspicioned our second pregnancy. I felt good, and Nathan could use a playmate. Some couples were unable to have children. I was grateful when maternity snuck up on me naturally. One more blessing to count.

Since our arrival in June, while his dad and I dealt daily with new experiences, so did young Nathan. We made mulberry jelly and he could sit and eat one little piece of jelly and bread after the other. He ate bananas like a monkey and we usually had a stalk of eighty or so outside the kitchen door. He regularly rearranged cupboard items and loved to play hide and seek. He often tramped around in his dad's big slippers. Always, we were glad we had Nathan to add sunshine to our days.

With no grandmas or aunties down the street, most missionary wives took in two young native girls and trained them in child care and homemaking. I started with Kuala and Bo. No birth records were kept, but I guessed these girls to be maybe fourteen years old. Kuala had three years' education so could read her hymn book and Bible. Bo was completely illiterate. They slept in a little one-room dormitory house in our yard and took their food from our supply.

The first thing I taught them was how to take a shower. Bathing in the river was all they knew so far. Attached to the side of the cook stove was a two-gallon reservoir for heating and storing hot water. To take a shower, a kettle of that hot water was mixed with three gallons of cold water and poured into a canvas nozzled bucket. It was hoisted up above the head by rope and pulley. The rope was fastened onto a nail in the wall. The sprinkler part was opened slightly. We could then wet the body, soap down, scrub and rinse before the water ran out! This was standard bathing procedure for all of us. The girls needed reminders how to wash personal parts for good hygiene practice.

Being used to cooking only over an open fire outside, the girls learned the use of our cook stove for various tasks. They learned the practical skills of simple food preparation, setting of the table, dish washing, clothes washing, and whatever I was doing around the house.

When everything is foreign, misunderstandings happen easily. I had a tea kettle half full of water on the stove. This was the large kind, like the pioneers in America used. I asked Bo to cut up some cabbage and boil it, but I failed to set out a saucepan. While I left the kitchen to tend to Nathan's needs, she stuffed my big tea kettle full of cabbage! While doing laundry, my girls mixed a new piece of blue clothing amongst the white, so we had a bleach job, and some of us just started wearing more blue!

Over the years, many girls worked with me and were a great help. I always prayed that they would find Christian husbands and could live an improved lifestyle when they returned to their village. (On our 2006 return trip, I met three of those girls. They gave me gifts and nearly hugged the life out of me. I was truly thankful to see them.)

In women's classes, we tried to teach basic literacy. Imagine being adult, and even old, and never being able to read a single word! To this day, I can cry when I think about it. Reading is a great love of mine.

It was said that over 700 languages were spoken in New Guinea. English was the school language. Vernacular tribal language (Tok Ples) was spoken in the village. Each tribe spoke differently; it would be as if within every thirty miles in the United States, people spoke another vocabulary. Many languages made a big problem. I spent hours working on Medlpa, which belonged to the Kotna group of people. This is a sampling of words from the language:

| manga | - | "house" | ambugla | - | "girl" |
| tikera | - | "hurry" | kang | - | "boy" |

A trade lingua franca known as Melanesian Pidgin (commonly referred to as Pidgin English and today known as Tok Pisin) developed for everything else. The latter was, of necessity, a mixture of local tongue, German and English and we quickly learned to speak this on the job. Some parts of Pidgin English are just too good to lose. In our family, we still use these terms:

| muski | - | "whatever; forget it; never mind" |
| picannini | - | a cute word for "baby" or "child" |
| lapoon | - | "old person" |
| susu | - | "milk" |
| kisim | - | "go and get it" |
| kaikai | - | "eat" and/or "food" |

On October 2nd, we rejoiced in our one-year-old's birthday. I made a meatball supper, and the other missionary families on the station came for a birthday meal. Nathan enjoyed the limelight and the presents. One of his gifts was a large inflatable toy, which he could punch. It took him a couple of days to accept the challenge this toy offered.

Among our guests were Dave and Laura. The big talk of the evening centered on the excitement and sadness that Dave had experienced that day. One man had slashed another during a bride price argument. In the bride price process, the groom's tribe had to negotiate and pay a fee of money, shells and pigs to the bride's family. The girls were often hardly into their teens and had little to say about the tribe and groom's choice. I often felt heavyhearted over these situations.

Two tribes wanted to fight over this. Dave had cared for one man and locked the other up in a building until the police came. Axes and arrows were collected, and the crowd dispersed. We prayed for all parties concerned.

As far back as I remember, and as long as she lived, my Mom had a Maytag wringer washing machine for laundry. My Maytag arrived in October. Doing laundry for our family, the single teachers, and two house girls—how blessed I felt, and how fun it was to have a real washing machine! Otherwise, the girls and I used a scrub board and tub with a hand wringer. (I would get my first automatic washer and dryer when we moved to the farm in South Dakota in 1976.)

Norris made a big cardboard house for Nathan out of the Maytag washer crate. There were doors and windows for toddlers to crawl through with ease. When 100 baby chicks were imported from Australia, this became a fowl house. Nathan and the other station kids had a lot of chicken chatter! Marge and I joked that they were talking Medlpa, the local language, as we couldn't understand it all.

Our trunks and barrels finally arrived in October. Shipped in May, they had been on a long route by truck, held on a United States dock, going on the ship overseas, sitting on the New Guinea dock, and finally coming by plane and truck to Kotna. Sometimes, cargo would get mixed up or lost, even going to a different continent. We were blessed. So, this was time to celebrate. This was a ceremony of thanksgiving. Laura was homesick and asked if she could just sit and watch me for a while! As I lifted each precious item from its tightly packed niche, I found that only one item had broken. So, we gave ourselves an "A" on the packing job.

The immediate and heavy workload took its toll. By mid-October, Norris was run down, and strep throat hit. Weakened, he had the first malaria attack. (We took anti-malaria tablets thrice weekly all nine years we were on the field.) He was a very sick man, with high fever and chills for many days. I was glad we had two nurses on our station.

Knowing that my Christmas cards would have a long ocean-crossing trip by ship, I mailed them out in October. Doing so early saved on postage.

I had never roasted a turkey, but as Thanksgiving Day drew near, the other two American wives at Kotna said that they had already done it, and I could have a turn. So, with a wood-burning stove and an oven with no gauge, I cooked my first bird. Norris had butchered a beef that month, so we could have had roast, but being 10,000 miles from home even small ties of tradition seemed important.

Reflecting back, I seemed to have been on a never-ending cooking, baking and hosting routine. I was young and aiming to please. One month, my notes mention making mulberry pie, hot dog buns, soybean soup, French pastry, sugar cookies, animal cookies, angel food cake, chicken, rye and white bread, lamb chops, eight dozen rolls, donuts, and chocolate fudge. On November 19th, twenty-four people came for supper. In my youth and single life I thought cooking was a waste of time. Now, it seemed a pleasure and necessity. I had to learn fast!

One day, a student named Aro refused to do gardening. It was called "community work" and was part of the daily schedule. The food supply depended upon everyone's cooperation. Norris reprimanded him. Aro ran away. We felt badly and prayed for Aro, his family, and his church congregation. A couple weeks passed. One day, Norris was coming out of the classroom and he was met by Aro and his father. They had walked nearly 100 miles to get Aro reinstated in school. Garden work was not a problem after that.

One evening, lots of pounding could be heard from the dormitories. Norris went to check on the sound. The school boys had heard that there had been a murder of a young lad twenty-five miles away at Banz. In the custom of pay-back killing, student Mundie (from Banz) was a rumored target who needed protection. Windows were being nailed shut and bunks pushed against doors. The night was tense, and prayers intense. Angels must have been dispatched, as no revenge event occurred. Many incidents like this occurred over the years.

As I worked with the women, Norris was always zeroed in on providing good food for the school boys. He saw the need for protein. The Sunday School at New Effington had sent $37 with us to be used where we felt there was a need. Norris decided to buy and plant peanuts as a protein source. One day, he gave each boy a cup of peanuts to plant during the gardening hour. Shortly after, a torrent of rain came over the mountain (before the peanuts got planted). Students gathered in their cook huts, and Norris ran for our house. When the downpour was over, he rang the bell to assemble the students in the classroom. He announced that planting would be done tomorrow. Heads went down on desks, and the student body was suddenly stone still. After minutes of silence, Kui raised his hand and stated simply, "We ate the peanuts!"

With the seed gone, Farmer Norris dismissed the kids and returned to our house. He slumped down into our woven plastic bucket chair. This was unusual behavior! I said, "What's the matter?"

He answered, "They ate the peanuts," and declared that he would reprimand them in the morning. However, overnight, he mellowed. Their protruding stomachs were evidence of the malnourishment that made the peanuts irresistible to them. He would try again.

We used a mission-organized short wave communication system. Norris asked if any station had peanuts. We never knew who answered, but a replacement came at no charge, which was much better quality than the first lot. From this point on, peanuts were propagated throughout the valley as the students took seed home to the villages.

In world news, Russia was sending forty ships with missile-launching equipment to Cuba. The United States was blocking them. Being "down under" in the southern hemisphere, we still kept up with the world news via the Armed Forces Radio network. On November 22, 1963, I was outside when the girls came running to me saying, "Your President got shot!" Kennedy was assassinated that day. Kuala and Ka heard it on our short-wave radio and mourned with us.

I wanted to see what a night in a village was like. The children and I went with Norris to Kumidle for an adult baptism. We observed much preparation on Saturday and a beautiful ceremony for candidates of all ages on Sunday. Bedding down in a village house that night, I heard both mosquitoes and rats, so guarded my children and hardly slept. After a long Sunday service in the language of Medlpa, I came home very tired. I also had a whole new appreciation for our off-the-ground wood house containing real beds. My sympathy for those in Stone Age lifestyle was very deep.

Some school boys were neither baptized nor confirmed when coming to our school. Indigenous pastors would conduct instruction classes with them. Seeing 46 of them make their sacramental vows made it a pretty special Sunday. In addition, Laura and Dave had their baby, Terry, baptized that same day. My heart ached for his grandma back in Ohio, a recognized writer in the American Lutheran Church Women's *Scope* magazine. How she must have longed to be in New Guinea about then!

Diary entries for the period of time we were at Kotna are included in the following reflections:

*"November 30th. Geta and Kuala not here. I had a nice, peaceful day just caring for my house and children." (Having girls to help and train was appreciated, but my need for personal family time was often slighted.)*

*On December 1st (1962), I turned 27. One thing that made it significant was that after they hosted the Sunday evening worship, Laura brought out a cake with candles and decorations for a birthday party. It seemed our religious and work life was all intertwined; and looking back, it's amazing how well we meshed. We were three families working with church, school, and hospital assignments. We became lifetime friends.*

*"December 2nd. I typed the Conference Report until 10:00 p.m." Once a year, missionaries gathered. Individual reports were completed in a book ahead of that gathering time. Norris' comment that evening was, "I never dreamed we'd be this busy."*

*"December 5th. Norris worked on a Pidgin sermon because the missionaries take turns speaking on Sunday with the indigenous leaders."*

*Sunday mornings, we worshipped with indigenous congregations in their language; but Sunday evening, we came together in each others' homes for worship in English. (I really missed this close fellowship when we returned to the United States.)*

*Another note later on in December said, "I think there were 10,000 interruptions today. I'm tired."*

Each Wednesday, I gardened for the first half of the day. Besides nutritious vegetables, I enjoyed beautiful gerberas, tubular roses, amaryllis, calla lilies, dahlias and roses. I used Wednesday afternoons for answering letters. I felt then, and still do today, that people at home who give to missions deserve to know what is going on at the field.

Winter was setting-in back in the United States. I had never been a fan of cold and snow, so I did not miss it. New Guinea, located five degrees south of the Equator in the South Pacific Ocean, enjoys a year-around tropical climate. The two seasons are wet and dry. The dry season is rarely over two weeks in length. Rainfall was over 100 inches per year, so when December brought downpours thirty days in a row, I realized the idyllic weather of earlier months was seasonal. The volcanic soil was such that most of the water sank into the ground, but mud was still plentiful. All the natives went barefoot, so shoes could not be left at the door. Every evening during these months, we washed our bare wood kitchen floor.

One nice part of the rain was the cozy sound it made, falling on the corrugated steel roof of our house. This made me feel lucky and secure. The bamboo-woven walls of native homes were roofed with kunai grass, which was laid in a shingle effect. I thought it strange how grass could shed the rain. However, the problem was that the roofs had to be replaced every few years. Thus, our mission home had a metal roof.

December was upon us, and I set to making something out of Christmas. Norris cut down a small pine-looking tree from the forest and made a stand for it. What could be the decoration? I used left-over gold paper stars from a German missionary who had terminated service. As we received Christmas cards, I hung them on our tree. And I had brought six candles along from America. The school boys were each given a t-shirt after we had stamped the Kitip logo on them. They wore them home to their villages for the holidays. I was glad that Marge and I had made fruit cake the day after Thanksgiving.

We were following the Australian school year, which ran February through November. Norris was out on an end-of-the-year school trip. The final testing of third graders in each of the eight circuit schools would determine which students would form the new 4th Grade class. Also, students would be selected for 1st Grade in village school at this time. The evening of the 23rd, Norris got home from school testing just in time for "Lille Julaften" (little Christmas Eve in Norwegian). Worship was the main part of Christmas on the 24th, 25th, and 26th. I had baked lefse, and we ate it with pork roast on Christmas Eve, just our little family of three.

Groceries, meals, and other necessities came from the supply house in Madang each Wednesday by Cessna or a DC-3 plane, depending on the load size. One of the station men would drive to the airstrip at Banz to bring the supplies to Kotna. Mail that year was so appreciated, especially at Christmas! The people whose lives we had shared in the past were very good at writing. It took a week for airmail to come from the United States to New Guinea. Letters usually arrived at noon, but rather than squeeze their reading into the day's hustle, I saved them until evening for savoring.

For ten days of school vacation that Christmas, we had six single teachers with us. They were hosted between the three families on our station. They had assignments on the coast, and wanted to experience life with us in the mountains. Our mission family varied from twelve to twenty people, including children. We were then a family-in-Christ of fourteen adults and four children. Someone got the idea of pretending we were on a world cruise. Sharing kitchens, recipes, and other imaginative resources, we enjoyed a Chinese Day, Time in Mexico, Down

Under in Aussie Land, and Back in the U.S.A. Every day became special. Besides exciting menus, there were thoughtful discussions on spiritual matters and work concerns, games, music, and playing with the pre-school crowd. We were all young and fun-loving!

By New Year's Eve, the party was over. Marge and I spent December 31st looking at a Montgomery Ward catalog, selecting fabric that we would order from Australia and sew for the additional house for the next teacher on the station. Bob and Norris made a ping-pong table.

The rest of the month was not usual fare, either. We flew to Madang for a one-week vacation, of sorts. Nathan began to talk. He said, "Mama" clearly, a special sweet sound to my ears. Mom and Corinne wrote that Dad had a heart attack. This began the fifteen-year decline towards the end of his earthly life.

Norris had experienced many severe sore throats over the year, plus malaria, causing loss of twelve pounds of weight. So, during this school vacation, he had his tonsils removed. The missionary doctor at the hospital in Madang at the coast told him a year later, "We almost lost you from hemorrhage." Dr. Theodore Braun was a forthright man, saving life but not fearing death, who often spoke with bluntness. His comment woke us to the fact that God was hearing prayers for our protection, even when we were unawares. Dr. Braun had grown up in South Dakota and, along with 150 other Protestant and Catholic missionaries, had been a prisoner of the Japanese in World War II. (An account of this jungle internment can be read in the book, *Walk Softly in the Darkness* by Esther Wegenast.)

Under the title of "This Vacation," I also had a prenatal exam. The first six months had gone just fine. Another prayer of thanks ascended. The full moon shining on the harbor waters, which we crossed several times, reminded us we were indeed in the tropics of the South Pacific.

The pastors, teachers, medical workers, construction and supply people all met for the annual ten-day conference at Wau each January. This was 120 air miles away from Kotna. It seemed to be a lonely sort of time, as the women and children were left alone on the station. I always prayed that nothing tense would evolve. An untamed Kuija River ran by our station and, some afternoons, we three young mothers let the children play in an area of that water. Some wives were home alone on outpost stations all of this time, so I didn't complain about our setting. However, as Nathan walked around saying, "Da-dee, Da-dee" repeatedly, I, too, longed for ten days to come to an end, even as I asked our Heavenly Father for guided discussions and right decisions at the field "bung" (Pidgin English for gathering).

## Chapter Thirty

# Welcome Steven
## — 1963 —

The new school year began in February. School was mainly scholastic. We had a minimum of books under Australian syllabus; thus we needed much teacher input. Students worked with notebooks. An occasional sports event was really appreciated. One Saturday, Norris took the tractor and a trailer with forty boys to Banz for a sports meet. They were very good athletes. They especially loved soccer. Often, I saw them even bounce the ball off their heads or kick it with precision during practice.

Besides substitute teaching, I was enjoying setting up a nursery. We had studied and selected names. I knew by internal kicks that our baby was alive and well. The night of April 16th was my last night at home. I would fly to Madang the next morning, ten days ahead of my due date, to be near the Yagaum Hospital when Baby #2 would arrive. Sleep did not come easily. Nathan had come down with

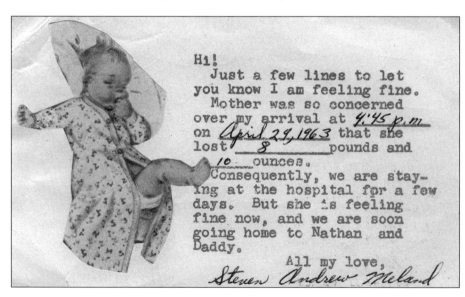

Hi!
    Just a few lines to let you know I am feeling fine.
    Mother was so concerned over my arrival at _4:45 p.m._ on _April 29, 1963_ that she lost _8_ pounds and _10_ ounces.
    Consequently, we are staying at the hospital for a few days. But she is feeling fine now, and we are soon going home to Nathan and Daddy.

        All my love,
        _Steven Andrew Meland_

chicken pox two days earlier. Dad and the house girls would be in charge. It was comforting to think that the rest of the pregnancy had gone well. The finale probably would, too.

In the morning, I flew by mission Cessna to Madang. I stayed with other missionaries and filled my time with reading, embroidery, and doing volunteer work. The wait lasted twelve days. That, at least, was better than delivering out at a lone station with only a husband to preside, as pioneer missionaries had done.

On April 29th, Steven entered this wide world. I said, "Thank you, God, for another beautiful, healthy child" and repeated my soul song of Psalm 103 over and over again. To avoid nine months of parental concern in South Dakota, this birth had not been foretold. I had made announcements before I left Kotna and I mailed them on May 3rd.

A DC-3 plane was bringing cement, fencing, five-gallon drums of flour, some chickens, and even a tied up pig—all strapped to the floor—to Banz. Steven and I were the only passengers. We had a seat hooked to the side wall of the plane. The most interesting air ride I've ever had! Norris and Nathan met us on the grass airstrip, and the reunion felt so very good. Being able to snug my tummy close to the sink again felt really good, too.

By May 22nd, our baby news had reached our moms and dads. Congratulations and New Arrival cards began coming by mail. Aunt Irene scolded me: "Don't ever do that again! It's hard on us old people. Shock could cause a heart attack."

Now, I was really glad for trained house girls who helped with cooking, laundry, and general homemaking duties. My home was like a castle, with a little bit of hassle, but joy and contentment permeated every room.

Since the Ialibu Mission Station eighty miles away had built a permanent house, the aluminum shelter they had used for a start-up was now available for someone else's use. Norris always had his antennas out for practical deals, otherwise known as "bargains." Willing always to work hard and make something out of almost nothing, he decided on a twelve-hour tractor trip to Ialibu to dismantle, load and haul the pre-fabricated home to Kotna. He made a toilet and shower facility out of it for the school.

To travel curves and mountain roads, dual wheels had been put on this tractor. Having loaded the complete house and securely tied it down, the eighty-mile return trip started. En route, he discovered an unforeseen problem. About one-fourth of the way back to the school, he ran into a heavy thunderstorm. The roads became very wet, and the heavy load could not be pulled up the steep hill. The tractor would spin out. Always the way-ahead planner, Norris had some shillings

(English coins, about the size of a quarter) along for an emergency. He told two of the school boys, who spoke the local language, to go back to the village they had passed and hire some help to pull the tractor and trailer up to the top of the hill by manpower. The boys came back in about fifteen minutes to report that the people would not come because they had just had a big fight with the village up the road. Some people had been killed, and they were afraid for their lives.

Norris then asked the boys to go to the village in the other direction and get help. The boys returned and reported that those villagers were at war with the other and would not come.

The next step was to send one boy to each village with twenty shillings. The goal was to get a group of young boys to come. One village could pull on the long rope in the front, and the other village could push the trailer from behind. Money talked, and the young boys came! Not looking at one another, they pushed and pulled, collected their money, and ran back to their villages, heroes in their own eyes. This was another moment of answered prayer. Norris and crew were back on the road again!

Another never-seen-before experience came when Norris got to witness hundreds of people being baptized. Natives lived very much a communal style of life. Mission strategies made use of that practice. The whole village had decided; they wanted to be Christian and to have a congregation. Mostly illiterate, they worked several years memorizing thirty Old Testament and thirty New Testament stories, the Lord's Prayer, the Apostles' Creed, and the Ten Commandments. Then, the commitment service came—a very special day with a long worship and the baptismal sacrament.

Gift packages from the home churches of Goodhue, St. Pauli and Zion started arriving. The contents made

*Some of the villagers being baptized were very old and this was the most joyous day of their lives. I'm sure we'll see many of them in heaven.*

112

a unique shower in absentia for Baby Steven and me. I could dress him in finery every day, even if we didn't go anywhere. At night, the quilt of handmade monogrammed squares kept him cozy. (I'm sure the Lord remembers the kind deeds of those dear folks—many of them having gone Home by now.)

On September 1st, Steven and ten other native babies were baptized by our New Guinean pastor. Marge and Bob were his sponsors, and they have been faithful godparents. Their third daughter, Miriam Ruth, had been born June 27th on Norris' birthday. We were her baptismal sponsors. On August 16th, when Miriam Ruth received the sacrament, Marge's parents were there to honor the day. I wished so much that my parents, who were so supportive of missions, would have visited New Guinea for Steven's baptism.

By December, Steven powered his little walker everywhere. Christmas was nearing and I had, by now, acquired some shiny ball decorations. Bad combination! Baby attempted tasting one. I washed crushed ornament pieces out of his mouth and worried that some may have been swallowed. Station nurses sent Steven and me on a Cessna to Yagaum Hospital. Fortunately, nothing came of it, but I felt as if our baby had been lost and came back. It could have been a sad ending. Angels intervened on many occasions.

*Steven's baptismal service was in three languages, Medlpa, Kate and Pidgin. Pastor Bob Jamieson is holding Steven and Pastor Bunubun is to the right.*

## Chapter Thirty-One

# Continuing Adventures
## — 1964 —

In January 1964 we took a one-week vacation at the coast. We had made plans to go to Karkar Island. It happened that Myrna, a less stoic gal from Chicago, was on the same boat. On boarding the Malalo, she announced the likelihood of sea sickness. She proceeded to prepare for fulfilling the prediction by sprawling on the lounge on center deck. Sure enough! The winds blew. The sea was rough. Waves lifted six feet above our vessel and sprayed over us. Our little family was drenched. Myrna wasn't. Oh well, we were tough. When a tinge of fear crept in, I thought of Peter being afraid on the Sea of Galilee when Jesus went to sleep on the boat; they were safe, and so were we.

Dave Lange and his wife were our hosts on Karkar Island. Dave managed a coconut plantation, and the profits went to sustaining the mission schools and hospitals. Most stations had a little two-room guest house, and that was where we were staying.

The next day, Dave suggested—and we agreed—that we should do the walk up to the volcano. His wife, Lucille, would watch our boys. Dave, Norris, and I would go for the walk. Myrna wanted to go along.

We left at 7:00 a.m. and walked steadily upward until noon, between and under shade trees. Being an island, there was no road traffic or other noise of civilization: only bird sounds, enlivening the forest and giving us pleasure. At the top, we looked down into the crater where, on the bottom, small eruptions were smoking. The cavity was big enough that a small plane could fly around in it. I'd picnicked in a variety of places, and now a volcano deck was added to the list.

In the afternoon, as we stepped downward, body brakes were needed to hold us back. Myrna, however, was less physically prepared and enlisted Dave and Norris, one on each side, to stabilize her descent. It was a humorous situation, but we restrained laughter until we were back in the guest room with our two little boys that night. Once again, we were thankful for physical strength for all of these experiences.

Dave Lange offered us another venture. He had a little dinghy and two oars. He, Norris and I would do a little fishing. The kids would stay with Lucille and their children. After a brief time on the sea, I noticed water seeping onto the floor of our boat via a small hole. Soon, rivulets were forming by my feet. I decided that bailing out water was more important than baiting a hook. A castaway coffee can came in pretty handy for scooping out water. I suddenly wondered why both Mom and Dad were out in a leaky boat. I wished I'd stayed home, even as I prayed that we would get back home. (I now could identify with my mother who once sat on a South Dakota lakeshore, watching my non-swimming father standing in a boat and casting a fish line, while her two young daughters—also non-swimmers— sat in the boat. At that time, life jackets were unheard of.) So, the men rowed on. We arrived back at shore, bringing no fish with us.

On our vacation, we also shopped in Madang, saw a movie and looked at some other mission stations.

January was coming to a close. Station carpenters, other indigenous staff, Norris and I were committed to clean up, paint, wash windows and make the newly built classroom ready for use. Also, two new teachers needed to be oriented. I sewed new curtains for their rooms.

Life was not boring, so we really didn't need the dramatic occurrence of the tractor driver's wife going to the river to drown herself. Before heading to the water, she had cut up her husband Bora's clothes and broken some dishes. It took some counseling sessions to restore peace to that household. Then, we could continue school term preparation.

After investing eight months with my house girls, Kuala and Geta, I had what I thought was a good rapport with them—and they had some good skills developed—yet they both decided to go back to the village life. I was so disappointed. I prayed and cried most of one whole night about it. Almost instantly, I developed cold sores from the stress. I felt bad that they didn't tell me they were leaving. Instead, they asked a teacher to inform me. I learned later that this is proper in their culture.

When they left, however, they took several items from the little house. I felt quite betrayed, but had no time to mourn. Hoping they would remember some of the good things learned from us, I set about finding new girls. Temba and Rangild were hired. After a few days, Temba's father wanted her back, so she quit. By then, Kuala wanted to return. I liked her a lot and was glad she came back. Hulda came on board because, meanwhile, Rangild had left. I had two little sons to care for, was doing a lot of teaching, and was providing our family and two single teachers with meals. With no babysitter, neighbors, or grandparents around, I depended on these girls for help.

Suddenly one night, school boy Andop began chopping branches off trees, running around with an ax, kicking dirt and acting generally crazy. I always shifted into prayer gear when new kinds of incidents evolved. I knew God heard our prayers, plus those of parents and other people at home in the United States who were remembering us. Norris and the school chaplain/teacher, Pastor Merrill Clark, got the ax away from Andop and calmed him enough so that nurse Margaret Voigt could give him a sedative.

Andop's second infraction came later that year when he was found under the bed in the house girls' house. This incident terminated his schooling and Hulda's work in my house.

By now, a new worker couple from Australia showed hints of not fitting in. In fact, there were obvious red flags. The wife, who came to serve as a teacher, was tiny and frail and stayed in bed rather than teaching a class. The husband, who came out to New Guinea under the title, "handyman," couldn't fix a thing. He would wait on his wife. We wondered if she was pregnant rather than having the flu. One day, they were both in bed! Two months later they were moved on and, yes, she was intentionally pregnant, even though she came up to teach for two years.

All our furniture was handmade by native carpenters. I wanted a corner cupboard in the worst way. Kinganro made one, but not quite ninety degrees, so it didn't exactly fit the corner; but I used it and loved it, anyway.

I also thought that a small, lightweight portable pump organ would make my house complete. Norris ordered one for me for Christmas, using gift money from the Bergh family of Goodhue church. We used it for school and church, as well as at home. I liked our home and our furnishings a lot. I crocheted an afghan of fall colors to hang over the wood sofa bench. I wish now I'd had a camera and taken a few pictures inside.

The women missionaries gathered for a Ladies' Retreat once a year, rotating hosting. I remember varnishing all of my living room and dining room furniture and the floors in preparation for when they would meet at our station. Seventy-three people came. It was hard work, but fun to visit with women from many other stations. Four of us Kotna women had done all of the organizing and purchasing ahead of this time. Sluffers, we were not! We had canned chicken to serve with chow mein for one meal. We had Bible studies, culture lectures, music and skits. Katie Clark, wife of Chaplain Merrill, Marge and I also sang a trio. I led a song fest with the accordion as part of the entertainment.

*I took this picture of the happy saw crew on the ridge behind our home.*

Norris was in charge of getting a new classroom built: one per year. To get needed lumber, he set up a VW-powered chain saw several hours' walk up near the tree line of the mountaintops behind our house. I had never seen it operate, so one Saturday when Norris walked up to do maintenance, I walked along. When the local people saw us both, the bush telephone began to function. People along the path yelled ahead, "The white woman is coming! Watch for the white woman coming to see our saw!" For a brief period of time, I was a celebrity.

Trying to help the people to a better life seemed a never ending challenge. Customarily, native women wore only covering from the waste down, even though temperatures at night went down to forty-five degrees Fahrenheit. Marge and I tried many varieties of sewing classes, using fabric provided by the ladies from the United States home churches. We helped the women hand sew shirts, blouses and skirts. Nutrition, Bible, child care, and gardening classes were offered in conjunction. The women joyfully participated. They laughed and talked as they learned, usually sitting on the ground in the shade of a bamboo tree.

When Norris went to Wabi to test for incoming students for Kitip, the children and I went along. We flew in on Monday morning, worked that day and Tuesday, and planned to return on Wednesday. We packed and then waited at the airstrip. However, the mountain airstrip stayed under clouds all day. Back at the house, we put sheets on the bed again and stayed another night. On the next day, we waited at the airstrip for an hour and a half, but made it safely home in the afternoon. My house girls had nine bouquets of flowers adorning our house when we returned! This is representative of tropic hospitality.

On our second end-of-the-year vacation, we went to Finschhafen and were hosted by Canadian and Australian missionaries. The change in temperature from mountain to coast was too much for baby Steven. The doctor said he had salt deficiency. I stayed by the ocean all day, coaxing him to drink salt water to replenish the dehydration. I wept and prayed, as many mothers have done. God must have heard because the next day the fever dropped and he began holding soft food. I think now, we lived grace-filled days beyond our recognition.

During our week's vacation, it was fun for us to tour the hospital and seminary and get acquainted with ten families serving there. Conversing with new people was stimulating and uplifting. Back in Lae, I wrote in my diary concerning the last evening of that vacation, "We rode in a real car, just us. We went to a movie." The kids sat straight up, completely engrossed, reaching up for airplanes, making noise with them and laughing heartily at Woody Woodpecker. We bought ice cream cones at a shop downtown. This was a big-treat-evening!

## Chapter Thirty-Two

# More Busy Days

Before starting the new school year in 1964, twenty-seven local teachers from village schools came for a refresher course. Four single missionary teachers were leaders. For me, it was like college dorm life again: sitting up, talking seriously about all sorts of things until midnight.

I was always on the war path with cockroaches. We prayed and powdered against them as much as we dared, without being in danger from poison. The pantry and office needed regular checks. A couple of my favorite books still wear the bugs' autographs. They ate on the binding.

A new class was added each year, which also meant that a new classroom had to be built and new teachers oriented. We now had 160 students.

With rainfall, puddles were often available and inviting for young children's fancy. It seemed as if the water had magnetic force, beckoning waders. Some days, my children needed three changes of clothes.

We were preparing a farewell for a family who had been working in New Guinea for thirty years. I needed to bring three dozen rolls, fruit salad, a vegetable tray and a cake. Maybe that's why I overlooked the United States observance of Valentine's Day. Since we were 10,000 miles away from America, Lincoln and Washington birthdays weren't as important either. We listened to the Vietnam War news and wondered if the Communists might have come south towards us had they not been stopped there.

House girl, Ka, stole peanuts from a neighbor. When I talked to her about it, she said that she didn't think God saw her do it. Not having grown up with Biblical teaching, the knowledge about God's omniscience was new to her.

One April day, the house started shifting, like a boat on a rough sea. I glanced out the window where Norris was mowing the playground with a tractor. It seemed to be convulsing over a rippling lawn. Things started tumbling from our medicine cabinet. Nathan cried out, "Tell Daddy to quit shaking this house!" We were experiencing our first, and only, major earthquake. A few of our water storage tanks split at the seams. My son's comment of trust in Dad seemed like a spiritual illustration of how we should trust in, and call on, our Heavenly Father.

Two nurses, Dave Kulow and Margaret Voigt, conducted regular baby clinics in many villages. They would see up to 200 children with their moms. They gave Triple Antigen shots, scabies medicine, talks on nutrition and a Bible story. This was all administered from the back of a Land Rover. Native "Dr. Boys," with some training, assisted. I went along one such day and felt thankful for their very worthwhile work.

On Saturdays, I had a planning session with up to ten school boys who would then each walk to a vil-

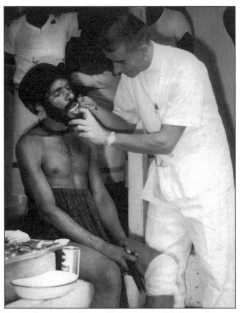

*At the hospital, Dave Kulow also did dental extraction as needed for the local people.*

lage and conduct a Sunday School class. Some Sundays we went along, usually driving the Land Rover part way. One Sunday, we walked with Funkawec to a village not reachable by vehicle. I wore old tennis shoes because we would cross a little winding river over forty times before reaching our destination. The joy of eighty cheering children and many parents made us feel very welcome. The children would bring in sweet potatoes for offering. These would then be used for food for the sick people in the Kotna hospital.

December was a flurry of end-of-the-school-year exams for our own students. Also, 300 village elementary children came on campus for games and the Christmas program. Some of our students brought vegetables to our door in gratitude for another school year completed. They then left for their own villages for two months' vacation.

Santa Claus came to the small town of Banz each year, but no snow meant no sleigh. Over the years, the jolly man in red arrived by helicopter, motorcycle, or jeep. That year, Nathan got a train. Steven got a pyramid cup set.

By then, DeGroffs from Minnesota had sent me irons for making Scandinavian goodies. Gradually, I baked spritz, rosettes, krumkake and sandbakkelse, and enjoyed keeping the delectable tradition from our Norwegian heritage.

On Christmas Eve, the local students—boys only—did a Bethlehem drama. Unusual effects were that the angels were boys with tinsel on their heads, and the star was an actual flash of fire.

Our little family had each a gift. I had sewn, with a hand sewing machine, flannel pajamas for Norris and the boys. The fabric had a candy-cane design. Nathan got a toy airplane. A few days later, he hid in the office and proceeded to take it apart to see "how it is made and what is inside." The next day, I hosted the station people for a turkey dinner.

(As I write this in our Texas winter trailer, I read in my diary that forty-two years ago, we had dinner at Hartungs in Madang. Christian bonds are as strong as iron. Just recently, I got a letter from Esther Hartung, now 85 years old, living in Pennsylvania. Now, back to the '60s.)

The next year, 1965, was much the same. I'll merely state the most significant event: we ordered a baby girl!

## Chapter Thirty-Three

# Karen's Year
## — 1966 —

The first big event of 1966 was the wedding of Wendy Span and Ed Hartung. Wendy was from Australia and had been a teacher at our school for two years. She was marrying Esther's son, an American. The Jamieson's daughter, Bobbi, as flower girl and Nathan as ring bearer, were a darling pair walking down the aisle together. The wedding was in Memorial Lutheran Church in Madang. I enjoyed the finery and joy associated with the marriage of a loved friend. Nathan didn't want to go to church the next day, fearing that he would have to "stand up front" again. (Wendy is still a dear friend, and we visited her in Australia in 2006.)

I went along to the annual conference of all the field missionaries at Wau. It was my first, and only, turn to do so. With many pastors present, the singing was so beautiful! I juggled caring for our three and five-year-old sons, helping make morning and afternoon lunch, and listening to some reports and discussions on the floor.

A short term teacher in his late twenties, who came from Minneapolis, became a source of frustration. He lived with us. He was deeply into some beliefs, like extrasensory perception, flying saucers and ghosts. He had no motivation and was slovenly dressed, and kept his room the same. Eventually, he left the mission.

By now, Nathan seemed so much older. He wanted to know, "Do flying saucers have men in them?" and "What in the world is a honeymoon?" He was into mechanical binges, and would, for days, work on pieces of old toy cars and planes. He was used to seeing his daddy fix things, and they would work. "Why," he wanted to know, "wouldn't they work when he fixed things?" In frustration, he would turn to Daddy, beseeching him to make his projects drive or fly; and when even that didn't work, Nathan would break into tears.

Steven had a bout with tonsillitis, something I realize now we put up with way too long.

We had thought that, within the grand scheme of things, a second female in our family would make it perfect. Finally, a planned pregnancy! Pondering the promises of Psalm 37:4 (ESV), "Delight yourself in the Lord, and He will give you the desires of your heart," we asked God for a girl, if it could be within His plan. This time, we had written home that we were expecting, so it wouldn't be a shock. Maternity clothes—my own and borrowed—were in vogue. I had some vein trouble, but otherwise, felt fine and grateful. I could carry on with normal duties even as we looked forward to family expansion.

Bob and Marge Jamieson were expecting at the same time. On April 5th, Norris and I were at their home in the evening to wish Marge well. She was leaving the next day to go to Yagaum Hospital at Madang and wait for delivery time. Later, that same night, we heard a hefty pounding on our bedroom door and Bob shouting, "I got a boy! I got a boy!"

Norris leaped from bed. We thought that a school boy was bothering their house girls—a big taboo and commonly suspected problem. The reality was that Bob was bringing an elated birth announcement. After three daughters, his son, Matthew Grant Jamieson, had hastily arrived at home! Mat-

*The Jamieson Family, Marge and Bob with their children, Rebecca, Roberta, Matthew and Miriam.*

thew's mom didn't have to go to Madang after all.

My house girl, Kum, finally broke down and left via the back way. Her father had stood outside our house for several days, wanting to bring her into marriage to an older man. I tried to prevent it, but couldn't. Again, I cried and prayed over the situation. That same afternoon, I wrote a story about it for the *Public Opinion* back in Watertown, South Dakota. I mailed it as soon as possible. It turned into a half page printed comparison of forced-versus-voluntary marriages.

I sewed two darling royal blue sailor suit outfits for Nathan and Steven. For Steven's third birthday, I made a four-layer white cake with lemon filling and white animal crackers atop. The neighbor kids and moms came, and he received toys and gifts. When I tucked him in bed that night, he said, "Thank you, Mommy, for the nice party. It was very nice!" He always was a grateful and happy kid.

On May 27th, I went on the weekly chartered supply plane to Madang to start the baby wait. Elva Hopkins from Canada was at the guest house also, waiting for their first child. (Thirty-nine years later, Elva and her husband, Lionel, came to South Dakota to visit us. Of course, their baby was now an adult.) I spent nine days reading, sewing, shopping, cooking, and visiting, all undergirded with the ardent wish that our baby would soon be in my arms instead of locked in the womb.

The baby was due June 5th. That Sunday evening, after the hospital devotion, Dr. Erwin "Butch" Heist asked if I wanted the baby the next day; he would induce me. At 4:00 p.m. Monday, we began the process. At 11:30 p.m., the head presented. The attending nurse ran to get the doctor, and he came on the run to help. I could hear the sound of his flip flops coming down the cement floor of the hall. At 1:00 a.m. on June 7th, I heard the cry of a healthy girl. This was a holy, miraculous moment. I could hardly comprehend the truth that we now had a daughter, too! Thanks and praise to God swept over me all day, Psalm 103 once again my theme.

The mission women were at the Annual Retreat in Madang at that same time. Five of them came to visit Karen and me. They agreed: She was a little angel! On Friday at 2:00 p.m., Norris, Nathan and Steve walked into my room. Surprise is an understatement! They had caught a ride on the back load of the supply plane to come and rejoice in our new addition. It was intensely meaningful and worth the money to me. The boys seemed so big now, in comparison to the baby, and I hoped I'd be strong enough to manage caring for three.

On Sunday evening, I attended one session of the retreat and, again, sang in a trio with Marge and Katie. We had practiced this before I left Kotna.

On Tuesday, our family flew back to Banz. My house girls had our home nice and tidy, with flowers in several rooms and food prepared.

Melands and Hagens had sent baby clothes in a package with a letter from home. I wished that they

*Lawiami, Kugla and Kelebe, house girls at Banz, knew how much I loved the many varied flowers in New Guinea. We must be dressed for a special occasion.*

124

could hold their new grandbaby. I was still spotting blood and felt a bit depressed, which I had never experienced before.

At 11:00 p.m. on June 26th, our sixth anniversary and more than two weeks after Karen's birth, I started a real hemorrhage and lost a half pint of blood. I remember my body trembling from head to foot from the trauma. The station nurses, Margaret and Marie, came immediately and gave me a shot of Ergometrine. I felt no fear for myself if I should die, but told Norris to be sure and find someone to look after our children. He said that I shouldn't talk that way. Sunday night passed.

We went to Mt. Hagen in the morning. Margaret was along. We had a barbeque dinner at the hotel for ten shillings apiece. Karen and I checked into the hospital to see what would happen next. On Monday night, Norris came on a motorbike to see me. I told him that I felt inadequate for mothering and hoped I'd be emotionally stronger soon.

On Wednesday, I went back to Kotna and tried to live normally, but on July 3rd, Sunday, I hemorrhaged again. On Monday morning, Karen and I were flown back to Madang and Yagaum Hospital. I was given a shot and a pill to relax me as Dr. Braun did a vaginal exam. He decided on a D&C (dilation and curettage) for Wednesday. I guess they had urgent operations scheduled for Tuesday. Norris flew down to be with me. I was feeling blue, but he was firm and optimistic, as ever, so I was glad about that.

On Wednesday at 7:30 a.m. he flew back for the district meeting dealing with teachers and school problems. My surgery was begun at 8:00 a.m. and done at 10:00 a.m. I had a needle in my arm until late afternoon. Dr. Braun's wife came to see me every day. She was a dear lady, and brought an orchid the first day. I thought, "In America the doctor's wife would not bring me flowers."

The spotting didn't stop, but at last—days later—on July 13th, Karen and I went home anyway. I stayed in bed at home. This was puzzling to Nathan and Steven. Mustering his five-year-old maturity, Nathan told Steven that, "Mommy's going to rest all day. We'd better stay away." Marge and Betty came with cake and coffee to my bedside. Through all this I nursed Karen, and she thrived, off to a good start. During the ten days of home healing, bleeding stopped. We praised God, and I resumed my regular schedule.

Karen was baptized at three months of age on September 18, 1966. On Friday evening, Pastor Bunubun came and told us they were planning a baptism for Sunday. Pastor Vern Severson had said via letter that he felt happy and honored to be asked to be her sponsor. Karen held her head up, with eyes open, as if answering the baptismal questions that were asked, and made her own sweet infant responses. It was a very meaningful event for all of us.

Another teacher and his wife, whose baby was baptized, and Manis Habu, our carpenter, were our dinner guests. Larsons gave her a gold locket bracelet and a New Effington family had earlier sent her a gold cross. This, together with the gorgeous gown that Corinne sent, made her a real princess. I am still awed that she really is ours!

## Chapter Thirty-Four

# Bits and Pieces

The children often entertained us with cute things they said or did. These "bits and pieces" are taken from my diary:

Left to right: Karen, Steven and Nathan

### Christmas 1966

*The boys love their new cowboy hats. We bought a small English-made two-wheel chain-driven bike for Christmas. Was five-year-old Nathan ever surprised! He learned to ride it in one day and continued riding all day, off and on, from breakfast until dark on December 25th, 26th, and 27th.*

### Nathan - 4½ years old

*This was Nathan's version of what happens when people die:*

*"God is on the inside of Heaven, and the angels are right on His side. He tells them to go down and get someone who has died, and the angels obey Him. They quickly fly down and get that person and bring him to Jesus. But, Mommy, what kind of clothes and food do they have up there?"*

*Norris had collected a box full of old broken watches. Nathan had a big time tinkering with the pieces, trying to make his own version of a new watch.*

*Nathan and Bobbi Jamieson were great playmates. Each had a plastic horn and they would giggle like crazy, running after each other inside the house and out. One day they put papaya in the toilet, and threw ground corn in each other's hair. When Joyce and Gerald wrote that baby Ann Meland had been born, Nathan wondered if his cousin came in the mail bag.*

## Steven - 3 years old

*Speaking of kids and eating, Steven had amused several hostesses, where we'd been guests, by exclaiming, "Mmm, I love that!" when they served the dessert. He also told one of the kids where we were visiting to "wait until the hostess sits down before we start to eat."*

*I was reciting rhymes with the boys one evening and Steven remarked, "Why did Humpty Dumpty sit on a wall anyway? Didn't he know that was dangerous?"*

*Norris was helping Steven pick up a box of straight pins that he had spilled. "You're a good helper, Daddy!" he said.*

*Steven loved to suck on raw sugar cane stalks. He slobbered its beloved juice all over his face and down his hands.*

*During evening prayers, Steven asked God to "Bless the kiaps (police) who lock up the humbug people and let the good people be." He also told me that evening that Mrs. Ayers had called him "a little gentleman" in church.*

## Karen - 1½ years old, December 1967

*Karen was delighted by the bright Christmas lights.*

*She was really quick. She walked and ran and got inside, underneath, or on top of most anything. If a rug was messed on the floor, she sat down to straighten the corners.*

*People were impressed with her big vocabulary and how clearly she spoke. I enjoyed her every day. She worked with her dolls and blankets, talking all the while. "Dolly, sleep nice. Mommy, come and see."*

*When our Australian co-workers Max and Ann Braunack left for furlough, she sang, "Auntie, bye-bye in the plane; Uncle, bye-bye in the plane; Carol, bye-bye in the plane."*

## Chapter Thirty-Five

# From Kitip to Banz
## — 1967 —

*The Kitip campus as we left it in 1966.*

Looking back, maybe 1966 could be called a "bombshell" year. Norris had given 100 percent of his energy to building up Kitip School at Kotna, adding four double classrooms, two dormitories, two houses for teachers, a toilet/shower and a laundry facility. In addition to building projects and new classes each year, he was also juggling maintenance and teaching.

Then, in the space of three closing months, one incompetent teacher left for the United States. Ralph and Betty Larson, both great workers and friends, also left for the United States, where Ralph would begin Lutheran Seminary. We were re-assigned by the executives to move to Banz and develop the Agricultural School there. It was all quite heartbreaking. Now, Kitip School, though built up physically, would be left as an infant with a brand new staff.

We celebrated Christmas, had a week's holiday in January near Madang, and finished our work at Kotna. I wanted to leave a clean house for Norman and Lola Auricht, the new headmaster and his wife, assigned from Australia. I packed necessities in the trunk and a barrel, leaving two drums in storage, because we would be moving from a five-room house to a small, three-room temporary one at Banz.

On February 11th, the locals sat on our lawn all day. I finally had a good cry with a native teacher's wife who understood the pain of sentimental people moving. In late afternoon, we drove to Banz.

The physical shift was done, but we knew that the school/farm roles Norris had grown into were too much for a teacher lacking an agricultural background. With part of our hearts left behind, we would dig into the new task of building up Banz Ag School, but still serve as Kitip's advisors. Our dog, Rusty, jumped out of the truck on the way, but later, heard Norris' motorcycle and ran eight miles to get home to Banz and be with us.

Norris' new title was Headmaster of the Banz Ag School, which, up to this time, had only eight students. This year, the school enrolled forty-six new students in a three-year course. Some boys left Kitip and followed us to Banz. There was a genuine need for agricultural training in this country. Eight subjects were taught by four teachers from various countries and nationalities, but they all spoke English.

Norris was responsible for station management, financing, curriculum development and staff assignments. In addition to his supervisory role, Norris also taught vegetable production and shop mechanics, which included welding, application of tools, and basic mechanical skill. Norris had twenty-four boys in his daily mechanics class. He has always been an organized guy. Here, he could use this skill to the fullest.

Reinhard Tietze, of German descent, taught and managed the dairy and poultry production and conducted daily afternoon woodworking classes. One of many items his class constructed was plywood boxes which local people bought for the burial of their dead. One such casket was always kept ready above the rafters in the woodworking shop. When Christians died, other believers did not eat for two days. Then, they would wrap the body in a white cloth and place it in one of these caskets. After burial, a cross was placed on the spot where the person had been laid to rest. Heathens simply buried the body, wailed and mourned—put mud on their bodies, pulling out hair or cutting off a finger to symbolize the loss—and then made a feast so bad spirits would enjoy the good smell and think kindly of them.

Theo Stiller, an Australian, was instrumental in the beef cattle operation. He taught fencing, pasture development, breeding and genetic selections. Using former U.S. Air Force landing pads, he and his students constructed a cattle holding area (which was so sturdy that it stands yet today).

Lorenz Uthardt, from Finland, was the expert in the piggery. He had owned a piggery in Finland and liked this area of agricultural science. Pigs were the only large domesticated animal that the indigenous people of New Guinea raised. Lorenz developed a plan for the cross-breeding of European pigs with the local swine. His class transported a good quality Ag School boar to selected villages for the breeding of their sows. This produced a larger, hardier animal with better meat quality. Lorenz also was in charge of coffee and tea production.

All staff members taught agricultural basics in a scholastic setting in the morning during regular classroom hours, followed by hands-on practical applications in the afternoon. Selected third-year students cycled through all of the sections as managers, preparing for government employment as agricultural development officers.

Our little house in Banz had a cement floor in the kitchen, which I painted gray. One wall was peach. I made curtains to cover up the open pantry shelves in the entry. This had been only a guest house before, but I would sew curtains and make it a home for seven months. We worked until 10:00 each evening, and we were soon settled. However, this house was only a few rods from the animal grain storage. Mice, which lived in the granary—and in our house—soon let us know that they disapproved of us as new tenants. We declared immediate war! Our nightly trapping numbered forty casualties from their army—two in one trap in one battle! We declared victory, and acquired two cats to keep it.

In May that year, Karen learned to walk, and by July she talked with a good vocabulary of nine words. I loved to listen to children trying out new words, and she was very good at it.

*Karen at eleven months of age and just starting to walk.*

Marge and I had started Bobbi and Nathan in a kindergarten course at Kotna. Now, at Banz, Nathan would go with the Braunack children to the local public school.

131

A missionary from Holland returned to his homeland, and we bought his Dutch made DAF car. Gorobe, who had been their house girl, came to work for us, and I loved her immediately. Over the years, many girls came and went. She turned out to be one who stayed.

I started literacy classes with the women. Twenty-eight enrolled. I incorporated hygiene, Bible, and social studies, as we had done at Kotna. We would meet weekly. People here were a bit more advanced than they had been at Kotna. One who had gained a degree of spiritual maturity was Tolem, a Christian village woman. She told me, "I will pull the others to come to Bible study, but when I go to heaven, I can't drag them inside the door. It will be up to them."

In July, Norris and four other men climbed the 14,880-foot Mt. Wilhelm, Papua New Guinea's highest peak. On the first day, they got three-fourths of the way up and slept in a crude hut, which climbers jokingly dubbed "The Hotel Hilton." On the second day, they reached the top. Heavy clouds blocked their view, so they had to descend just 100 feet short of the summit. This was an adventure I felt bad about missing. It sank in deeply that I was no longer as confident in my physical strength as I had once been.

The Hagen Show was a Western Highlands feature, something like the South Dakota State Fair. Native dancers attracted thousands of people, many from different tribes, as well as tourists from other countries. Produce was displayed and judged. On August 8th, we were up at 6:00 a.m. and worked steadily until 11:30 a.m., getting vegetables, flowers, poultry, pigs, calves, forty school boys and ourselves off to the show. We camped out, eating kaukau (white sweet potatoes) and singing around the fire that night. For church service the next morning, my School Boy Choir sang, "God's Son Has Made Me Free," a beautiful anthem.

September came and Braunacks moved into a new house on the station. We, after another round of cleaning and painting, moved into their old house, which was a mere stone's throw up the slope. The floors were the nicest I'd had and I enjoyed the screened-in veranda where we ate noon lunch. I sewed checkered curtains on my hand-driven sewing machine. How ironic that, as I was playing queen of that nice residence, we would also be planning our furlough whereby we would leave it and travel to the United States.

On October 2nd, Nathan got a carpenter's set for his sixth birthday, and right away, began building a bird house. By now, Karen could say many words and could also enjoy Nathan's party.

That October, we also sent the order for tickets to go home in May of 1968 on the S.S. *Oriana* (the last flagship of Orient Steam Navigation Company's ocean liners).

Vic and Fran Sandager, with their four older children, had traveled from their home in Hills, Minnesota, and arrived at Kotna to serve as caretaker for Kitip School. This was good news and uplifting to our hearts. Vic seemed like a wise mentor/dad for Norris, and Fran became a senior friend to me. We enjoyed two turkey dinners together, celebrating Thanksgiving and Christmas. Our other holiday guest was Phyllis Leifson, a fine violinist, who graduated from St. Olaf College. I savored our music moments together. (I later became her matron of honor.)

## Chapter Thirty-Six

# Furlough
## — 1968 —

At the completion of our six year term of service in New Guinea, it was furlough time. On May 14, 1968, we would start our journey to the United States.

In March that year, I was invited to Lae for lectures on religious curriculum development. Upon completion of the lectures, our assignment was to create lessons, based on the information. We revised, planned, set objectives, and typed from morning until night.

I stayed at the guest house and ate evening tea at other missionary homes. I found it mentally stimulating to be away from the many domestic duties back home, and the coastal atmosphere felt good. After ten days, I was very happy to return home to the home routine, and the family was glad I was back.

Two days after the Lae trip, I shifted gears and began packing even though our actual departure would occur two months later. Much had to be done in preparation. I went through the house, room by room, deciding what would be shipped home ahead of us and what would stay and be shipped next year—if we didn't return. We separated what could go for a rummage sale or be given away and determined the clothes we would need for the suitcases en route. We set trunks, foot lockers and barrels for the different categories in several rooms. It was my job to gather the items to be put into each. It was Norris' job to compactly pack these containers for shipping. This included packing a ceremonial ax, bow and arrows, bark belts, and student-made bamboo arts and craft items. We would drive through Australia, go on the ship and be home before the heavy luggage would arrive.

We prayed about, and sent applications for, graduate school at SDSU. We studied maps and solidified our travel plans. We started realizing the emotional impact of saying goodbye to students, co-workers, and local people. Many, we would never see again. However, this was not the only thing on our minds; a one-and-a-half-day retreat for village women was about to take place. The local pastors' wives and I met in devotions, Bible, literacy and health sessions. A young native teacher played basketball with them. I was surprised how limber those old people were after a lifetime of gardening. Songs, dance, eating, gifting, and planning for their future filled the time. I knew that God looked down from heaven and smiled, because I really sensed His spirit covering us with blessings.

April 14th, Easter Sunday, was grand in simple ways. In the early morning, Theo Stiller had snuck into our living room and set out a basket of candied eggs and a real live hen for our kids to wake up to and enjoy. We had hot cross buns for breakfast. Amy, a single teacher from the United States, played the trumpet and I played the organ for church. We ate ham and eggs for dinner.

A never-to-be-forgotten surprise farewell party took place on May 5th. Many mission friends arrived at noon with a potluck meal, followed by a "This Is Your Life" skit. Afternoon tea, coffee, and goodies just happened to include "trick" food. We were served Australian lamington bars—cake wrapped in chocolate icing and rolled in coconut—except these had a sponge in place of the cake! The afterglow went into the evening, and I remarked how fun it was to have a party that didn't end.

There were other amusing discoveries as well, such as these pranks: We went to bed, but since one plank had been pulled out from under our mattress, we sank! Sitting there, late and tired, we laughed and laughed. Then, we resettled in bed for sleep. Our slumber was interrupted twice more by alarm clocks going off in various odd places, such as in the top cupboard shelf. Mischief could be expected from the young single teachers living with us. They loved us enough to make fun happen.

This would be a week of goodbyes. On the next day, Theo and the school boys barbequed a pig and hosted a farewell. There were gifts, crying, hugs, prayers and songs. On Tuesday, I made a nice final supper for Amy, who was going on a retreat in the morning. Her head was full of wedding plans, so I gave her a yellow robe for her trousseau. Later, little school girls from Kotna arrived in a truck to say goodbye. Our next farewell was expressed by local women who each came with a handful of vegetables. Someone brought pieces of chicken. The women placed the chicken and vegetables into a ten-gallon urn, set it over an open fire, and honored us with this final meal.

We must have been quite crazy, because in the throws of these events, we were still finishing school paperwork, repairing a tractor for another station and hosting ten first-year students for supper. Workman, Daing, invited us to his kunai grass hut for a moonlight meal outside. It was lovely.

The emotionally draining week passed, and Sunday was here again. It was Mother's Day, but we were too busy to think about it. We did some last minute packing and ate supper at the home of a native teacher, Ginga.

On Monday, May 13th, our final day, we closed our suitcases and stopped one last time at Kotna, Kentagel and Ogelbeng Stations before boarding the plane at Mt. Hagen for Port Moresby. Theo, Gill (a carpenter), and a couple of representative school boys gave us one last send-off, and our bittersweet departure drama was complete.

Here we were, having completed six years of unsurpassed, unique experiences. Our time here was made even more sacred by the fact that two of our three children had been born here. Nathan was six-and-a-half; Steven had just turned five, and Karen was almost two. We were heading home at last! Weary, I sank into the seat, allowing some tears of gratitude to trickle down my cheeks as the plane took off. Norris blew his nose and whispered to me, "I think we'll have to come back!"

Our first Australian stop was at Cairns in Queensland, where we took a motel. In the morning, we had steak and eggs, a common Australian breakfast. This was time to just enjoy each other in this unique coastal city. We delighted in seeing the world's finest coral reef, swarming with tropical fish, which we viewed from a glass-bottomed boat just off Green Island. We topped the day with a nice shrimp supper.

This was the first day of a month of touring Australia. Over our six years' stay in New Guinea, we had become acquainted with many people from Australia who had invited us to visit them on our way back. We took advantage of their graciousness.

On the next day, we took a bus to Townsville, where we stayed with a sugar cane farmer. There, we learned about the various stages of planting and harvesting this crop. Theo had told us that we would see teens working barefooted in the wet soil of the cane fields, and sure enough, we did! Also, Theo had forewarned us not to be surprised if we saw a living green frog in the bottom of the toilet bowl. Good thing, because sure enough, we did! Instead of screaming at the sight, Karen and I just laughed about it.

Having stopped briefly at Bundaberg and Brisbane we arrived at Canberra, the capitol city, and were hosted by a gracious Christian Indian family. There, we rented a Ford Falcon and drove westward. The thrill of seeing the Snowy Mountains and the Aussie country side, with its sheep farms, was diminished only slightly by the cold winter temperature. We drove to Adelaide for visits with various mission-connected people. There, at Shirley and Owen Borgelt's home, we celebrated Karen's second birthday. (Shirley had been the first teacher who lived with us at Kotna. We would meet again on a riverboat ride in Brisbane in November of 2006.)

On June 13th, we returned our car to the Hertz rental company at Melbourne. Having seen hardly any movies during the last six years, seeing the movie, *The Sound of Music,* was a special family treat. The following day, we boarded the

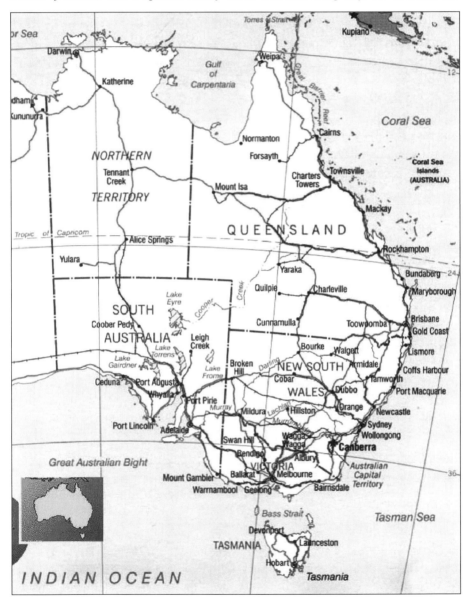

*Oriana.* During this month of travel, Karen, who was in toilet training stage, had been greatly motivated by being allowed to flush the toilet every time we went to the restroom. No matter if this required pulling a string, pushing a handle, or poking a button, she figured it out. Looking back now, I'm utterly confounded: how did we go to so many places and see so much with three children along?

We sailed all night on the *Oriana* and arrived in Sydney by the next morning, Saturday. We debarked and went to the zoo. On Sunday, we walked three blocks from the ship to an Anglican church for worship. We spent the afternoon sunning on an *Oriana* deck. On Monday, we headed out across the big ocean. We experienced our first bon voyage, whereby those on the ship were connected to loved ones on shore via colorful streamers. As the ship departed, and the streamers broke, a fanfare of beribboned color filled the air. We felt quite lost in the crowd because we didn't know any of the hundreds of people who stood with us on the ship, and we were leaving no loved ones on the shore.

We soon learned what being seasick means. While laundering our clothes that night in a lower deck, I washed in one tub and vomited in another beside me. Unbeknownst to us, we passed through a storm. The ship's capacity was 2,000 people, but most did not come to breakfast: they were seasick.

The ocean liner's library, play room, shops, theater, swimming pool and recreation rooms all provided ways to pass time. We would be in this floating village for thirteen days, so we began scheduling ourselves into a routine. After forty-eight hours, we were at Auckland, New Zealand. Maori dancers entertained us. A highlights-of-the-city tour was next. The kiwi birds wondered who we were.

The sea journey continued the next day. Norris and I set goals for the constructive use of our time. We worked daily on a memory course. I don't think it did much good, but we tried. Norris edited our New Guinea films for home showing.

When we crossed the International Date Line, we realized we'd have two Saturdays; one on each side. The ship's staff hosted a tropical celebration with a Crossing the Line ceremony. One of the highlights for children on the *Oriana* was initiation into the Kingdom of Neptune by being slathered with ice cream before jumping into a pool to rinse off. I had brought along outfits from New Guinea for Nathan, Karen, and Steven, who dressed up and participated in a costume party. I mixed lotion with cocoa for their face and hands, turning them into little brown natives. They took first prize in a very confident manner and looked really special.

It felt good to set foot on American soil at Honolulu. I remember touching the ground with my hand and thanking God that we had come this far. At the

Arizona Memorial at Pearl Harbor, we walked on the site with our fellow travelers, all of us respectfully voiceless, hallowed by the nearly 2,500 deaths. We also saw pineapple fields, and they were vast.

At Woolworth's, we ate a real American hotdog! This was our 8th wedding anniversary celebration. I remembered the comment at our wedding about the first ten years being the most difficult. We only had a couple years to that mark. I reflected on our compatibility. Anything I could do, Norris could do faster. Yet I was blest because, though he was ready to go first when preparing to go the many places we went, he patiently announced, "I'm ready when you are."

I'm forever impressed with the enormity of the Pacific Ocean. Our journey continued and Vancouver, British Columbia, Canada appeared visible on Sunday, June 30th. It was ten o'clock in the evening, but broad daylight. Stepping onto the firm North American mainland felt good and brought tears. As one lady on the ship had told us, "You are a privileged family." I knew we were.

I had always wanted Norris to meet part of my Canadian family, especially my Dad's brother, Paul, who was a gentle man and reminded me of my Dad. His son, Paul, Jr., met us and brought us to his parent's home. There, Paul, Sr., and Aunt Beth greeted us warmly. We were all glad to see each other, and they loved the kids. The next day, young Paul showed us the city, while Beth and Paul, Sr., roasted a turkey. We sat until late into the night, talking.

On Tuesday noon, we were on a train rolling eastward. It had been big fun being with, and watching, our children through all of these new experiences. The total stress of it all had settled temporarily in my back, however, so I took a few naps en route. Destination: Fargo, North Dakota.

## Chapter Thirty-Seven

# Home in the U.S.A.

Our parents were at Fargo to meet us upon our arrival, Wednesday at midnight. I don't recall any long, lingering hugs, but I know we were all totally thankful to be together again.

(I didn't realize, until I had my own grandchildren, how much our parents' missed out on during our children's early childhood days. However, I think we all should be commended for letters going both directions each week for six years! Maybe heartfelt thoughts were better expressed in written aerogram than in person?)

We six adults and three children rode home to the farms in Norris' dad's 1968 Chevy Biscayne. We arrived home for 5:00 a.m. breakfast and then went to bed for a beautiful rest.

Norris' relatives from Wisconsin—Clara, Alex, Molly, Norman, Gill and Gigi—were at Melands. The house was full. Only Corinne and her husband, Mike Colon, Sr., were at Hagen's house, so we slept there. It seemed that right away we were part of an extended family again.

On Saturday, Norris and I went to Watertown to buy clothes for the children. Sunday was the big 40th wedding anniversary celebration for his parents. Goodhue Church was full of well wishers. There was a program, I know, but the only part I remember was that I sang a solo, but I have no idea what it was. That afternoon I met Norris' cousin, Cheryl Larson [Huntington] (whose motivation and skill aided me in writing this book).

*Agnes and Art Meland, celebrating forty years of marriage, June 27, 1968.*

140

On Monday morning, it was farming full force, as if no break had ever occurred! Norris began plowing down the South Dakota soil bank acres. My dad's health was not good, but he still wanted to farm, so my mom was kept busy running errands. Mike was really nice with our kids. He shot left-over firecrackers and did other fun activities with them. During that week, Helen Leen and Betty Lou Kuklish came from New Effington to see me. When my dear friend, Helen, saw my children she declared, "Three living dolls!" In my mother heart, I felt the same.

I showed slides at Goodhue WELCA. We worshipped at Egeland Lutheran Church in rural Waubay. I took Agnes, Art and our children along to Clear Lake for swimming and a visit with Kirk and Carol Hansen and children.

At every occasion, people asked us if it was hard to adjust to life back home. Right then, it wasn't, but if asked six months later, I honestly replied, "yes." Everything had changed so much in six years. For instance, instead of a few choices of cereals, now there were many!

The next week, we headquartered at Meland's home. It would be so for the entire summer, switching every week between the Meland and Hagen home fronts. Socially, we reconnected with friends, both in New Effington and Minneapolis. In one week alone, we either dined and/or stayed with Fossums, Leens, Clarks, Jamiesons, and DeGroffs.

My dear friend, Trudy, by now was married to Bob Ender. They had adopted Tina and George. They arranged for a babysitter for their and our children and treated us to an elegant evening at the Edgewater in Minneapolis. Norris and I took the mission-required physical exams the next day at Rochester, and then we went home to South Dakota.

Agnes' brother, Ed Larson, and his wife, Kaia, were celebrating their 50th wedding anniversary in Montana. This was a must-attend for Agnes and Art. While they went there, we stayed at their home for a whole week and did the chores. Wow! Being just our family of five in a place by ourselves was such a treat! I washed the milk separator, did laundry, sold Agnes' eggs for 25¢ a dozen to the neighbor ladies, and enjoyed my own kids every day. Betty Bergh came to buy eggs and commented, "Looks like Agnes herself is here!" I considered it a compliment, because my mother-in-law kept a neat house at all times.

Life was full of the usual variety, the only difference now being the inclusion of the three little Melands in our midst.

- Norris showed pictures at Wallace Family Night.
- Cousin Carol Dale came for coffee.

- We attended a Sunday parish picnic at Ne-So-Dak. I had a solo. We all had fun in the water.
- Helen Leen and I just had a quiet retreat and played with Karen. Norris and the boys went fishing with Pastor Severson.
- We had an old time music fest with the Fossums.

Who said, "The more things change, the more they stay the same."?

Our mission deputations continued while we were on furlough salary. We shared our New Guinea experiences with congregations in Watertown, Claire City, Wallace, Hayti, Hazel, Bradley, Webster, Lily, and many other places. Our children most often went along and sang. We were a featured family at mission festivals.

While Norris helped on both farms, I joined in with our mothers' activities. We canned string beans, beets, peaches, plums, corn, pears, and apples. We also attended several church, community, and family events, such as Elsie Chilson's Circle at Goodhue, an Extension Club picnic, and a 4-H Dress Review. Our family took part in the Dale Family Reunion, held at Lake Kampeska. After leaving the lake, Norris and I went to St. Pauli Church and showed slides. Many of the relatives came along, and their interest brought us joy.

At one point, Norris' brother, Arvid, and his family came from Sturgis, South Dakota, for a visit. Hosting both our family and Arvid's at one time was too much for their mom, Agnes. She ended up in the hospital for a brief rest.

One day in July, Norris and I went to Brookings to line up housing for the school year. We picked up an ads paper. I think that the Lord had a house marked for us, as we very shortly found a nice place near campus. It was only three blocks from where Steven would go to kindergarten and Nathan, the 1st Grade. The owner, Warren Williamson, was on the athletic staff at SDSU and would be gone one school term for sabbatical leave to secure his doctorate. This suited us perfectly. Our children were enjoying farm life and grandparents at two places, so the actual move would wait a month.

When rain comes, farmers go to town. Norris and I went to Zimmel's Furniture and bought a davenport (I think it was second hand), a mattress to fit a bed frame, and a china cupboard. (It seemed I always had a need for a china cupboard wherever I lived.) The total cost of our purchase was $300.

On August 28, 1968, Merlin Hagen came with his cattle truck. We loaded it full with our stored and bought items. He and Norris took it to Brookings, and I drove the car. Unloading went fine. The three of us ate at a café, and then the men went home. I unpacked until midnight, and then happily fell into a sound night of sleep. It was so fun to have a house of our own again. Norris and the kids came the next day with Bunny Boy, our white rabbit, his cage, our clothes, and a lot of energy for settling in. They then proceeded to get acquainted with the neighbor's kids.

I never doubted that God had picked this house and location for us. A few days after we had moved in, Jack Laschkewitsch strolled across the yard and introduced himself. We found that we had a lot in common.

Knowing that we would again be going to New Guinea and returning after another three years there, both Norris and I turned our attention to educational pursuits. In mid-September, Norris started classes at SDSU to work towards his Master's degree in Guidance and Counseling and Administration. I renewed my teaching certificate so as to be qualified to work upon our return. I enrolled in Art, Choral Conducting, and voice lessons. I auditioned for choir and was accepted.

By now, both Nathan and Steven had attained school age. This was a very significant time. They would be attending public school in America! I enrolled them at Hillcrest School. On the morning of their first day, since Norris had gone back to the farm to help his brother Jerry plow, I walked them to school. Nathan, having had a bit of New Guinea schooling, was not impressed with formal education. I prayed that he would have a good year here. Steven cried when I left him at kindergarten; I cried, too. Seeing a child start the road to independence seems such a defining thing for moms. His teacher resonated with warmth, and the room was nice. I thought he would have a good year.

When October 8th brought fall hunting, Norris' desire for a hunting companion was realized and he introduced both of his sons to their first hunting adventure. Good luck. Eleven birds.

On November 12th the first snow fell. It was such a tender moment, sitting by the window, sharing the children's wonder. For the first time we watched the flakes land softly on our lawn, turning fall greens into winter white. I hoped the children would always have an awe and respect for the cycle of seasons in God's creation. We went out and made small snowmen and played Fox and Geese before breakfast. Before that winter was over, eastern South Dakota had received over 94 inches of snow. Cars in Brookings wore red flags on the antenna to ensure safety at intersections.

Tasting lutefisk and lefse again was a treat. We feasted often. We bought and decorated a Christmas tree, but most of the holiday time and activities were at Meland's and Hagen's, with a lot of family eating, gifts, games, and programs. For many of the years past, we had spent New Year's Day with the Myer Hagen family. This January (1969), Harlan and Maribeth Hagen invited us, my mom and dad, Merlin and Thea for dinner. We played Scrabble and other games inside. Even though the temperature was below zero, Harlan's kids took our kids for a horseback ride.

The next day we were back in Brookings, but we stopped en route for coffee with Norris' Uncle Randy and Evelyn. It seems that wherever we are, we find good friends. Mary and Sam Hatlestad stopped by our house in the afternoon, and Mary and Jack Laschkewitsch had a lovely steak dinner ready for us in the evening.

That January, Norris and I and Jack and Mary spent early mornings together completing a series of weekly Bible studies, before breakfast and school, while our kids were sleeping. We also stood as witnesses to their baby Sherri's baptism.

Bunny Boy had been the family pet since summer. Cold and snow found him living in our basement. We took him out of his cage daily for a while, letting him hop about. He ate the food that rabbits are supposed to eat, but also, he enjoyed exotic desserts, like ice cream and strawberries. Eventually, fecal remains became a problem. By mid-January, we advertised him on the radio, and he got a new home.

Television was part of the United States culture our kids enjoyed. Norris and I should have made more time for sharing it with them than we did. We went to one movie, *Doctor Dolittle*. Karen was developing a fantastic vocabulary for a 2½-year-old. She used words like "necessary," "certainly," "satellite," and so on. One day before she and I went shopping, she said, "Mom, do you have the coupons ready?"

Since four of us were student status, report card time for each of us was important. I was busy thanking God that we all had enough ability for earning good marks. By mid-February, Norris was making plans to graduate on August 2nd and fly back to New Guinea on August 6th. We were careful not to become too confident in our own plans, remembering James 4:15, "Instead, you ought to say, "If the Lord wills, we shall live and we shall do this or that."

On February 24th, Corinne called to say that their first son, Anthony Todd, had been born. My first thought was that it would be good for Mom and Dad to have a grandchild nearby. Norris and I became godparents for my first nephew.

On March 7th, we had a 75th birthday party for Dad Meland. At home for a weekend at the farm, Nathan and Steven took old car radios apart, shot the BB gun, and chased rabbit tracks for amusement. On Sunday, we were at Hagen's, and Derald Holden came and gave us snowmobile rides.

Easter that April was really muddy. Nearly 100 inches of snow, to run off or soak in, resulted in floods all over South Dakota and Minnesota. Steven got one of his boots so stuck in Grandpa's slough that his dad had to go and retrieve it.

Throughout the winter and spring, I had spoken at conventions, mother-daughter banquets, garden clubs and various other functions. Norris addressed the Agronomy Club and the Lions. The newspaper, *Brookings Register*, ran a story on us. I sang in the SDSU Oratorio Chorus. We wore long blue velvet gowns and elbow-length white gloves. We performed locally and, in April, went on a two-day tour to Minneapolis.

When school was out in May, I started cleaning and packing again to prepare for shipping whatever we would need the next three years in New Guinea. The kids stayed with their grandparents. Norris started summer school. Mary Laschkewitsch and I prayed about selling the second-hand furniture we had bought last year. I held a rummage sale, and it sold for a profit! The Williamsons would be coming back to their house, so we lived in the Laschkewitsch house until we actually left the United States. Jack was an audiologist, working in other smaller towns that summer.

I remember one little neighbor girl who came over in the midst of our moving commotion, and in childish profoundness, sighed and said, "School is out, and everybody's moving; but I guess I'm staying." I, on the other hand, was about to cry, as I told Norris how I hated to move and leave Mary because we had shared so much in just nine months. He replied, "You'll just have to find a new Mary over there."

A neighbor helped us move. Some things would go back into storage at the Meland's place. I waxed the floor and left our Brookings home on June 21st.

Meanwhile, my social calendar remained full and interesting. My cousin, Carol Dale, married. I sang two songs at the ceremony. A close group of Norris' SDSU classmates, who had resided at the Lutheran Student Association (LSA) house, held their annual reunion at Dora and Leroy Spilde's home in Volga that year. (Our reunions with this group have been ongoing since 1960.)

We borrowed Laschkewitsch's camper and spent a weekend at Enemy Swim Lake, trying to fish. We were low in practice and experience, and the wind was blowing non-stop. This all added up to bad luck. Not enough fish for a meal! So, Grandma Meland made a fast walk to the bait and goodies shop and bought a can of sardines.

The summer was speeding by. On August 2nd, Norris was in the SDSU graduation ceremony having earned a master's degree. It was a lovely evening, with outdoor stage and setting on the campus. Norris' mortar board had a blue tassel.

Looking at it, Karen emphatically declared, "When I graduate, I will have a pink tassel." (Nineteen years later, her prophetic wishes were fulfilled in maroon and gold.) After the ceremony, our parents and we ate TV dinners together in the basement of the LSA Center, proudly honoring the occasion.

Anticipating our leaving, I didn't sleep well the last two nights. Once again, our parents would be brave in seeing us off. My mom and dad were 66 and 69 respectively; Norris' mom and dad were 66 and 75 respectively. We left on August 6th. We asked the Good Lord to take care of them until we would return, and we thanked God that we were given health and ability enough to be a blessing to family and beyond.

Some folks say it is impossible to travel with children. I think missionaries prove that isn't necessarily so. Our kids were very good travelers, joining in the adventure of new people and places with ease and confidence wherever we were.

After twelve hours of waiting time here and there, and twenty-four hours in the planes, we were safely back in Lae. A friend had a nice supper ready, but we were all too tired to do it justice. I vividly remember walking from Myrna's home to the guest house for the night. Norris and I carried Steven and Karen, and Nathan walked between us the whole block without waking up.

## Chapter Thirty-Eight

# Back to Banz
## — 1969 —

Returning to Banz felt truly like coming home. Pastor Mugang bowed almost to the ground. Pastor Basananke joined fingers with us and just hung on. Urum remarked that she had thought she wouldn't ever see us again. Polem had wondered if we'd had any more children. Daing yodeled; Norris echoed back in reply, and Daing came limping to shake hands. Mitita said, simply, "Mama came back." Little school girls came to welcome us. A truckload of former students, who were en route home from Asaroka School, stopped to give us welcome-back hugs. That was at 10:00 p.m., but time didn't matter. Kudjip Village, down the road, made a feast. Everything felt good. We knew we were right where we were supposed to be. And it turned out that my new "Mary" was Karin Tietze, a co-worker who became a friend.

We came back to the same house. Needing groceries to start out, Norris and I went shopping in Mt. Hagen. My flower garden was in need of tender loving care. Nathan and Steven started school. Mrs. Nicol was the teacher. She seemed wise and mature. Unfortunately, the United States school term ran from September to May while New Guinea's ran from February to October. Grandma Meland and I had tried to keep our boys' math and reading skills alive over the summer at home, but how fun was that for six-and-seven-year-old boys, especially mine, whose energetic genes superseded the scholastic ones? Basically, they used September and October for review, then had two months' holiday before starting the next grade in February 1970. By then, they were ready for learning and took off, doing great at Banz Public School. I was so happy.

During the year we had been gone, the curse of alcohol and drunkenness had increased in New Guinea. I visited two single mothers who lost their husbands to alcohol. Pastors and women came to discuss the problem. We knew then, and know now, that this is one of Satan's tools. Domestic and community violence was on the rise, too, as shown by these incidents:

- Vandelim's husband beat her because she was cleaning the church and didn't have dinner ready for him.
- One village tried to raid another, and a mud fight ensued. Good thing it wasn't spears.
- A merchant from India accidentally ran into a little New Guinea girl as he was driving his car on the road near our station. The tribe wanted to kill him as a "payback" because they thought the girl had died. The merchant came running to our door for safety. Norris hid him in the classroom under the teacher's desk. Norris convinced the father to give up his ax and go along to take the girl to the hospital, leaving the tribe wandering around the school. Two other teachers called the police, who came and picked up the merchant. The little girl recovered. A few days later, the father came to get his ax from Norris, and they talked about how good it was that he had not killed that man. Life went on.
- Two tribes fought over the price that should be paid for a bride. Tradition was that the groom's tribe bought a wife with payment of money, pigs, and gold-lipped sea shells. These arrangements were usually made by the clan's leading men, not by the young people. In this instance, they settled on a bride price totaling $1,100 in value. This eventually led to rules that would govern the bride price. Below is an article from the 1972 New Guinea *Post-Courier.*

### "Upper Limits" Placed on Bride Prices by Councils

*Two Highlands local government councils have passed rules to curb inflation in the cost of marriage. The rules impose upper limits on the amount a man may pay for his bride in a customary marriage settlement. The prices are based on a sliding scale.*

*The councils are Mendi in the Southern Highlands and Dei in the Western Highlands.*

*In the Mendi council area, the maximum bride price for a single girl has been set at $100 cash plus four pigs and four pearl shells. For a divorced woman or widow with no children, the maximum settlement is $50 cash plus three pigs and three pearl shells. For a divorcee or widow with children the maximum payment will be $30 cash plus two pigs and two pearl shells.*

*If the man comes from outside the Mendi council area he is not allowed to pay more than $200 in cash and items for his bride.*

*In the Dei council area, the bride price for a single woman must not exceed $300. For a woman who has been married previ-*

*ously the maximum price is $80. The council has ruled that if the woman is marrying for the third time the man need not pay for her.*

*Under the rules which are now in force, marriage settlements must be witnessed by councilllors for the wards in which the bride and groom are living.*

*The marriage must be registered by the councils.*

We continued to grow deep friendships with coworkers at Banz Ag School. Max Braunack, a fruit farmer from Australia, was the caretaker. His wife, Ann, added luster to my days because she loved reading, flowers, and music, just as I did.

Having lived and worked with Australians, we had gotten used to "supper" meaning the snack one eats before going to bed. One night, our American friends Al and Dellene Stucky, who were Wycliff Bible translators at a nearby station, invited us for supper. We had forgotten that to them, "supper" meant the evening meal. So, we ate our evening meal at our house and then went. Dellene had supper ready, so we ate again.

I turned thirty-four years old on December 1, 1969. My memories of this day are absolutely beautiful, from a sentimental mother's viewpoint. Norris had given Nathan, age eight, and Steven, six, a dollar each to buy something at the Trade Store for my birthday. On the way home from school, I waited in the car while they went shopping. As they came from the store, they carried "it" behind them. They sat on "it" on the way home, hiding "it" so I wouldn't know what "it" was. When at the house, they collected paper, tape, string, and pencils from all directions, and they began a wrapping frenzy. They claimed the porch and I was told to, "Stay out."

At supper time, I unwrapped a cute little two-quart aluminum saucepan. I still treasure it. Characteristically, way ahead of time in planning, Norris' Mom had sent a birthday package along with us in the summer time in our trunk. So, now I got to open that gift and wear the soft green nightgown. Norris gave me a record of western songs to spin on our new player he had brought home from a school trip to Lae.

Advent that year in our home was special. By now, our kids knew some carols, so we sang as a family. I set up candles and a wreath. We prepared towel and soap gifts for twenty-five Bible school students who would be baptized at the church. Norris and the boys built a doll house for Karen. It was kept a secret until the 24th when we presented it to Karen wrapped in rag rugs. We had packed Lego and Spirograph sets in our barrels from the United States, so I wrapped and placed them under our tree. Steven gave me the most original and tender gift of all: three little match boxes, taped together, with a piece of candy in one drawer, an "I love you" note in the second, and two pennies in the third. I still have it in my dresser drawer.

*Karen, taking a first look at her dollhouse, which became a memorable childhood toy.*

Christmas worship at the church was a program in three languages. We ate turkey dinner at Jamieson's on the 25th. Since it was holiday time, there were lots of games and eating with on-duty school boys and other station people. We would soon be starting the New Year, 1970.

A friend from New Effington wrote that, "This is some of a winter." Once again, we thought we were lucky to be in the tropics! Nathan wrote to his South Dakota grandparents, "If I was there, I would build a snowman so high you couldn't touch the top." He also claimed that he could milk a cow faster than the first year students at the Ag School. Confidence was growing. Being nine seemed like a landmark for him. He learned to solder his own broken toy, how to make pancakes, and he walked the two miles from school with the Braunack children.

I've always believed that letter writing builds relationships, so will include several in this chapter, including samples from our children.

A Nazarene missionary terminated service at their hospital station. He gave our boys a pony named Rhee, so now, Nathan could put on his birthday Stockman boots and be along on rounding up cattle. He and Steven had already practiced riding on our station pony named Soldier.

We had a beautiful Bougainvillea bush growing between our laundry house and a shed that Norris wanted to move. Practicality took precedence over aesthetics. The building was moved, and the flower-covered shrub was torn apart. I cried. Steven asked me why I felt so sad. When I told him, he cried with me. Just then our dentist, Mr. Wilson, from Mt. Hagen drove in. He asked what was up. We said we were crying for the bush. The doctor understood our sentimental feelings and joined the mourning party. We decided a replacement should be planted, sat down for a cup of tea, and then we each went on with our day.

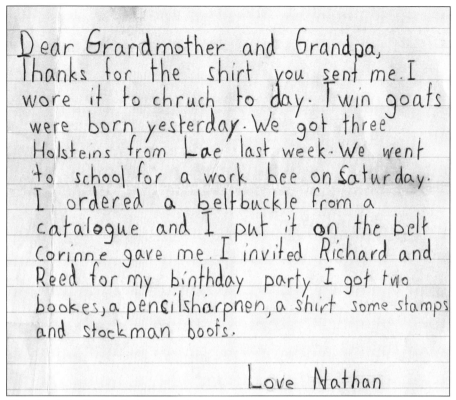

*Above is a letter Nathan had written to his grandparents.*

Norris' mechanical and other fix-it skills became known amongst local and mission people. Some missionaries planned a break at Banz Station, in their longer trips, so as to receive Norris' Good Samaritan services. Natives would bring him a wrist watch, a flashlight, a radio, hand-powered sewing machine, bicycle or the village-owned truck. There was more than one way to be a blessing as we lived amongst and loved the New Guinea people.

Udal was our station carpenter. While he was working at another station, a Banz Ag student spent the night with Udal's wife. Norris and Reinhard attempted to admonish and reason with the student, teaching that this was not right. He, in turn, slugged Norris and broke his glasses. This was not his first offense, but it became his last. My house girl, Tun, also was involved. Both were dismissed. School was a privilege (and misconduct would not be tolerated like it is in current America).

The Stuckys were with us for Easter dinner. The kids played croquet, rode horses and swam in the dam. The adults watched them and enjoyed it. We also

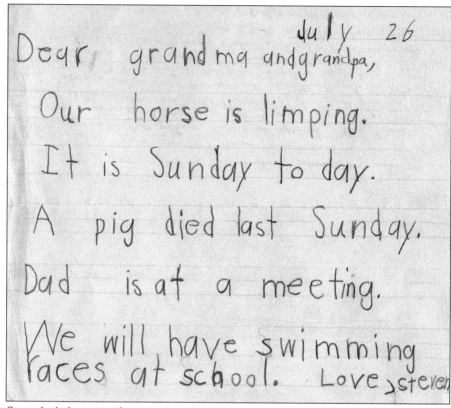

*Steven had also written home.*

played Password and discussed our work concerns and news from home. Very faithful people to this day, the Stuckys served in New Guinea for forty years. We had a lot in common. Dellene was a South Dakota girl.

South Dakota, as my home state, is like a very old friend. It has some strengths and some weaknesses, but I love it in its totality, both for what it is and for what it is not. Sometimes cold in climate, South Dakota is warm in personality. We felt this in our welcome back from New Guinea.

Back at home in South Dakota, my Dad managed the Williamson eighty acres. We had started buying this land for $37.50 an acre with our teachers' salaries in New Effington. One day in 1971, I asked Norris what he thought our total financial worth was. After eleven years of marriage, and in just a few minutes of figuring, we decided about $17,000.

In writing this, neither Norris nor I can remember much about our pay during those years. We know the basic allowance was $263 a month. Everyone got the same amount, from the Bishop to the newest support staff member. We don't recall much money talk at all. The common joke was that to increase salary one needed to have another baby, because the scale went by how many children were in hand.

Through my connections with the indigenous primary school, I noticed one bright little girl with an almost constant smile. I checked into her family. Her parents had both died, and she was being raised by an uncle named John, who was a Bible School teacher near our station. Pursuing our hearts' desire to bring someone from New Guinea home to the United States with us, we asked John if he would permit us to groom his niece for this opportunity. He consented. We sent her to Wau for two years of immersion in English, modern living, and learning at the boarding school for missionary children. At the same time, a successful publishing couple from Circle Pines, Minnesota, John and Eleanor Yackel, came our way and offered to pay the cost of her airplane ticket. That is how God works behind the scenes, and that was how Dongau, later, spent a year with us in America.

The annual Women's Retreat that year was at Nobonob, a high altitude mission station perched above the Madang coastal valley. In memory, I still rank it as a mountaintop experience. We were sixty women led by a missionary with forty years' experience in Africa. Galatians 5:22 was the theme. The wonder of God's creation and love, once again, filled my heart. I got to help lead a sunrise communion service overlooking the sea, a closing highlight.

Our VW hatchback was often the means of morning transportation to the elementary school three miles away. One morning, as I was taking the neighbor children and our sons to school, a very pregnant, stressed woman and her husband stood at our door. The mother had been in labor several days, and they needed a ride to the Nazarene Mission Hospital five miles beyond our Banz Public School.

The couple got into the car with us. Just as we neared the school, the mother's water broke, and the baby's head presented. The father was very happy, stating, "Now, we won't go to the hospital! We can just go home." Rather than do a delivery in the car, I firmly declared, "We now will be going to the hospital... really fast!"

I did not stay through the birthing, but some days later the family came to our house with the new baby. Apologetically, they explained to me that they wanted to name the child "Mrs.," because I had helped them, but that this name wouldn't fit a boy. They wondered if it would be okay with me if they named their little boy "Meland." I told them we would be honored.

We were later invited to a naming party in their 100 square foot home. Twenty people were there. I was presented with a hand-made bamboo tray with a New Guinea mother and baby design. I think the brother, Joe, who was in school, had made it.

Our mothers were very good at sending birthday and Christmas gifts, and sometimes packages in between, from home. One contained a swim suit for Joe, the big brother of Baby Me-

*Norris and I held our namesake, Meland Kabuk.*

land. (An addendum to this story is that in 2005, after being away from New Guinea for thirty-three years, we got a letter from the grown-up Baby Meland. In 2006, when we visited New Guinea, we met Meland and his mother. Big brother Joe now works for a Toyota business in another town and drove seventy miles to see us. He and his wife gave us a $40 gift package of New Guinea coffee. We have so often been so very blest.)

Continuing with the theme of writing letters, the following is an excerpt from one I wrote home in September of 1970:

*"We got back from our school camp-out yesterday about 3:00 p.m. It seemed I spent most of last Thursday packing up and organizing. At 10:00 a.m. Friday, we left. We stopped midway for a sack lunch. We were thirty-one children, aged five to twelve, and five adults in one truck and two pickups. We arrived at a bird sanctuary about 2:00 p.m. It is located forty miles beyond Mt. Hagen. Altitude there is only 3,000 feet, and the vegetation is like a rain forest, with high, straight trees as the tall layer, shorter shrubs and bushes underneath, and then three-foot begonias and ferns under that. The men and boys put up two tarp tents, one for the men and boys and one for the girls and women. There was a bush material shelter, with a fireplace near it, where we girls set up the cooking. The kids were rostered out for helping. We were blessed with absolutely gorgeous weather: sun and slight breeze in daytime and full moon every evening.*

*There must have been two dozen kinds of birds of paradise, crowned pigeons, and numerous other birds and an equal number of tree kangaroos and other little forest animals in cages. We spent one forenoon looking at them and also taking evening walks, led by a ranger, seeing the activities of the nocturnal animals.*

*Each afternoon, we all went swimming in the river. Between times, we played games. In the evening, we had planned activities. The first evening was spent on song fests around the campfire. On the second night, the children had a spontaneous skit program. Australians call these "concerts." The kids sang, recited poems, told jokes, performed dramatizations, or whatever they could. Norris auctioned off the teacher's coat. I sang "Old Shep." Karen acted out "Old Mother Hubbard," all five verses. Nathan and Steven did a song about their teacher who killed her dog because he stole a sausage off her table. Everyone had a good time.*

*Norris made pancakes for everyone on Sunday morning. I had mixed the dry ingredients at home. They really hit the spot. Every kid looked after his own cutlery, plate, cup, bed roll, clothes, and so on. After breakfast, we had an outdoor Sunday School hour and then went for a long mountain hike and swim. At the swimming hole was an old tree protruding from the water where all the kids went diving. Nathan worked on his belly flop and turned it into a dive. Karen built sand castles with the five-year-olds, and told me, "to keep an eye on that one little girl, because she's pretty small, you see." Actually, the other little girl was older, but smaller, than Karen.*

*When we came home yesterday, Nathan and Dou heated water and got the clothes washing going. Steven and I unpacked and put things away, so today, we're all back to normal."*

So that we can appreciate anew the thought and forthright innocence of children and their thought, language and development, I will share some glimpses and gleanings from 1969-1971 at Banz.

- One day, Norris came from a meeting at Asaroka. He handed Karen a shoe box. It had holes punched in the side. Inside was a small, silky, black kitten. Karen played with Midnight and mothered it almost non-stop until one tragic day; a native dog killed it. So, we got a less beautiful tabby cat for replacement. Dogs did not allow it to live, either. The kanakas (a Pidgin-English word meaning the less learned people) would eat cats and dogs. Sadly, when seeing the firm dead body of Tabby, Karen reasoned that maybe, if we put her in the oven, she would thaw out and could live again.

Our third attempt for a pet was a kapul, a cat-sized, fur-bearing tree kangaroo, which Karen dubbed, "the cute little fellow." However, he was a marsupial, so he slept all day in his cage and could not be a good daytime playmate.

Then we tried a bird, a pretty little parakeet from the forest. It became quite tame, would sit on our shoulder, and could eat from a hand. We did not have a good enough bird sitter when we went on vacation. When we came back it was not alive.

I guess we were not good pet keepers, so I'm glad my grandkids have been able to have Bella, Toby, and Buddy.

- After reading a bedtime Bible story to the children, Steven remarked, "It will be fun when I get up to heaven and see Abraham, Noah, and all those other guys."

- I had the rare find of a package of Scandinavian bread in Madang during January vacation. Nathan, in 1st Grade, was eating flatbread with 2nd Grade friend, David Braunack, as an after school snack. Nathan explained, "This is Norwegian bread, so now we are little Norwegians." This was followed by "Butte, Bitte" (German for "Butter, please"). I was amused how German, Norwegian and English all fit in this little boy's conversation.

- Karen was talking to her doll: "You remember last year when you were on the farm, when Grandma was driving Grandpa's tractor, and I was along?"

- A quote from my letter to my Mom in 1970: "Steven is a real charmer, cute and at ease with new people and places. He has a smile and something to say to everyone..."

- The childrens' heights on March 30, 1970, were: Nathan 4'4"; Steven 4'; Karen 3'2."

- There was an annual Sports Day for about 500 students from eight schools in the Hagen district. Two-thirds of the participants were white and the remaining third were native children, all in 1st through 6th Grades. They wore uniforms representing their different schools. In the parade, they carried banners. There were competitions, games, and lots of fun. They also had ball throwing, broad jump, high jump, and so on. Steven won 1st place out of seven sack racers in a fifty-yard competition. That evening he said, "The parade was very good, and my teacher told me I am the best little marcher in her room."

- We were invited to a baptism dinner at a New Guinea home. They gave the guests gifts to share their happiness. We got a rooster. It was quite tame. Steven was feeding it and came in and said, "I think he's going to lay an egg." Nathan explained, "Now, whoever heard of such a thing?"
- I kept Tietze's baby Aias for a day while his mother, also named Karin, went along to Mt. Hagen. Our Karen loved it. Gazing at the tiny creation, her conversation went like this: "He's just as sweet as I was, isn't he, Mommy? I'd like to keep him two days. Why can't we have a baby, Mommy? I'll bet he'll be a worry when he grows up. You know, his big brothers are sort of humbugs."

*Reinhard and Karin Tietze and their potential "humbugs," Johannes, Markus and Aias in a family photo mailed to us after we returned to the United States. A daughter, Susanne, completed the family when she was born later.*

- Karin Tietze made a great forty-year birthday party for her husband, Reinhard. There were balloons, flowers, cake, music, and the three station couples as guests. At breakfast the next day, we told our kids about it. "I can hardly wait until I get that old," declared Steven.
- My Mother wrote that the Florence parish was putting new carpet in the parsonage. I usually read the letters from home out loud. Steven heard about the floor cover project and, typical of his generous nature, offered to "give five of my dollars to start buying a carpet for our floor. Would that help? I really wish we had a fluffy floor." (All floors in Mission homes were varnished wood.)

The cute things my children said and did are rich treasures for me now. I'm glad for memories of activities in which we were involved.

## Chapter Thirty-Nine

# Work and Family

In 1971, Banz School set up a little agricultural store to improve the subsistence farming of the community locals. Some of the items sold were: worm medicine for hogs, staples and wire for fencing, sprayers and weedicides for the coffee gardens, garden seeds, fertilizers and hand tools.

Students worked in shifts at the store, hopefully learning a few business principles at the same time. Once, the students sold $250 worth of sweet potatoes to a village that didn't plan six months ahead, and so ran out of their staple food. The school did about $700 of business per month, including the sale of eggs, milk, and vegetables to the coast where the temperature was too hot for these foods to be produced. With these funds, they ran the station and also built new classrooms. By 1972 the goal of creating a self-supporting school was achieved and enough funds were generated through the sale of milk, eggs, pigs, chicken, coffee and vegetables to pay a New Guinean staff.

Life on the mission field was exciting—something different every day.

One student took the horse and dehorning shears to the village to dehorn a cow for a "onetok" (a tribal person who speaks the same language). This was done without permission. He had a record of prior disobedience, so this act terminated his studies at our school.

Norris woke up one morning with a case of mumps. At age forty, this was no picnic. When the system is weakened, malaria sets in as well, so over the next nine days he was very sick and lost fourteen pounds. As usual, we called on the Great Physician. God heard and healed. Steven caught mild mumps, but Karen and Nathan remained healthy.

I had never attended a District conference, so I asked Norris if it would be possible to attend one before we returned to the United States. The following letter was written on July 26, 1971.

*Dear Mom and Dad,*

*Now it is 10:30 a.m. Norris and I are seated outside under a grass thatched roof with about eight other missionaries and 100 delegates from eight circuits (like a parish at home) for a district conference. Each circuit gives a report on their work for the year. Most of the talk is done by New Guineans, in preparation for their own leadership later. Questions are asked and discussions are informal. Around the outside of the shelter are a couple hundred village people dressed in leaves or nude. Delegates are fairly well dressed. Locals are seated on bunches of leaves as we had a heavy rain yesterday and with all these people tramping around the ground is very musky. The sun is nice and bright, but at an altitude of 8,000 feet it is still cold, so I have my slacks on under my dress and two sweaters on top.*

*The chairman of Bible Schools and the seminary is making a report. So, I have one ear on that as I write. Everything is done in Pidgin-English. Problems all seem pertinent and brought forth in sincerity.*

*I've never been to one of these conferences and figured this was my last chance. I thought there wasn't room for me, but just in time yesterday morning we decided there was and I asked the kids what they thought.*

*Nathan said, "Why not, mom? You don't have to worry about us. We have plenty of stuff we can do around here; if I didn't have to go to school, I'd go." Steven and Karen agreed, so I talked to Karin Tietze whose three little kids we had kept for 10 days awhile back and she said she would keep an eye on them, too. After school and for supper they will be down there. For the night and for breakfast they will be with Dou. So, I think they are getting along okay, God willing.*

*Love, Lorraine*

After giving my perspective, Norris added his portion to the letter. In New Guinea, transportation was always shared and vehicles were often full of people on different errands. Norris' description of the District conference includes the trip to Alkena in a Toyota Land Cruiser and the ensuing events:

*We left Banz at 8:00 a.m. with one student who is doing ag extension work at the Bible School twenty-five miles away; twenty dozen eggs, twenty-five pints of milk and ten half pints of cream for Mt. Hagen, which is fifty miles down the road; one boar pig for a station up the road sixty miles; one bag of concentrate for the station eighty miles away, and also one teacher's wife and newborn baby for that same station; and, finally, the five of us who are delegates to this conference. Oh yes, we also had along one student who is to get a fan belt in Mt. Hagen for the missionary's car and return to Banz.*

*After making the necessary stops we arrived at our destination. There, I set the brakes on a tractor they were using to haul food and people to the conference from thirty miles away. Then, I shot the bull which they would use to feed the conference gathering. The next morning came and the tractor battery was dead. They had dressed out the bull and taken the stomach to the river a mile away to wash it, long after dark. When they returned during the night to get some people to push the tractor, other people had stolen the stomach. Since the tractor generator was not working, I took the truck battery and put it in the tractor, then put the tractor battery in the truck and pulled the truck to get the battery charged. Now, at the conference, I will change the batteries back again as theirs is charged up.*

*We will leave for Banz again tomorrow morning at 7:00 and should be home by 4:00 p.m. Thankful for a weekend of fellowship and activity with these people.*

*Love, Norris*

It seemed there were always people at our door. One morning right after Christmas, when Norris was gone, I decided to count who came by and why.

1. Jana, a student, came to get keys for the poultry house. Everything was kept locked because of constant stealing.
2. Yawe, a new West Irian refugee teacher, asked where the tire patches were. He was in the workshop fixing someone's tire.
3. Jim, a student in charge of gardening, wondered if Norris had more cabbage seed.
4. Mugang, a native pastor, wanted to buy a little alcohol for starting his primus, a kerosene single-burner stove.
5. Vui, a woman from the village, wanted to give me six cucumbers.
6. Gary Marks, a Scotsman and manager of a church-connected major marketing company, needed Norris' advice on his truck.
7. Tera, a student, wondered who would drive the milk, eggs, and vegetables to the air strip to send them on the plane to market in Madang.
8. Yawa, a village woman, wanted to sell me some potatoes.
9. Mrs. Major, the wife of a coffee plantation owner, came to pay the bill of $40 for 200 of our used, empty feed bags, which they would fill with coffee beans that they bought from the natives.

10. Karin Tietze came to get camoquin (malaria pills), sugar, flour, cough syrup and mayonnaise which I had brought from Mt. Hagen on our trip the day before. We didn't get home until evening, so I hadn't delivered them yet.

By then it was ten o'clock, and I had seen ten people, so I quit recording.

Another morning, there was a sudden revelation that the students were having a strike. The school boys got to comparing government schools with mission schools and decided that work at our school was too hard and things just weren't quite fair. Thus, they stayed in their garden and houses, so classes and Ag departments would shut down for a couple days.

The government did provide more benefits, but their training wasn't nearly as thorough, so Norris, Reinhard and Lorenz took it in stride. They did the necessary work and then chose to sit in visible places by the bamboo tree, like many village people did, to visit, drink coffee and pray that peace would return to the campus. This was much easier than doing lesson plans and teaching classes anyway, and kind of a reversal of roles from the white man's 20th century ambitious drive to a "take it easy" way of tribal men.

The students shyly observed from a distance. On day three, they sent an ambassador to say they would like to have a meeting. Without television and structured jobs, the culture loved meetings—the longer the better. This was sometimes hard on missionary patience!

A letter came, addressed to the student body, followed by a visit from one of the members of parliament. Discussion ensued, and agreements were made that led to studies being resumed. The mission staff appreciated the intervention of concerned leaders as it represented lasting, changed attitudes toward education.

The women's work continued. The class sewed fifty-one blouses for wives of native student pastors. These would be given to them at Christmas. Four of my women had perfect attendance for weekly classes, going from February to November. I considered that a great record.

It seemed we had a constant run of guests, maybe for a meal, a day or an overnight, or a couple of nights. They came from many places and backgrounds and various connections with the mission. This ministry of hospitality included:

- A World Brotherhood exchange man from Hecla, South Dakota.
- Mr. and Mrs. Roberman from Holland. He was serving as an agricultural officer with the New Guinea government.
- Banz 6th Grade girls and their mothers for a send-off to their high school at Goroka, seventy miles away.

- Theo Stiller's sister and husband from Australia.
- A music teacher from South Carolina, who worked at another station.
- A family from New Zealand on staff at a nearby Christian Leaders Training College.
- The mission accountant, on vacation from the field headquarters.
- An American mother, brother, and sister-in-law of a single teacher who had worked with our mission for ten years.
- A student from the Lutheran Seminary in St. Paul, Minnesota, who was doing a year of internship in New Guinea.
- A New Guinea man who would be the organist at my friend Phyllis Liefson's wedding.
- A young native man from Ghana, Africa, who was a speaker at a neighboring Christian Leaders Training College conference, spent a supper hour and evening with us. We talked long into the night, comparing his country and New Guinea.
- Soloman Islanders came one weekend. Their skin was black as coal, and their pure white souls committed to God. Oh, Boy! They really could sing and preach!
- Pastor Paul and Janine Jordahl, originally from Wisconsin, now from the seacoast of New Guinea, sat with us on the steps of our home under full moonlight, singing in parts and sharing stories. They had an active sense of humor, so healthy laughs were interspersed.
- An on-and-on breakfast service when Vic Sandager and sons, John and Mark, from Hills, Minnesota, returned from a several-day walk-in trip to the Jimi Valley. This remote area was only accessible by plane or foot, being locked in by steep mountains. Vic had now served as a volunteer for one year as station caretaker at Kotna. Their adventure brought out the appetite of teenage boys. We had lots of eggs at Banz Ag School, so I fried one after the other, and all were relished and devoured.
- Basanu, sister of our Kotna carpenter, Manis, was a memorable guest. She had smoked home-grown tobacco rolled in newspaper since the age of seven. Now, she was a very committed deaconess type of single lady. She related how God told her to give up the cigarettes. She quit smoking cold turkey, and now, even the thought of her old habit made a putrid taste in her mouth.

At the end of each year at the Ag school, we had a graduation ceremony. I re-wrote the words for this well-known song so that we could use it appropriately for such occasions.

*I saw the highlands with crops prolific;*
*I saw the ocean, the South Pacific;*
*The Wahgi Valley with water rolling;*
*This land was made for you and me.*

*The sun was shining, and I was working*
*Out in my garden, but rain was coming.*
*A soft wind blowing seemed to be saying,*
*This land was made for you and me.*

The end of the year holiday was a week at Graget Island off the coast of Madang, near where Dongau was born. This was a vacation taken for needed rest. Come with me to relive a coastal day via a December 17, 1971, aerogram that my mother saved:

*We had sandwiches and coconut milk for noon lunch at the beach. The boys are swimming. Karen is picking up shells. Two big ships sit in the harbor, one from China and one from Japan. We can travel across the bay into Madang by a small motorboat that families here use, like you use a car there. Our boys have tried to snag bait fish with a many pronged pointed spear. So far, little luck. One story was that a sword fish took the bait! There are big tuna and mackerel jumping nearby. Yesterday, Nathan was down at the dock by 7:00 a.m.*

*The serenity of a quiet sea creates an all pervading feeling of rest and calmness, good for body and soul. Every once in a while a hollowed log canoe goes by, paddled by one or two New Guineans, much more plain and simple than the noise and speed of civilization's boats. Around the corner, the land juts toward the ocean at large, so breakers of foam rumble against the rocks. I sat on that side for a twilight-close to yesterday. The beam from a lighthouse blinked every couple seconds. Now, a sailboat is coming into view. I love this location!*

Now, for a few more quotes and glimpses within the family:

• Karen wanted me to read to her that night, and I was doing something else at the time, so Nathan said, "You bring me your little chair in the

163

bathroom, and sit down nice, and I'll tell you a story while I'm having my bath." So, he sat in the little plastic shower tub and went on. "Now, I'm going to tell you all about Florence Nightingale..." It was so cute! I sat in the living room and listened to the whole thing and learned quite a lot. Language was very contemporary, like "so, she came down to the place where the wounded were in the hospital and saw how messy it was and saw all the suffering and she said, 'Well, we gotta do something about this!'" In social studies at school each kid had to give a report on something, so he had gotten the information there.

- August 1971: Norris couldn't figure out how the Briggs & Stratton gas engine on the Maytag washing machine just kept going, one or two times a week, three or four hours each time, for nearly eight years and he'd only changed the spark plug and serviced the engine.
- October 13th: I was teaching Karin Tietze to play the lightweight upright pump organ. She played the guitar and was naturally musical, so learning was going fast. Meanwhile, Norris was having a hard time teaching one of his students, Walta, to plow and had written home about it:

> *"He has no feel for it at all. I take the welder to the field to repair so it won't take so long. We got stuck last night, so Nathan, Steven, and I went down at six this morning to get the tractor out. We're just getting into the wet season. Nathan says, 'I want to plow when we get home. You never let me plow here. You say the students have to learn.' It's eight o'clock now, and we're having boiled eggs and toast for breakfast. We eat the cracked eggs because we can't sell them."*

- One Sunday we planned a fishing picnic. It turned out to be hilarious! Nathan forgot the worms. The river was too swift to net. Lorenz Uthardt and his wife, Dagmar, were along and wanted us to hike twenty minutes to the best spot. Our feet got mired with mud. Karen spilled the lemonade jug. Norris heated beans on an open fire in a tin can without opening it. It exploded, and beans flew everywhere. The can landed in the river. We laughed and laughed and decided we must all be newcomers.
- Nathan and Steven sat by the river with Lorenz, waiting for ducks to fly in. Lorenz was a wonderful new adult friend. The boys were mesmerized by his hunting and fishing stories. Later, Nathan and Steven went with Lorenz to the Ag School classroom where he supervised the school boys' evening homework. With imagination fueling their minds, our boys sat in one corner with head in hand and elbows on the desk,

for two hours, experiencing Lorenz's tales. This was something far superb to Hollywood and TV, moonlight episodes from a loving, infectious, enthusiastic personality!

## Chapter Forty

# Homeward Bound

As January 1972 rolled around, we knew the next year would be a time of transition. We had submitted the following letter of termination on June 28, 1971:

*Norris Meland*
*Box 30, Banz, W.H.D.*
*Territory New Guinea*

*ATC World Mission Office*
*Church Council*
*President, Rev. Pech*
*LES, Don Ruthenberg*
*Ed. Sec., Ray Blacklock*

*Dear Brethren,*

*In our service and furlough record of September 3, 1970, I stated that we were uncertain as to our plan of service. We now wish to inform those in concern of our intent to terminate our missionary service in New Guinea.*

*With the approval of those in authority we request this termination take place at the time of our three months optional furlough, mid-May 1972.*

*This decision is not because of any dissatisfaction with our work here at Banz or with the mission organization. The Lord has certainly blest and provided for us in every way, and we are grateful for the privilege of working nine years on this field.*

*We would like to offer some of the reasons for our decision to conclude service here:*

*1. Both Mrs. Meland's parents and my own are in the 70-80 year bracket. We will have been in mission service nearly ten years by departure time and feel the need to share in caring for our own parents in their old age.*

*2. In our opinion, civil order is breaking down fast in New Guinea, and the probability of remaining here until retirement seems unlikely.*

3. *Lessening employment opportunities beyond the age of forty have to be considered, as well as the possibility of taking over one of our parents' farms.*

4. *The work being done in our boarding schools among young people demands considerably more than ten hours per day, six to seven days a week, and an additional resource of physical and mental energy and stability. From my viewpoint, it is a job for a person between 20-40 and not the forty-plus era, which I am entering.*

5. *We feel there is a great need to be a Christian influence in our own country at this time. We wish to leave the field here in good standing and, should the Lord call us back in the distant future, may we be ready to obey.*

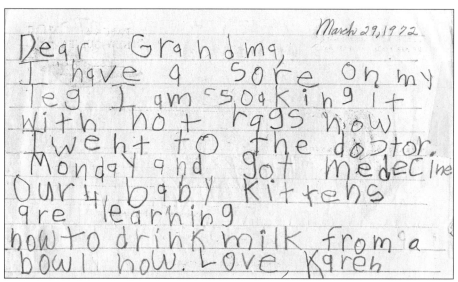

*My Mom loved her first real "Grandma letter" from Karen, written on an aerogramme.*

It was a new year, and Norris and I were making decisions for winding up our New Guinea term and re-entry to American living. Meanwhile, our children's world of play needed no prior organizing. Our kids lived one day at a time and always helped us keep the right perspective on life. One Sunday review reads like this:

*"The kids went swimming twice in the stock dam today and had five native kids here with them for picnic dinner and playing most of the afternoon. They made a campfire outside, fried fish fingers and roasted bamboo shoots;*

*then, they made bamboo flutes and ran around, blowing on them. Karen is
such a playhouse girl! I think I'll have to fix my old playhouse between the
two evergreens behind our house at home for her this July. She would just as
soon take over my kitchen here sometimes; she makes up new recipes, plans
dinners, feeds her dolls, straightens the place, and oh, my! So busy, talking
the whole time about all what is going on in her little world."*

Following the Australian-New Guinea school year, December and January
are holiday months. The American school year (September–May) never jibed for
missionary kids. We planned ahead, having United States home school materials
with us for our children, February–April, 1st, 3rd, and 5th Grades. This was a
more flexible schedule than regular school, so they also got in on station activities. For instance, Nathan started his farming career with one sow, and practiced
salesmanship getting rid of the piglets. Steven was catching minnows from the
dam. Karen, age five and a natural scholar, zipped into writing.

My parents often sent money "to be used as needed." The paragraphs below
show how easily it could be spent.

*One pastor's son had hepatitis since before Christmas, and our carpenter
worked in the same village, so it just turned out for me to send some food over
every day to get him strong more quickly. He is back in school just this week.
Seems a bright young boy, so would be a pity to have missed the year.*

*Also, the widow of the funeral we wrote about last fall nearly talked
herself into dying last month, so we got her to the hospital, washed, fed, and
clothed her, and convinced her that God decides when our time on earth
is up. Stoic people, these are. Last Friday, she came to my door. She had
been released from the hospital and walked the five miles home by herself,
so we had a cup of tea and sandwich on our kitchen floor to celebrate the
homecoming and thanked God together. They all prefer floor-sitting to using
chairs, because that is their custom. 'Em tasol' (that's all for now).*

Flowers were at prime beauty after the rainy season. In March, I started wondering how I would ever adjust to winter again. Our folks wrote about blizzards
and minus zero temps. I had eight colors of roses from my own garden on my
table. This might never happen again.

Some days were bitter-sweet as I sorted through our personal things and
spilled a few tears amongst them. Much would be disbursed. Some items fit the
take-home category and were sent off in a barrel on a truck for shipping to the
United States. Five outfits apiece would be saved for living from the suitcase

during our journey home. Housekeeping now was very easy—just the bare necessities.

We applied for jobs in South Dakota schools, near our parental homes, Florence and Redfield. We learned about openings there from a Teacher Vacancy List. After much talking with God about the matter, we did like Gideon in Judges 6:36-40—relied on divine guidance. If we were hired, or not, we would be okay. We mailed our letters of application on April 6th and then bought a plane ticket for traveling home in May. Required cholera and typhoid shots were taken. Norris bought an international drivers license. All the while, we continued work with our people as normally as possible.

Norris bought travelers checks at the bank, and when he did, the boy who sold them, Kui, had been one of our smallest students way back when we were teaching at Kitip School. Both Norris and Kui reflected upon the incident at Kotna Station nine years earlier, when a rain had stopped the peanut-planting process. It was this Kui, now a banker, who had raised his hand and bravely confessed to Norris, "We ate the peanuts!" That had been a depressing time years ago, but now, God had worked grace and this boy behind the counter shook hands with Norris and thanked him for coming to serve in his country.

On April 23rd at 5:00 p.m., I was thinking about making supper. The phone rang. "This is Mr. Likness from Florence, South Dakota," said the firm, clear voice. "It is midnight here. I just came home from a long school board meeting. They directed me to call and hire you two immediately."

I was so excited that I nearly dropped the receiver, but calmly stated that we would quickly respond. I did not realize an undersea cable had been installed, opening the phone service to the outside world. I thought our communication system was just between Mission Stations in New Guinea. Isn't that just like God, to answer in such a dramatic way we would never mistake or forget?

I was thrilled to be the bringer of good news and ran to the classroom. Norris, Lorenz, and Reinhard were having a Friday night staff meeting, sitting outside the building on the lawn. Together, we rejoiced and gave thanks. We telegrammed back that the Florence School should send contract with details. They did. We signed and posted them back.

Days from then on, until we left, were filled with deep emotions. Women came and cried with me. Their goodbye feast was again a chicken soup, cooked in a five-gallon cauldron over a wood fire outside. Each woman added some vegetables. Affection was liberally shown. A spirit of pensive thoughtfulness permeated the air. We ate together on the lawn for the last time. Blessings of small deeds done in God's strength were returning one hundred fold—all very humbling.

On Friday, two villages hosted us. Saturday, the school boys gave a farewell with dramatization, music, food and farewell gifts—all very touching. Lorenz and Dagmar, his wife, invited twenty other missionaries for the last Sunday afternoon together. Some of those people would be our lifetime friends in the United States. Some, we would never see again.

Sleep escaped me completely that last night. The next morning we arose at 5:30 a.m., did last minute pick-up and pack-up, and clamped shut the suitcase lids. We had a scant breakfast and then were taken to Mt. Hagan to fly to Port Moresby.

With us, was Oscar Natara, a coastal man who would stop off in Germany for three months of Ag studies and would return to work at our school, Banz Ag. He was to become the headmaster. Also with our family was Dongau, our long-planned-for girl, who would come and spend a year with us in America.

Even after eight months of arranging for this, Dongau's passport had never reached us. In desperation, we had wired the Embassy. They promised to meet us at Port Moresby Airport and deliver the passport. During our wait to transfer planes, no one came. We had prepared Dongau and ourselves to face this reality if it had to be. Without an important little booklet called a Passport, she could not go with us; she would simply return to Banz. Frantic last minute prayers flew heavenward. (I can feel the tension yet today, as I write.) As we were on the tarmac to board for Hong Kong, a stewardess came running and waving the Passport for Dongau! Praise and thanksgiving! Amen! And WOW!

Dongau said, "I feel like jumping ten feet into the air." With almost wobbly legs, we climbed the steps and looked for our seats. Just then, a Qantas Airline stewardess came to inform us that the economy section was overbooked, and since we had bought tickets early, we would be switched to First Class. Situated there in a special cabin, just behind the pilot's space, we were given blankets, slippers, eye masks, perfumed washcloths, juice and snacks. We could finally relax and revel in the mysterious serendipities God sent our way. As a bonus, this was Mother's Day. Our family of seven was finally off to Hong Kong!

Dongau had never been on a big plane before. I took her to the restroom to demonstrate how the gadgets there worked. Her response was, "My Uncle John will never believe me when I tell him I went to the toilet up in the sky!" We just stood together in the 3x4-foot lavatory and giggled for a long while before emerging.

While we lived in the international community in New Guinea, we rubbed shoulders with people who had traveled from many places, in various ways, who were glad to give recommendations and suggestions. Conversation there often included places seen, routing, costs, and other travel hints. The church paid for a direct flight plan, just to bring us home. We realized that this might be our last chance to see the world. Checking with the airlines, we had found that for a reasonable personally-paid expense, we could break the trip into stops along the way. I had bought a couple books on how to journey on a shoestring, then wrote ahead for reservations for beds at pensions. These were plain, but clean dormitory-type buildings in Europe and Asia. I also noted ideas about food and sites. We knew we had a place to sleep each night. The rest, we left in the hands of our Lord.

Chapter Forty-One

# Trip of a Lifetime

Our first view of Hong Kong came in evening darkness. There seemed to be an unbelievable never-ending vastness of lights below us. After landing, we were brought to a plush hotel, courtesy of the airline, for an overnight. Efficient porters scuffed down the hall quickly—so swiftly I could hardly see their feet move. Seeing a telephone mounted in the bathroom triggered a burst of laughter. After a long, hot bath, we tumbled into bed. It was my best sleep in weeks.

The next morning, we walked down the hotel street, which was solid with orderly people walking quickly. Their workday had begun. There were many jewelry places. We had budgeted for wrist watches that Norris and I needed, so we let ourselves be lured into a business place full of time pieces. A man at the door, offering a can of Coke, was also bait. Oh, yes, he could give us the best deal.

We walked out with new watches on our wrists. These would be well used in fast track living back home. In fact, I think we bought watches for Nathan and Steven at that point also.

Oscar bought a bracelet with green jade stones in it. Between the stones were Chinese characters, wishing the wearer health, wealth, and long life. With a kiss, he placed it on my wrist, a touching gesture. He had bought one for his mother and one for me.

Why not tour Hong Kong on our brief stop? We'd probably not visit here again, either. Foreign cab drivers were plentiful, knowledgeable, and charged reasonable rates. We told one when we needed to be back and what we wanted to see. He agreed on the price, and off we went. He had been born Buddhist, but went to Catholic and Protestant schools, and now followed Confucius' teachings, he said.

He took us past twenty-storied apartment buildings with laundry hanging out of the windows. It looked rather like cloudy flags in the breeze. These apartments evoked sympathetic feelings in this South Dakota girl from the open plains. I guess if 4,000,000 people are to live in one city, there has to be some layered living. Still, the city seemed clean and neat.

We saw a lot of boat homes, 10 to 20 feet long. Some Hong Kong people are born, live, and die on the water for several generations in these small vessels called sampans.

We were shown a hillside with many semi-buried urns, the average size being that of a two-gallon jug. They hold the bones and ashes of loved ones. From there, we could look across a strip of water: freedom on one side and Communist China on the other.

From Hong Kong, we flew to Delhi, India. A hot, dry, furnace-blast of heat hit us as soon as we deplaned. Ground personnel here were less friendly and less organized. We had been six hours in the air and were again glad to flop down and sleep. We had three double rooms, $4 each, breakfast included, at the YMCA. The next day we would visit Old Delhi, viewing New Delhi in a separate trip.

Old Delhi had numerous 7th Century dynasty buildings. Some of the 4.5 million residents had lovely homes, but the gap between rich and poor was huge and very evident. Many people slept on mats between $6,000,000 marble buildings. There were tiny hole-in-the-wall shops. Copper, ivory, and cloth were the most common products. Bartering for price was expected. Ninety rupees equaled one U.S. dollar. Old, white-haired, ragged men were laboriously carving ivory pieces from elephant tusks. I bought a set of ornate fruit picks. They wouldn't take much suitcase space. There seemed to be little sense about making things to help make daily life more comfortable. Well-worn bullock carts rumbled everywhere.

Eighty percent of India is Hindu, so cattle and all animals are sacred. They walked or reclined freely on the street.

Children were on the street, too, begging. The ground looked like gray and yellow clay. We saw precious few blades of grass and hardly a flower. With temps up to 109 degrees, that was understandable. A lot of water was needed for our bodies to stay hydrated.

Our next goal was Israel. We flew over Afghanistan's enormous areas of striated desert, interrupted by raises of rough land. The plane made a pit stop at Tehran, Iran. We spent an hour with vendors at the airport. A nicely trimmed, brown wool vest jumped out and grabbed Norris. I bought a teaspoon for my collection. (When we passed over Iraq, we had no inkling concerning the ugly war to come, thirty-five years later.)

Landing at Tel Aviv, we found Customs people to be prompt. We switched immediately to a bus and heard English being spoken in the seat behind us. A Jewish family, who had lived their working years in California, was now retiring in

Jerusalem. I thought of Biblical prophecies, saying in the latter times, this would happen en masse.

People were dressed like the folks back home. Cars whizzed by us. We saw orchards, wheat fields, olive groves, poultry houses, all possible only because of irrigation in an otherwise very barren land. No wonder Jesus often referred to contrasts between wet and dry, smooth and rocky. The sources of His parables and illustrations were vivid here.

We went to a German-Lutheran Hostel in Jerusalem. The buildings along that street were all stone construction, and the streets were very narrow. Having traveled westward across four time zones, we were tired again. Oscar and Norris went down the street and bought peaches, apricots, dates, figs, oranges and bread. After eating, we showered, had devotions, and went to bed feeling thankful.

The next morning, we made some phone calls and decisions on how we would spend the next three days in the Holy Land. An Orthodox Christian taxi driver was contracted. For $17, he would show us the sights we requested to see. Along the road were goats and sheep, tended by shepherds, dressed with wraps on their head, like our Sunday School Christmas programs portray.

Farmers were winnowing wheat by hand. Camels and donkeys were laden with water pots and all sorts of other cargo.

We saw the place of the Good Samaritan Inn and the Temptation Wilderness where Jesus spent forty days and overcame the temptations of Satan. We looked at the Qumran's red rock crevices where the Dead Sea Scrolls were preserved.

Our outdoor lunch in Jericho consisted of six plates of various breads. They were served with mixtures of ground up spinach, beans, sesame, cucumber, and eggplant. Of course, Coke was the beverage. A walk around the place where Joshua marched and blew the trumpet before the wall fell down seemed appropriate. The new Jericho was a small, but rich, area full of date palms, because of a spring that feeds the city.

Sycamore trees, like Zacchaeus climbed, were pointed out. People everywhere were very friendly and spoke some English. We passed The Garden of Gethsemane, Herod's Tomb, the place where Mary Magdalene is buried, and the place in Bethlehem where Jesus was born.

The last stop of the day was at The Holy Land Christian Orphanage that my parents and we had helped support for many years. The children were cute, and the workers dedicated. Space was very limited, however. A staff member said, "We are poor in everything, but faith. In that, we are rich!" Norris and I wished that we could magically transport the 400 children to a big, lush, green foliage area in New Guinea and watch them run. They would think they were in paradise!

The second morning, we slept late. After all, this was supposed to be a holiday, but we were always aware of limited time. Actually, this WAS a holiday in this country, so in keeping with tradition, a lady from the Israeli Tourism Bureau brought us six rose buds. Dongau and our kids played hide and seek and soccer with the Israeli kids down the street. Steven helped put rivets in a camel-skin hassock (footstool) that Norris bought. Karen was learning to whistle, and she practiced every spare moment.

Norris and I walked to the Dome of The Rock, where Abraham nearly sacrificed Isaac, also the spot where Solomon's Temple stood. Guards stood on the wall around Jerusalem. A local restaurant man told us, "There will always be war in Israel, but I hate it."

After eating out that evening, we went to a folk music concert. Antiphonal lines I'll always remember were:

*"Of what do we have too much? ROCKS.*
*Of what do we never have enough? WATER."*

On the third day we drove north to Galilee, stopping at Nazareth and The Sea of Galilee. We drank from Jacob's Well, Nathan and Steven swam in the Jordan River, and we sang with a Christian youth group on the Mount of Transfiguration. At the end of a long day, we arrived at the Mt. Carmel Retreat House. The smell of a good, hot Western meal was wonderful for us. Tired sojourners needed a hot shower, too! Everyone slept well.

On morning number four, we had a cereal and toast breakfast. A lovely piano in the parlor welcomed us to a two-hour song session. Oscar would always harmonize. A nice treat was sharing a ten o'clock coffee and devotion time with the staff. Then, we all practiced ping-pong until noon. Dongau and I washed clothes that afternoon, and then Oscar and I sang for a couple more hours.

An Assembly of God pastor and his wife, from Wales, England, lived and worked there. Also staying there, an Arab Christian married to a Canadian was working on Christian broadcasting into Africa. Oscar, Dongau, and I joined them for two more hours of evening song. At last, my soul was full of music again! I prayed I would find a soul mate in Florence to sing and play with. (So far, that prayer has not been answered.)

Dongau and I could hardly believe we had walked the places where Jesus walked. I couldn't think of anything I'd rather spend money on than to have had that experience. Over the centuries, there have been cycles of destruction and rebuilding, but it was still The Holy Land.

Expect the unexpected when traveling: the plane bound for Istanbul, Turkey, was seven hours late! The girl at the airport who confirmed our ticket had four rings on each hand, but very little in her head. Flight times had changed, unannounced to us. So we people-watched, did some reading, bought comics for the kids, and then let them scamper about using their own creativity. Anyway, we made it to the mid-point between Europe and Asia.

Located on the Black Sea, Istanbul is one of the oldest cities in the world. It was called Constantinople until 1453. Land and sea routes to Istanbul had been main streets for history.

The Topkapi Palace Museum displayed 1,200year-old swords, armor and helmets, as well as a lock of Mohammed's hair. Muezzins (Muslim prayer criers) were out on the minaret (tall slender tower) at regular intervals calling the people to worship. I assumed our guide was Muslim and told him that we were Christian. He said, "No problem. Some Christians good, some bad; Some Muslims good, some bad." We removed our shoes before entering the beautifully tiled Blue Mosque. The music playing inside was very dissonant, all in minor keys, and performed by one musician reclining on the floor beside a two-octave keyboard. This music evoked sad feelings for me, as I compared it to the harmonious, rich choir sounds in America.

After a night at the Zell Hotel, we were out on the street trying to select breakfast pastries from a towering display of many different kinds. Tea was served from beaker-like glasses. The streets were filled with cars dating back as far as 1947. Roses flourished everywhere. Hundreds of doves shared the marketplace.

The bazaar had so much jewelry, it hurt our eyes to look at it. People were like beasts of burden, carrying huge loads of cargo on their backs. These loads included vegetables, paper, furniture—most anything that they could mount and carry. Dinner was a meat based plate of vegetables.

The next day, we moved on to Athens, Greece. We flew by Air France. The plane had sophisticated blue upholstery, and the stewardess called me, "Madame."

Athens is surrounded by three mountains and the Mediterranean Sea. The marble in the columns of the Parthenon were carved from one of these mountains. We stayed at the Orion Hotel

We walked to the top of the hill where the aged Parthenon still stands. Construction began in 47 BC, and took fifteen years. Also, it was built by free men, not slave labor. Here is where old philosophers sat and discussed the issues birthing democracy. One spoiled American tourist in our group complained that there was no restroom at the top!

Our kids were too young to understand or appreciate all this history and geography, but they had plenty of energy for climbing the rocky hillside. The weather was glorious: a warm temperature, clear skies, and no mosquitoes. A sound and sight evening performance was delightful: girls in long skirts with pretty aprons, men with balloon-legged pants and puffy sleeves, guitars, dancing, songs, and effective lighting.

Pastries and black coffee cost 180 drachmas (six U.S. dollars). The escalator by the subway station entertained the kids as they went up and down many times. Cars were parked upon the sidewalks all over the city. Athens was a city of unique sounds, tastes, and sites.

Our stay in Athens was nearly over, so we returned to the airport. This was the busiest airport in which we'd been. We noted planes for Syria, Austria, Switzerland, Egypt and Iraq—all coming and going. With the cacophony of announcements, we nearly missed our plane to Rome, Italy. By now, we were seasoned enough to rush to the right queue and make it on time. (On this plane, Dongau forgot a coin purse. A kind stewardess sent it to our American address so it was there when she arrived home.)

There were no numbered seats so we picked window seats if possible. I sat by a sailor from Pennsylvania. Seeing and talking with a clean cut young American was a treat.

After disembarking, we rode the airport bus into the city and took rooms at the Vittoriana Pensione. Norris and I brought pizza and orange drink to the room for our evening meal.

The city of Rome was built on seven hills and served as governmental headquarters for a vast area. We hired a local cab driver (as suggested in the *Companion Guide to Rome*) who would guide us to the places we wanted to visit. At its time of glory, 117 AD, the Roman Empire stretched from Northern Britain all across Europe and into Northern Africa, covering 2½ million square miles! The Empire fell apart 1,500 years ago, but the principles of civil law developed there are used in the United States today.

The driver took us to the ruins of the Colosseum, a world famous amphitheater. It had been built by 35,000 slaves during a period of eight years and held 80,000 spectators. I could sense grief and anger well up within me when we stood where the crowds had watched lions kill Christians or gladiators fight for entertainment.

Another eerie experience was standing in a tunnel aisle of the San Callisto catacombs. Many thousands of bodies were buried there in enclosed shelf-like spaces, one above the other.

We walked the road Christians had walked to their martyrdom. Wild red poppies grew among the wheat along the side of the road.

While we were seeing the fountains and monuments, our driver said, "They're all going against the red light; we may as well go, too." We zig-zagged through several traffic lanes until we were safely delivered back to the pensione. We looked at each other with sighs of relief. Angels may have been dispatched on our behalf.

Our day was completed with hamburgers at an American restaurant and some very large strawberries that Oscar bought for dessert.

Sunday morning we went to St. Peter's, the largest Christian church in the world. It is built in the shape of a cross, 700 feet long and 450 feet across. The nave is 150 feet high. A huge statue of Saint Peter was the first thing noted. People kissed his toe as they entered, and it was worn thin! An enormous pipe organ began playing and choirs broke into song. Goose bumps spread over me as I stood, dazed, in one spot, not caring if I should see more or not. The aisles were full of standing people, quiet and reverent as mass was celebrated.

We left Rome by airport bus. The flight to Munich, Germany, included wonderful views of the Alps. Below, the mountains seemed enormous, powerful and endless. They were jagged, majestic, snow-covered peaks.

*In Rome, Oscar took a family photo while we were waiting for the city bus to take us back to our Pensione.*

Suddenly, it was announced that we would be stopping briefly at Geneva, Switzerland, a bonus surprise for us. That airport was very luxurious. We checked our luggage into a locker, and took a Swissair bus to have a look at the city. At the park, men were playing a bowling game in the spring sunshine and fifty-seven degrees Fahrenheit weather. Stores and houses displayed window boxes holding geraniums and pansies.

When we were back in the air, clouds surrounded us as we flew over Mont Blanc, the highest point in Western Europe. Before long, we landed in Germany. Waves of joy swept over us as we saw Reinhard waving to us. The ride to his home was two hours, smooth and fast in a Mercedes Benz. Karin showed us to a little apartment with a vase of fresh flowers on the table. We slept under eider down covers. The weather was rainy. We'd forgotten the uncomfortable feeling of being cold. Standing by their space heater was comfy. Long pants and sweaters were needed here.

Aias Tietze and our Karen (who would be turning six soon) were honored with a birthday cake. Dongau gave her an Italian souvenir doll and Oscar gave her a little red leather coin purse from Rome. Six years earlier I could never have imagined the trip we were on now. The day ended in devotions with Grandpa and Grandma Tietze. At their country acres, they were used to hosting city folks who came for rest at this peaceful place. We were so very blessed to have a week there.

Besides the hours of conversation, reminiscing, and wonderful German and Bavarian meals, we were taken to Munich and other areas. Reinhard showed us a real German beer garden, the site of the 1972 Olympics, and Oberhaus Castle. A day in Salzburg, Austria, where the movie, *The Sound of Music* was filmed in the Mirabel Gardens was very special to me. While there, we also went 200 feet under the Austrian Alps to see a salt mine and toured

*Our children, along with Markus (seated on donkey with Steven) and Johannes Tietze, enjoyed rides on one of Grandpa Tietze's pet donkeys.*

Mozart's home. The children had time to watch TV and play, enjoying the freedom of the farm setting, and our family enjoyed a visit to a Fairy Land park with life-size puppets, swan boats, and train rides.

Now we were preparing for land travel through Scandinavian countries. We considered renting a car, which led to the purchase of a small 1962 four-cylindar, four-door Fiat for $120 in U.S. currency. Norris put two new snow tires on the rear; purchased an International license plate and a month of liability insurance. Now the six of us were ready to travel for a little over $200. We agreed that if the car should break down we would use bus transportation as an alternative from that point on to Oslo, Norway.

It was a sad farewell again as we left Karin and Reinhard and their family, yet we were also eager to continue on our journey toward home. Oscar stayed on in Germany to receive training before returning to the Banz Agricultural School in New Guinea.

We decided to christen our little Fiat, "Experiment X." Autobahn driving was pressured, but we putted along—very often passed—at about forty-eight miles per hour, passing through forests of perfectly beautiful stately fir trees.

Before we left Germany, we heard one of the famous boys' choirs, sixty voices, singing in the Regensburg Cathedral. We had an opportunity (through a connection with a New Guinea agricultural teacher, Gunther Oelschlagel and his wife, Heidi) to stay in a 500-year-old castle at Warburg. We also visited with other missionaries, Pastor Dieder Menzel's family and the Walthers. We worked closely with Hans Dollinger while at Kotna, and were treated like kings during our visit with his family, touring picturesque Mespel Brunn Castle with moat and a textile factory. Their daughter, Kirstin, and Dongau had been students together in New Guinea and the two had a wonderful reunion. All of the families longed for New Guinea when they saw Dongau. As we approached the Danish border, we also stayed with a family from New Guinea, but now it was time to say, "auf wiedersehen," to Deutschland.

After getting the Danish stamp in our passports, we visited Odense, where a Dane in a gas station led us a few blocks to see Hans Christian Andersen's house. We drove fifty miles along the coast and then took a thirty minute ferry ride, driving the car up onto the boat, continuing toward Copenhagen. We stayed in a small hotel in Roskilde, eating open-faced sandwiches in a café.

We spent the next day sightseeing with a tour agency. Some of the sights included the mile-long "walking street," city hall, the changing of the guards at Amalienborg Palace, Tivoli Amusement Park, and the site of the then-pending Olympics. I noticed that many of the words here are the same as Norwegian.

After another half hour ferry ride, we were in Sweden. Our short stay in Sweden was with Lorenz Uthardt's uncle. He was a pastor who served in the largest Finnish immigrant church in Stockholm. He had indicated to us in a letter of invitation that the church had 21,000 members. The next day, Sunday, Norris had a speaking date in that huge, beautiful cathedral built in 1648. When he climbed the steps from the back room to the pulpit and looked out over the congregation there were twenty-one people in attendance, mostly women, with five of them being our family members! Norris spoke and Pastor Uthardt translated into Finnish. Following the service, Pastor Uthardt humbly mentioned that attendance was low because most members, except for the very old, had gone to their summer cabins.

We had planned to stay in the pastor's home, but one of their children had chicken pox.Arrangements were made for us to stay in the Salvation Army hotel. Across from where we stayed was a nice park, but whiskey-bottle bums and addicts claimed it as a resting spot. Police came and cleared them away once, but they were back within half an hour. We had also noticed long-haired, ill-clad hippies reclining on the capitol steps as well as by famous fountains and at intersections throughout Europe. This evoked feelings of pity in me. God never gives up on anyone, so I always prayed that they could change.

We spent Monday, June 12th, with a group of women on retreat at a church-owned summer house in the woods outside of Stockholm. It was good that we could be a blessing to them. They absolutely loved Dongau and our children, giving Dongau a $20 collection. On the envelope it said, "As the Father has sent me, so I send you." The retreat had a sauna, a form of cleansing and entertainment that was brought to Sweden by the Finnish. The sauna was an enjoyable novelty to us, and the kids and Dongau got a kick out of going from the hot sauna to the cold lake! We ended the day with a soup and bread supper.

We left the city on an evening ferry to cross the waters over to Finland. We drove our little Fiat onto a lower deck and went above to have a delicious smorgasbord. We had never seen so many kinds of fish in one meal! After a sleep in a cabin, we arrived in Turku in the morning. After debarking, we journeyed north to Vaasa where Lorenz and his wife, Dagmar, met us with open arms and a cup of strong European coffee.

Next, we met his sweet mother in Malax. We immediately dubbed her, "Mama Uthardt." Until her death in 2006, she was a wise and entertaining mother figure to me via letter exchanges. She was fluent in Finnish, Swedish, and German, but when we went with her to the village bookstore, she bought a thick English book. It was a western cowboy novel. Mama Uthardt had fish fixed in four different recipes for dinner that evening! We savored knekkebrød, cheese cake with currrent sauce, and wonderful hospitality. She was much like Lorenz, gifted in clever humor and story telling. She had taught English in schools there for twenty-four years. Using our stored up energy, we took pleasure in cleaning her garden, raking her lawn, and then mowing her lawn on the second day.

Norris noted, on June 15, 1972, in a letter home:

*We have now slept on paper sheets, and Lorraine was given a paper dress. I hope it doesn't rain when she wears it! Lots of small Ford tractors here. Paper and timber are the chief exports. Farms are small, and most rural families have one wage earner employed in town. Roads have been good all along. Germany had the best, so people could drive sixty miles per hour, and there were lots of trucks. In other countries northward, it's more a community sort of driving, with not much speeding and passing.*

*These lands of the midnight sun are for real. We could easily sit and read by sunlight at 3:00 a.m. We were both awake when the clock hands were on 12 last night. We went outside Mama Uthardt's house, in our pajamas, and took pictures.*

*Crops in Germany were heading out. We are now far enough north that wheat and barley are just being planted. We see very little corn. Karen is jumping around in the bed as I write, which explains the squiggles. We had coffee at the neighbor's house. The house was built in 1912, so not nearly as old as the 300 to 500-year-old ones in Germany. Vaasa Village is about ten miles from the sea, so many fishermen earn a living that way. Time to get up now.*

*Love, Norris*

From Finland, we crossed by ferry boat past northern Sweden and drove through Lapland's tundra on our way into Norway. Lakes were shimmering blue and plentiful. The mossy ground carpet was soft beneath our feet when we stopped. Curious reindeer were within forty yards, looking at us. People were out planting potatoes. A firewood stack was by each of the sparsely spaced homes. The windows have flowers in them and curtains that are all lace and ruffle. Just like South Dakota, all Scandinavia is speckled with persistent, yellow-headed dandelions.

Following a curvy mountainous road with snow on both sides, I thought how good it was that Norris had driving experience in New Guinea mountains, as well as in South Dakota winter snow. There were tall Willow tree stakes in the snow marking the edge of the road! Waterfalls cascaded from high peaks. Dongau and

*Our Fiat, dubbed "Experiment X," parked in the Norwegian countryside as we take a break from travel.*

Steven took a one-mile run down the road for exercise. White wood churches with the same architecture as the rural ones at home dotted the village and country-side. Our goal was Balestrand, and we were all happy to get there safely for a night at the hotel. We knew that Norris' ancestors came from Balestrand. The cemetery stones had all the same Norsk names that we see on grave markers at Goodhue and Saint Pauli at home. Anders Meland lived on the same land from which Herman and Kari Meland (Norris' great grandparents) emigrated. He took the Meland name from the land, but was not related to us. They served coffee and cake, plus desired information with gracious hospitality. I gave his wife a New Guinea netbag and she gave me a tapestry off her wall. The inscription was in Norwegian, "There is none like Jesus." After quick bonding, we parted, all eyes moist.

Back on the switchback roads heading south to Voss, we saw sheep nibbling grass beside the mountain crags. We ate lefse at all our picnic meals along the way. Marta Egdeveit, my Mom's relative on her father's side, welcomed us to the home where she lived with a bachelor son. Their house had been bombed in the war and rebuilt. It was small and made of unpainted weathered wood. Marta was an elderly widow, but alert and agile. She served us Rømmegrøt—cream porridge, and Spekekjøtt—brine cured and dried meat, her traditional everyday food. She had no refrigeration. Butter, leftover sardines, and cheese were all placed in an under-the-table drawer. (We had such a table when I grew up, and the drawer was always called a "skuffe.") At breakfast, the skuff produced the same food. I whispered to Norris, "Do you think it's safe to eat?"

He whispered back, "It must have been okay for her." We all partook. In the forenoon, she took wool from Johanne's sheep and demonstrated the use of her spinning wheel.

Living on a mountain between the fjord waters, these folk were private and almost isolated, but so very warm hearted towards us. When we left the next day, she said, "These kids of yours are getting a wonderful start in the world." She gave me 100 kroner so I would always remember her and Norway. On the way to the road, her son Olaf, visiting her from Oslo, pressed another 100 kroner into my hand, because it was so nice that we came and visited, and that we had helped other people. We left, overwhelmed with God's sheer goodness to us coming through in so many different ways.

The money gift turned into a beautiful hand-knit sweater, which I still wear with pride. Traveling up, up, up, and down, down, down, in this rugged beautiful land, we needed a stop at a gift shop. A local woman had knit all winter to make sweaters for tourists in the summer. I was one of her first spring customers. No, "Made in China," competition there. Norris also bought a pure wool men's sweater in the Norwegian style.

My second cousin, Conrad, and family lived in Stavanger. We bypassed Bergen and arrived there by evening. Conrad looked a lot like Uncle Meyer Hagen. He worked on the oil rigs in the North Sea. Conrad and his wife Bodil had a cozy, modern home overlooking the harbor. (All these towns were along the west coast of Norway.) The evening visit passed much too fast. In the morning, we saw him off to work and their twins off to school, and then we had an unhurried smørbrød breakfast with Bodil before continuing our journey.

By this time, we were longing for just a tiny stretch of straight flat road. As we rounded Norway's south and east coast, we saw only more mountains and more curves. I had always heard that my Mom's maternal grandparents came from Kristiansand in the south, but we had no leads for checking. Along the east side of Norway, south of Oslo, we were delighted to arrive at Sandefjord. My second cousin, Marit Febakke, married to Thor Stange, greeted us. They shared their home with us for the next several days.

Her mother, Konstance, and her Aunt, Martha (both were my dad's cousins), told us about when my Dad and Grandma had visited Norway in 1914. Martha and husband, Georg, lived in the same house in the Telemarken area where my Grandpa Lars had grown up. We had a fine Norwegian meal with them, as well as much reflective conversation and laughter. Martha concluded that we are, for sure, related because, "We don't get tired, and that's how you are, too!" We were shown the church Grandpa Lars and his parents attended near Holla. Gravesites of relatives were in the cemetery there.

I was reminded of the Norwegian-American folk song, "Kan Du Glemme Gamle Norge?" (Can You Forget Old Norway?)

> *How can you forget old Norway?*
> *Land of rock and narrow fjord,*
> *Where the mountains are like castles*
> *Stand like sentinels on guard?*
> *How can you forget old Norway,*
> *Land of everlasting fame?*
> *Can you ever find another*
> *With so glorious a name?*
> *How can you forget old Norway*
> *And its narrow fjords so grand,*
> *In and out between the mountains?*
> *'Tis my own, my native land.*

The afternoon stop was to see Alma, a third sister to Konstance and Martha, also Dad's cousin. Oh yes, here, too, we had coffee from china cups on linen table cloth. As we were leaving, she sent along a bag of apples for the children and a bit of money. She thought we were so young. "I see many people doing bad things on TV. It's nice to see people who have done something good for others." Alma and many other Norskies we met had personalities like my mom, happy and content.

Ragnar Berg, distantly related (or "around nine corners" as Silke Meland later taught us to say), took us touring one whole day. He had a County Agent position and was literally a living history book. He spoke English, showed and told us much about the area's agriculture, politics, people and places in general. Only four percent of Norway is tillable.

All the homes here have 10 to 20 family pictures on one wall, indicating close ties. Most window sills have flower pots sitting upon them. Ragnar took us to visit his friend. Christian Berg, 81, had worked on the sea from age 15 to 60, operating machines on a whaling ship. He said it took three weeks to go to the South Pole for whales. He sat with a whale tooth in each hand as he told us stories. They had a factory on the ship that processed whole animals en route back to Europe. He had fallen from the bridge to the deck at one time and broken his jaw and legs, and thus spent eight months in England at a hospital. Thereby, he learned English. He was a very entertaining personality.

Marit, our cousin with whom we were staying, worked in an oil company office. Her husband, Thor, sold Volvo cars. They had a cabin by the water, so we spent one afternoon there. Before getting in their boat, they bought a big bag of boiled shrimp. We peeled it, ate the meat and threw the shell to the seagulls. Their sons, Andre and Jan Tore, meanwhile cruised around in smaller boats. Teens there buy boats, instead of cars and pick-ups, in order to be, "cool." The second day, we had a very formal Kransekake—a crisp-on-the-outside and chewy-on-the-inside cake— made with almond rings that are stacked in graduated tiers. This was served with delicious coffee, of course.

Marit, a very gracious relative, would also become a precious friend. So would her brother, Arne. He is a wonderful Christian family man. He was a banker. His wife, Eldebjorg, was a homemaker and they had four lovely children.

The family hosted us for a pleasing dinner, so we got to know everyone. It was just a cozy afternoon. We hated to say goodbye to Norwegian kinfolk, but we also were looking forward to getting HOME.

It was time for our last stint in "Experiment X." We drove to Oslo and visited the Kon-Tiki Museum and the Viking Ship Museum. We spent the night at a Lutheran hostel. The car was simply abandoned along the street near our hotel. Norway, with its many curvy mountain roads, doesn't want too many cars. Therefore, an extremely high government tax is levied. No chance to sell our Fiat. Norris removed the license, but left the key in it, and we took the airport bus to meet our plane. Dongau remarked that some hippie would certainly be very happy to find the car.

Our flights took us to London, Chicago, and finally Minneapolis, bringing us home to the Midwest.

Chapter Forty-Two

# Adapting to U.S.A. Life

The first year back in the United States was, without a doubt, the hardest in my life. Life is rather like putting together our own huge jigsaw puzzle. This was a difficult piece to place. It's even tough to write about, because I have no diary or letters to which I can refer. Journaling stopped in 1972; the thirty-six years of memories between then and now—2008—must be resurrected and are intimate with my own personality, including life's joys, gripes, fears and dreams.

Our first realization was that we were returning to parents who had aged. My Dad, age 72, was trying to farm, but due to a heart attack and slowly worsening Parkinson's disease, physically could not do it anymore. Norris' Dad, age 78, was losing his eyesight. How should we fit in?

A house in Florence, owned by the school district, would be our home. This was part of the contract: "a principal must reside in the town." After a couple days with family back on the farm, we decided to go and see where we would live. The house itself was a big two-story structure two blocks from school. No need to commute; that would be a good thing. At the moment, however, this house was in a sorry state. In the middle of a shingling project, a big rain storm had done its mischief. Big pieces of wallpaper hung from the ceiling, like teasing banners. Two strong women were in the process of painting some of the walls. The basement had two feet of water in it, with fruit jars floating about. I came home to the Hagen farm, went behind the house, and just sat down and cried. After awhile, my spirit revived when I came to the understanding that someone was fixing things up. I would make it a home, no matter what!

There were five rooms downstairs, including a pantry that had been converted to a bathroom. There was a nice, big open stairway, which gave it a touch of elegance that I liked a lot. The bedrooms were upstairs; Norris and I had a big master, Steven and Nathan settled in the room next door, and Dongau and Karen had a bedroom down the hall. A claw-footed bathtub sat in an unused, unplumbed upstairs bathroom. Making sure that no one was below, and being unconcerned about antiques, we cast the old bathtub out the window and down to the ground. Thus, this room could serve as a little storage space. It was fun to unpack the things Norris' mother had so kindly stored for us and the items we shipped home. We sorely lacked furniture. Kitchen and dining room tables, a desk, piano and china cupboard were all we owned.

Norris immediately turned into a South Dakota farmer, helping both dads with work that neither could do anymore. He said that I should just go to Watertown and buy what we needed. In one day, at Zimmel's Furniture, I picked out three bedroom sets, a flowered sofa, a green velvet rocking chair, a living room carpet, six dining room chairs, and a hanging lamp. Now, our home would look just right. After traveling so long, we were anxious to feel settled in one place.

*Dongau's school photo was taken when she was about sixteen years old and attending Florence High School.*

Actually, it took four years and another move for this to really happen, but I did love our Florence house while we were there.

As we settled in, Dongau helped me a lot, and so did the children. They readily made friends with the Squashingroff and Rowell kids next door. They played Kick-the-Can and other neighborhood games until dark on summer nights.

We were thankful to have jobs; many people were without. Norris and I needed to spend time at the school getting familiar with upcoming work. He had science teacher and principal assignments; I had 5th and 6th Grade as well as music, both half-time. Views and attitudes had changed much in ten years. The turbulence of the '60s still seemed to reign.

I loved the warm welcome of the "dear hearts and gentle people" in St. Pauli and Wallace, where we had grown up and were well known. They accepted us as if we'd never been gone. Florence felt different. We would have to earn our place in the school, church, and community there. It was not easy for our children entering 1st, 3rd, and 5th Grades. Classmates were a circle of tight-knit children who had been together since kindergarten. Who were these newcomers? We knew we were called here, however, so were undaunted. We would do our best. Dongau was a well accepted novelty in school, and we were very glad about that.

We asked Pastor Hansen about doing a "Mission Emphasis Sunday" as we had done in many churches before, but he said, "People just aren't interested in that anymore," so we never did a program in the church we still attend. I was invited to join a circle of mostly young women, which I attended monthly, even though I'd worked out of the home all day.

Once into the school year, I enjoyed getting to know the students and their families. My schedule brought me to each of the four elementary rooms and the music room each day, so I needed to be super organized. The passing of the school year was measured by special events, Homecoming being the first. I bought an orange and black outfit to wear while marching beside my class in the parade. Under many different themes, with varying weather and class numbers, I repeated this march for 19 years, wearing the same basic uniform.

We all had a pretty minimum wardrobe. The upcoming carnival seemed to be a big deal, so-much-so that it merited a Watertown clothes shopping trip. I felt very proud of my husband—the Principal—dressed in a new green sport jacket. Barbecues, pie, ice cream, coffee and pop were sold. There were many games, from bingo to a fish pond. People went home late in the evening, 11:00 p.m. to midnight, content with prizes in hand and heads full of conversations. The floor was totally covered with confetti when the evening ended. Whoops! I happened to look at my left hand and noted that the diamond was missing from my ring. Panic set in! Then, reason stepped forward. I had not left the gym. The stone had to be here somewhere. I sat very still and talked to the Lord about my predicament. Next, Mary Ann Resen, mother of a number of our very good students, walked with me, kicking the paper bits. Lo and behold, about ten feet away, a sparkle was in clear view. God does look after details, even lost gems: whatever it takes to show love to His children.

Halloween evening brought nearly a hundred trick-or-treaters to our door. I was prepared, and enjoyed guessing who was behind each mask. It was another event in the "firsts" category here. No Halloween in New Guinea. It was an over-done one here, finished off with eggs being thrown at our porch screen.

The Christmas program included sacred and secular parts, featuring individual drama and choir; it was a big success. At the room parties, I received precious gifts. (Some of the 100 ornaments still used on our Christmas tree came from students from that class.) Those students started my collection.

I was always impressed by the merriment that came out of Valentine exchanges. Special little notes, attached gum or candy, decorated boxes or bags, some games, and cupcakes or Rice Krispy treats made for a perfect party. The excitement almost was equal to that of Christmas.

Mr. Ptak, the Band Director, was a good friend and co-worker. He exemplified patience and promptness. If a student didn't come for a lesson, he went and got him. Concerts started exactly on the minute. He started Nathan on the cornet, and since I never had a chance to be in a band, the idea of my children having that experience made my heart dance. Miss Jurgens, my 5th and 6th Grade team teacher, was known for keeping firm order, and we worked well together. We took turns on recess duty. Not used to the cold weather, I donned extra warm winter attire.

Language Arts and Social Studies were my part of the curriculum, which I enjoyed with the 11 and 12 year olds. Since I taught Vocal Music, Kindergarten through 12 Grade, I got to see my own children in regular classes. Coming from a New Guinea culture where kids were gifted with harmony and melody to United States high schoolers, in a setting where few could sing or simply didn't care, music was not fun anymore. A few students thought it was their job to be a distraction. Also, my ear for hearing parts with confidence was limited. At one point, stress caused me a spell of shoulder bursitis. Dr. Bartron, Sr., gave me an injection and pain pills. The euphoria the latter granted taught me how tempting drugs are for youth. I told Norris I would prefer a self-contained one teacher, one classroom, position.

Football and basketball seemed to take priority in most peoples' lives. Homework, confirmation lessons, music concerts and contests were on lower rungs. This was new. We had become used to the church and scholastics of school being of main importance, and sports were ancillary. Here, there seemed to be an ongoing battle for balance.

Mr. Aman was Superintendent of Henry, Bradley and Florence schools. He wisely visited regularly, but let the principals handle the daily goings-on in the schools. This meant that Norris had a very big job at school. He was also determined to help on the farm. Life was getting hectic: mostly work and little play. Contract time came and passed, but I had not signed mine. I wanted to have a year at home and try to carve out some quality family time. That might be more valuable than the $6,200 salary.

Memorable moments from our first year back in the United States follow:

- At the farm one day, Dongau had seen a squirrel peeking out of a hole in a tree trunk. She took a gunnysack and deftly held it over the hole. Sure enough, the little creature jumped right in! For a brief period, he was a Florence house squirrel, but one day, he broke loose and became an independent resident.
- Just before Christmas, a lot of people had the flu, including some of our family. Nathan's every evening prayer asked for health to return "so we

could have a nice Christmas." God heard, and we had a Glædelig Jul (Norwegian for "Merry Christmas").

- Finally, Karen could have a pet cat. In Florence, it would not be stolen or eaten. That was good. But, one afternoon, Bootsy was missing. We walked up and down the streets, looking for her. No result. However, someone had seen a cat curled up in the seat of a tractor at Lyle Thorson's Implement Shop. From there, her pet was retrieved. She later had a cat named Fluffy, who—as an inexperienced mother—delivered a small litter of kittens under an afghan on our sofa!

- Dongau was gifted athletically and was therefore appreciated in school sports. One cold, wet, windy day in April, after returning from a track meet, she came home to our house. None of our family was there. Her story upon our return went like this: "Oh, Mamma, you can't guess what happened! I was very cold, so I decided to put hot water in the bathtub to warm up. Soon after starting to soak, the phone rang, so I stepped out of the tub and dripped across the kitchen into the dining room to answer. Someone said that there were kids up on the schoolhouse roof, and I should tell Mr. Meland. Then I got back into the warm water. But very soon, the phone rang again. I dripped over to the phone once more. A lady wanted to talk to you about Sunday School. I decided to try again to enjoy my bath, but no! The phone rang a third time. By now, your floor was very drippy, but I did clean it up. This last call was from a person in another town who wanted me to come and speak to their Community Club. I told them that life was getting very complicated here, and I would refer it to you, Mamma."

So, the year ended, and two months later Dongau left. It was very hard for me to say goodbye. We had so many in-depth conversations. It had been fun to show her our people and country.

*Dongau, outside our Florence home in her track uniform, ready to compete at a meet with the Flyers.*

191

She would accompany a missionary returning to New Guinea. Pent-up emotions broke lose and tears flowed freely as we parted. Her absence left a hole in our family circle.

## Chapter Forty-Three

# Buying the Farm
## — 1973 —

The 6:30 Easter Sunrise Service was followed by a ham and egg breakfast. This had been a Goodhue tradition since 1951. Norris and I were a part of it from 1960-1962, and now again in 1973, with our children added. During the fellowship in the basement, Marie Sikkink asked Norris if he was interested in buying their farm, since it was the place Art Meland's parents (Norris' grandparents) home-steaded. He said that he would think about it. My mom and dad and his mom and dad were dinner guests at our Florence home that day. We mentioned that we might drive out to Sikkinks that evening (where Mike Bergh now lives) and have a look at the farm. Early evening, not long after my folks had gone home, our phone rang. If we were still home, they wanted to come back to town to talk about something.

We had been back in the United States nine months. They, and we, wondered who would operate the Hagen farm, but no one had talked about it. Dad was emotionally attached to the land and could not bring up the subject. Being born and raised there, and having lived on the same spot for seventy-three years, the thought of change was hard. Unable physically to work anymore, verbalizing became necessary. My folks always liked and trusted Norris, but there was Corinne and family to consider, too, although they were firmly ensconced in Sioux Falls life.

I have no idea what exactly was said that night, but before long Mom and Dad went to Watertown and, on their own, bought a nice little house. We started buying the farm. Dad envisioned our sons involved in agriculture, as well, so we budgeted for land purchase and started dreaming about remodeling the old home.

Since Mom and Dad had never moved, they had no idea how to go about it. Time passed. Neither one packed anything. Preparing for a move was old hat for me. We gathered cardboard boxes and began, room by room, putting in personal favorite items. What was not cherished could be left and added to a Florence neighbor's estate sale. The old farm machinery would be left with the land for Norris Meland and sons. Moving day was a family affair and went smoothly. Corinne bought a china cupboard to replace the built-in corner cupboard, two easy chairs, and a side chest for their new home. Thus, Mom and Dad began the last four years of life in a modern house at 513 1st Street SW in Watertown, South Dakota.

The next three summers, weekends, and sometime after school days were invested in the farm. A sobering shiver swept over me one Saturday morning, as I walked with Norris, still in my blue bathrobe, out to mark the spot where we would sink a couple thousand dollars into the ground. We needed to dig a well. I knew I would not be a farmer. I'd been around the world twice, and now, I'd settled on the same spot where I began. How had this happened? No more travel now. We would be tied right here.

My year off school hadn't accomplished what I had intended. I needed to learn that I am not in control. For example, I made a lush apple pie one Friday, thinking we'd all eat a piece together after school. Norris came from school, took two bites of pie, went to change into work clothes, and then took off without finishing his pie. He and the boys left immediately for the farm. This was a defining moment for me. My wonderful, energetic, achieving husband was not one who could relax, nor would he promote such luxury for our boys. I would seek school staff status again.

Aldrow Kinstad came the day after Christmas and sawed the wall out for an archway between the dining and living rooms. Steve Skinner and Randy Becking would replace the windows. Lawrence Benson and Herman Gulbraa would build an attached garage, and put vinyl siding on the outside of the house. With Norris as the Contractor, my growing-up home became a community project. None of us were carpenters. So, between times, we used the space in the empty house for various other kinds of projects, like Nathan's rebuilding of a small motorcycle.

Miss Rosenstein had been Karen's 1st Grade teacher. She was engaged during the year and, in June, she moved to be with her husband-to-be. This made a perfect opportunity for me. I was offered the 1st and 2nd Grade teaching position for 1974 and 1975. This was the start of nineteen mostly wonderful years teaching children the basic skills of reading, plus the rest of the curriculum. The parents were nice to work with, and I was feeling more a part of the community. Life was good again.

By now, some basic remodeling was done on the farmhouse. Karen and I were painting, varnishing and hanging wallpaper whenever the guys went to work outside. A Holstein cow came with the place. One lovely Friday afternoon in the spring, we came to the country just in time to see the mamma deliver a sprightly black and white calf. It was a perfectly timed birth for a family biology lesson. We carried the baby on a blanket into the barn, and the mamma followed, so they could be cozy out of the March chill.

Nathan started junior high that year, which involved changing classes and teachers, and having a chance to play basketball. I saw parts of some home games, but don't recall attending any of those played away. Steven moved from 4th Grade to the 5th and 6th Grade room, and Karen went from 2nd to the 3rd and 4th Grade room. The way things worked out, Norris was now principal and superintendent. This meant he was now on an 11-month school contract. It was a high stress job, but he handled it for two years.

In the spring of 1976, Norris declined his contract. I would teach, and he would farm. We had prayed about moving and discussed it with our children. It meant they would have to change schools again, because the farm was now in the Webster District. Wallace had closed in 1961. Our family decision was that we would go and live in the country. By now, our farm home was updated and inviting. Norris was forty-five; I was forty-one, and we finally had our own place. The kids would now become Webster Bearcats instead of Florence Flyers.

Summer turned dry. Not a drop could be squeezed from the sky. In July, I suggested to my mom that maybe the planet had changed; we would be under a drought for years. Without missing a beat, she assured me, "Oh, no, we'll get rain when we're supposed to get it." August came. No rain yet. The school board still had not hired a "Mr. Meland" replacement. Now, they offered him the job again, and this time he would not have to live in Florence. Feeling need for our family's financial stability, he accepted.

The first adjustment under this plan was a regimented daily morning departure. Nathan started high school; Steve entered junior high; Karen enrolled in 6th Grade. They would leave on the school bus at 7:15 a.m. At the same time, Norris and I left for school. We partially set the breakfast table the night before. Somehow, we managed to get through one bathroom, a meal, and a brief devotion asking blessing on our day, and still leave all at the same time.

Chapter Forty-Four

# Our Children at School

By now, I was comfortable with the established pattern of my job, but I felt sorry for our children, having to start all over in a new setting with classmates, who, again, had mostly been together since kindergarten. Kids can be cruel, and the newcomer's role is not easy. By and by, each found their niche with a few favorite friends, but I don't think the bosom buddy friendships were theirs to enjoy. At whatever cost, it made them more brave and independent.

Scholastically, they pretty much set their own pace. Knowing full well the range of natural abilities within a class, we did not pressure them to be at the top. They were simply encouraged to always do their best. I liked to take them out for hamburgers or ice cream treats after good quarterly report cards. I enjoyed meeting their teachers who, all along, from elementary through high school, said only good things. I never had a troubling conference. Giving thanks to their Maker and Sustainer was the substance of my personal conference with my Lord.

Other milestones pointing to their growing up were their Confirmation Ceremonies at New Helgen Church in Florence in 1977, 1979 and 1981. Foundations for this confirmation of their Christian Faith started at home and will be ever on-going, I hope.

Having to ride nineteen miles each way on the school bus can be a bore and a chore. This made it hard for our kids to be in extracurricular activities. Nathan dropped band, and became active in FFA. He found himself a welding-for-manufacturing job at Terry Gaikowski's machine shop in Webster.

Steven stuck with band and choir six years, right through his senior graduation. Being gifted with an ear for harmony and a musician's sentimental nature, I think he liked it (and I loved it) but memorizing notes and words and getting to extra practices was probably frustrating. I can still close my eyes and see him running with his trombone case in hand up the driveway all the way to the mailbox at bus time. He, many times, ran around the section, because he was an important part in the cross country team, going to several State meets. Being of compassionate heart, one time when he came in first, he returned to a less skilled teammate to run alongside and encourage this runner the rest of the way. It reminded me of a time in Florence when he came home late from a piano lesson because he had stayed to help his elderly teacher rake some leaves. He found employment at the Day County Electric in Webster. He also worked one summer with Keller Hardware in Wallace.

Karen spent herself generously in Webster School She earned excellent grades, was in the Future Homemakers of America, played clarinet in the band, sang in the choir, and was on the school paper staff. One of her editorials told how she had ridden the equivalent of once around the earth on the school bus! She was also a part of the cross country team, making it to the State meet as well. During wrestling season, she was a cheerleader. Karen was a disciplined student. She had a full vita.

The boys bought their cars when they were Juniors, using money earned on the farm and from their town jobs.

*Nathan's first car was a 1970 Plymouth Sport Satellite, and it cost $550.*

Karen had Grandma's second hand Biscayne. It had no air conditioning or power steering. Rain had leaked in. She and I hated the moldy smell, but her dad ruled that it had basic wheels and engine; we could forget about the odor.

Graduations triggered a new era. When Norris and I finished high school, the relatives came over, and that was the extent of the celebration. College was even more minimal. By 1980, full blown receptions were the norm for honoring

*Steven's first car, a 1975 Oldsmobile Cutlass.*

twelve years of education completed. For Nathan's graduation, I did not know how many guests to plan for. Buns with ham, salad, cake, nuts, mints, coffee and Kool Aid were standard fare. My grocery bill was $80, the most I'd ever spent for food in one crack. Lots of people came, but we had plenty of food left-over. Two years later, when it was Steven's turn, I decreased the quantity, but the bill was higher. Karen's party, two years after that, the same story, but food amount was just right!

Each of the three ceremonies was a reflection time for me. I knew they were as thrilled to graduate as I had been twenty-five years before, but it seemed to me that they had grown up too fast! Their dad and I had gradually let them become independent, so I trusted they were prepared. Yet, the ways of the world are often like a prowling lion. I pleaded with God to please take care of them and guide them.

Nathan decided to do a fluid power course at Granite Falls, Minnesota. The apartment he stayed in also had a couple of pot-smoking residents. One of the first weekends he came home, he brought a marijuana sample to show us. The antidote, also brought home, was a cassette tape he had bought at an evangelical service he attended. God is faithful. Mr. Wood was a wise teacher at his school, and tales from his class were often quoted at our kitchen table. My first look at this school was at the Open House for families, probably at mid-year. After viewing student projects, I was given a bag of machined small tops for my first graders to spin. (Much later, my grandchildren played with them.)

By May of 1982, Nathan was ready for a graduation ceremony from his two-year program and would leave immediately for an accepted job in New Orleans. Unbeknownst to us, when our family drove to Granite Falls, the Chilsons and Bergans were right behind. We enjoyed a meal and the ceremony together. They were a wonderful support party and surprise.

Nathan and a fellow graduate were capped and left immediately afterwards for the South, where they would work on the hydraulic machinery related to off-shore oil rigs. Having launched our first son, we left for a weekend in Minneapolis. The excitement of the occasion was too much for me. I could not sleep at all that night.

God dispenses His gifts variously. Steven was born to be a people person. Unfortunately, I or nobody else could convince Steve that his was a special talent. Farming is a profession that consumes the family. Not intentionally, but subtly, in our home this was the most affirmed way of life. Being a free spirit, brave enough for adventure, Steve had signed up with the U.S. National Guard at the end of his Junior year, when he turned eighteen. I knew he had prayed a lot about this, but I still cried when he told me, "I can't do things good enough on the farm."

Love of God, country, and fellow man is noble, but costly. Aptitude testing at school reflected his tendency towards a helping profession. This led him to do one year in Law Enforcement School at Alexandria, Minnesota. Not being sure about such work, he switched to Northern State College at Aberdeen, South Dakota. In the summer, he went to Army Schools in Alabama, Georgia, Washington, Kentucky, Hawaii, and other far-off places.

Steve completed a degree in Sociology and, on May 17, 1986, he became the first of our children to finish college. On graduation day, he was also commissioned Second Lieutenant through the Army Reserve Officer Training Corps. In typical free-spirited fashion, he showed up at the reception in a newly traded car. Friends and relatives

*I traveled by bus to proudly attend Steven's graduation from U.S. Army Ranger School in Fort Benning, Georgia, on June 4, 1987.*

joined us for a nice meal at a restaurant where we had reserved a room. It was a great day for our family.

That summer, both boys were gone, so Karen was the only kid at home. We were not good at it, but she and I tried to help Norris with haying and harvest. During combining on the Meland quarter, between the grain loads, we were so hot we went to the Goodhue basement and rested on the cool cement floor. Some farmhands we were! Another incident was that on the way to town with grain, I tipped the gravity wagon. I think Norris missed his sons. Other summers, Karen worked as a nanny in Connecticut, at a garden shop in Fargo, at ShopKo in Watertown, and at an art museum in Moorhead, Minnesota.

Meanwhile, Nathan had, after nine months, come home from Louisiana and put in the crop on the farm in South Dakota. To make use of extra time in winter, he transferred credits from Granite Falls and enrolled at SDSU in Brookings, seeking a degree in Agronomy. Nathan's aptitude was easy to read. He had a mind that told his hands how to create, design, and repair anything that even looked like a machine.

Karen's friend, Jennifer Bergan, was enrolled at Concordia College in Moorhead, Minnesota. She also had a friend at Webster who was thinking about going there. Karen and I went with Kathy Swift and her mother to have a look. Home Economics and Communication at this Lutheran school became Karen's choice.

I enjoyed special times with Karen during college. I would drive up for Homecoming, Christmas concerts, and Mother/Daughter weekends, and was treated royally. When the boys left for school, they took very few things with them. Karen, however, filled the car and made the dorm room or apartment homey. At Concordia, she found like-minded lifetime friends, including Thomas Asfeldt, who later became our son-in-law.

*One of the many mechanical innovations in Nathan's farming career was this 24-foot field cultivator fabricated from two 12-foot field cultivators.*

One October 2nd, we met at Sica Hollow near Sisseton to celebrate Nathan's birthday. The "kids" came from three different colleges that Sunday, and I fully understood they were now three young adults. It was a pretty low-key party, but for me, it was a significant day.

Nathan's SDSU graduation day was May 2, 1987. His cousin, Ann Meland, graduated the same day, so we honored the occasion with a special meal together in Brookings. It was two-down and one-to-go for Norris and me.

Karen's big final day at Concordia was dry, dusty, windy and miserable! I was so happy to see her smile at us as the class marched in. I took it as an omen that she would be positive and flexible enough to handle the twists and turns of her ongoing life. The families of her room-mate, Juliane Saxon, and her boyfriend, Thomas, joined ours and we rejoiced together with meal and gifts.

Throughout these years, ours never was an empty nest, just a sort of chang-ing, rearranging home base. One Christmas vacation, sev-eral young peers were house guests. Mixed with outdoor

*Karen and Thomas are pleased to display their diplo-mas from Concordia College following the graduation ceremony on May 11, 1988.*

farm fun were games, goodies, TV, music, and "hanging out" as kids nowadays say. I woke up at midnight, and they were popping corn. How wonderful it was to have a college dorm atmosphere right in our own house! I remembered how anxious I was to try my wings, and so I never tried to hold them back. Imperfect parents, as we were, we did the best we could to give them a firm foundation. Now, they would soar in their own directions.

Chapter Forty-Five

# Vacations

Ideally, I believe families should take a vacation each year. Norris loves farm work so much that he lives in vacation mode every day when he's out with a tractor and machinery. Therefore, I was pleasantly surprised in June of 1974 when he returned from a Watertown business trip with a brand new family-sized tent and sleeping bags for Nathan, Steven and Karen.

A Midwest trip resulted. We saw the historic Laura Ingalls Wilder home and school in De Smet, South Dakota. Stop number two was at Minden, Nebraska, at a very big Pioneer Village museum complex. Darkness came before we found a spot for the night. We didn't know it, but the one we found was near a railroad track. Trains full of wheat rumbled by all night. Erecting a new tent by flashlight, where the mosquitoes thought that we had brought them supper, was a beginner's mistake and initiation, but we would learn. Kirchhoffs, who had been neighbors in New Guinea, now were settled at Cedar, Kansas. Their kids were the age of ours, so a stop with them was lots of fun.

So began our list of United States vacations. My grown-up children, now looking back, may not look with fondness on our very active vacations, but I think they were better than none.

*This is a family photo of our lifetime friends Jack and Mary Laschkewitsch with their children Sherri, Scott, John and Ben, taken in 1978. We shared several vacations with them.*

- 1977 – Steven, Karen and I had some days with the Laschkewitsch family at a campground in St. Louis, Missouri. The Arch, Six Flags, and being by a lake were the highlights. Steve got a chance to water ski.
- 1978 – We had a look at the eastern states: Wisconsin Dells, Niagara Falls, New York and Boston. We stayed with Kulows a couple of days at Dover Air Force Base in Delaware.
- 1979 – We had a Christmas week in Texas. We enjoyed the holiday with the Laschkewitsch family in San Antonio and soaked up the warm weather.
- 1982 – The five of us took a fishing trip outside of Winnipeg, Manitoba. Driving a new Chevy Citation limited our luggage capacity, and this embarrassed our teenagers.
- 1982 – Norris and I traveled to New Orleans to visit Nathan for Christmas.
- 1984 – After Karen's graduation, she went with Norris and me to California. We drove through many states, with stops along the way, ending with Disneyland and the Sequoia National Forest.

Now, the kids were grown. I felt blessed that Norris was able to set work aside and the two of us could travel together.

- 1985 – Thunder Bay, Ontario, north of Lake Superior to see Cousin Annie, and her husband, Jack.
- 1986 – Fairbanks and Anchorage, Alaska, where Norris had served in the Air Force.
- 1988 – Germany, visiting Steven, and a return trip to Norway where we were with cousins Arne and Marit and family.

*Thor Stange and his wife Marit are on the left while Eldebjorg and Arne Febakke are on the right.*

- 1990 – Dawson Creek, Alberta, Canada for our 30th Anniversary trip. Thomas' parents showed us good times.
- 1994 – Florida with Kulows, and a five-day cruise in the Bahamas, as we began considering winters away from South Dakota.
- 1995 – Arizona, as another snow-bird possibility, visiting cousins along the way.
- 1996 – Donna, Texas, for five weeks. We bought our park model.
- 1997–2008 – We wintered in Texas from January–March each year.
- 2006 – Papua New Guinea and Australia for one month of travel with Karen. It was a joy to see so many friends from our mission days, and a thrill to be reunited with Dongau and her family!

It is truly a great, wide, wonderful world in which we live!

Not all of our travels are far away. Each place we have lived, we seem to have developed a web of connections. We have a guest book that was started when we were married forty-eight years ago. Running until now, we have 500 entries, ranging from hometown folks to visitors from twenty different countries. Meals and conversation together have been a blessed part of our ministry of hospitality.

*This is an earlier family picture of Dongau and Fua Singin with their children, Lorraine, Hendrik, Masu, Ioane and Danielle.*

## Chapter Forty-Six

# Parents Went Home

As time went by, we truly realized the excellence of God's foresight in bringing us to the United States in 1972. During the 1968 furlough year, the Meland and Hagen grandparents became more than just names to our kids. In the '70s, they had opportunity to develop relationships further by sharing holiday dinners, rural old-age experiences, confirmations, overnighters, and much more.

Arthur's decline came first. Glaucoma started, causing loss of sight. That led to an accidental slip off the porch, causing a broken hip. A few weeks in the hospital followed. A sore throat developed, which later was diagnosed as Hodgkin's disease. He lived a few months at Prairie Lakes Nursing Home in Watertown; then passed away on December 21, 1976, at the Watertown Hospital, at the age of eighty-two. In typical efficiency, the funeral for Norris' dad was December 23rd. He would want us to still celebrate Christmas.

Ever since my dad had a heart attack at age sixty-one, and Parkinson's set in later, he puzzled over the question, "Why did I get old so young?" He had a lot of goals and interests and the loss of physical strength cut them short. Corinne stayed with Mom and Dad for a week in late June 1978, while our family took a vacation trip to the East Coast and back. On return, I stayed some days with my parents. Dad was weak and mostly in bed by this time. He had fallen many times, but he had never broken a bone. I asked Mom if we should bring him to the hospital. She said, "No, he wouldn't want that."

That evening, we read the 14th chapter of the gospel of John, about the many rooms prepared for believers. We prayed The Lord's Prayer together. Mom, Karen and I went to bed.

At 6:30, July 10th, Mom woke me. With one hand held high, she announced, "Dad went Home last night!" I think they both saw this as a peaceful exit from a world where good health could never again be found. Somehow, the funeral arrangements got made. A comforting service was held in the St. Pauli Church, the one his Father, Lars, had helped build in the early 1900s.

The winter of 1980, my mom started doctoring for a bronchial cough. Dr. Clark at Bartron Clinic gave her a sulfa drug and told her to drink lots of water. No improvement. I suggested we go to another doctor. She insisted Dad's Dr. Clark was also good enough for her.

She drove out to our place for Nathan's high school graduation in May. When she refused to eat lunch, Corinne declared that she was taking Mom home with her to the Sioux Falls hospital. Within a few days, Sioux Valley (now Sanford) staff diagnosed her problem as an enlarged heart. She was in the hospital a few days. The doctor told Corinne and me that he could do surgery, but if it were his mother, he would not put her through it.

We talked it over and prayed about it. Mom was ready to go and meet Dad. En route to an x-ray, I asked her what day it was. "Yeah, in two days it will be two years since Lawrence died," was her immediate reply. In his absence, she had bravely carried on with usual activity, saying, "I have to get used to this." She never did. After forty-eight years of marriage, and never having lived alone before, the burden was too great. Corinne and I were there for her, but it was not the same.

Aunt Judy and Uncle Herald walked in to her hospital room at just the right time, unannounced. In that moment, I realized what the ministry of presence means. Corinne and I were both there. Mom was leaving us, and it felt so good to know someone cared enough to drive 370 miles to sit with us.

That night, Corinne and I thanked Mom for being a good mother. She told us she had always been grateful for us, and that we were what we were. We read John 14 again, prayed individual prayers, and closed with the Lord's Prayer together. That night, July 10, 1980, angels came and took her to her Heavenly Home. How marvelous this assurance of salvation is for those who believe in Jesus!

After making funeral arrangements, I talked to Helene Kinstad regarding lunch at the church. I said, "A piece of cake and coffee would be enough." This was not acceptable to her. She firmly responded, "Oh, no! We will also have ham sandwiches." The funeral day, July 13th, had a sunny, clear blue sky. The St. Pauli Church was full. Many of my cousins, and uncles and aunts were there, along with many local people.

Corinne and I wrote the following tribute to Mom, which we shared with close friends in the thank-you cards.

*There are many thoughts which we feel like sharing at a time like this, so we have put a few in writing. Since Mom was always hearty, her leaving us after only three weeks in the hospital (due to congestive heart failure) took us by surprise. However, as she said, 'God has a plan for each life,' so we rejoice that she was blessed with a happy and healthy life and did not have to suffer long in departing.*

### Our Tribute

*Our table is laden with cards from friends*
*Expressing love in beautiful blends.*
*The sympathy each one seems to bring*
*Gives us peace and helps us sing.*

*We had not thought of letting Mom go.*
*Our Father in Heaven knew this, and so...*
*He's shown us, little by little, His plan*
*Of taking her Home to a much better land.*

*She used to hum while pancakes she fried.*
*Encouragement, we were never denied.*
*A new dress to finish, she'd sew late at night*
*So for a special occasion, we'd look just right.*

*A great many memories come to our mind.*
*We were blessed with good parents: helpful, kind.*
*We knew Mom was lonely since Dad went away.*
*Praise God! We will join them in Heaven someday.*

*For them, all cares and pains are past;*
*But we, our burdens on the Lord can cast*
*And go on, forward, as they'd want us to:*
*Living each day in God's grace anew.*

*And pass on the heritage of faith*
*To the next generation walking life's way.*
*So that death can mean gain, and not a loss,*
*Because of the victory of Christ on the cross.*

*Daughters, Lorraine and Corinne*

When it was over, reality had not sunk in. As I was leaving the church, my rambling thoughts included, "I'll have to go home and call Mom and tell her who was here." A few days later, when in the garden, I waxed into a make-believe conversation with Mom, telling her about the sweet peas and the beans. At forty-five, I was now the oldest in my family.

Sometimes, I'd wish my parents could have seen their grandchildren grow up. Then again, maybe the prayers from Heaven for us now are even more powerful than would have been those sent from here to Heaven.

Corinne's son, Michael, was also celebrating a birthday on July 13th. So, back at the house, we honored his turning ten years. Both my parents died at age 77. Now, we needed to carry on.

Agnes, always characterized by energy and strength, had moved in with her brother, Randy, in Watertown a couple of months before Art died. There, she took a very active part in Ladies' Aid, Bible study, and congregational life. She went regularly to the nursing home and did mending "for the old folks" there. She and Randy had a host of friends with whom they played cards and other games and shared good, home cooked meals. Sometimes, they and their guests gave "organ recitals"—that is, each told about medical problems related to aging—discussing the heart, lungs, and so forth. She lived for seveneteen years with her brother.

In 1995, she developed pneumonia. While in the hospital, shingles was an added complication. Her system could not heal. After two years in the Jenkins Living Center, God called Norris' mom Home on November 15, 1997, at age 94.

Nathan and Steven both called on her that afternoon and read some Psalms to her. A hectic work schedule, busy toddlers and brewing winter weather kept Karen in Sioux Falls. Norris and I sat with Agnes in the evening. As she rose from the pillow, the heart stopped and the soul departed to a place with no pain and endless joy. It, too, was a peaceful departure. Norris' first comment was, "Those hands sure did a ton of work!"

The funeral was on November 19th at Grace Lutheran Church in Watertown, with internment at Goodhue Cemetary, beside her beloved husband, Arthur.

Chapter Forty-Seven

# A Trio of Weddings

Almost suddenly, wedding bells started ringing in the New Year 1989. Karen had taken work in Minnetonka, Minnesota, where she lived as a nanny in a wealthy home, but worked part-time as a writer. While still in college, she had told me one weekend that she and Thomas were quite serious in feelings for each other. Thomas also had chosen employment in the Twin Cities as a nurse at St. Mary's/Riverside Medical Center. Karen was concerned that one problem for our family was accepting that, "he is not a farmer." (I said, "Good!") Another consideration was that he had recently been diagnosed with Diabetes, something that would certainly impact their life together. I said, "What if it were the other way around?" So, she had my blessing.

As the boys came and went, Norris kept the farm going and expanding. School duties were full time for both of us, as well. Some years prior, I had asked Nathan what we should do about his dad. With all the wisdom and maturity of his nineteen years, his response was, "Let him run. You can't tie a race horse to a post." So, we did. Some wear-and-tear health issues were showing up, but they were not like brakes that could halt anything.

So, one freezing Saturday morning in January, Norris was up on a hill feeding cattle. Our phone rang. Thomas was planning to give Karen a diamond that morning and wanted our blessing. I said mine was granted. He wanted Norris' consent also. I ran up to the tractor and told the driver that he was needed on the phone. He said he was busy and instructed me to take a message; they could call back later. I informed him that this was an emergency call and bade him to come at once. He didn't like the interruption, but he did come. Was he surprised!

We had known Thomas for about four years, so felt that he and Karen would make a good team. Norris agreed to become his father-in-law, and then he went back to finish the cattle chores.

Several inches of loose, fluffy snow had fallen that morning. Sunrays and the laden tree limbs created a fairyland outside. I thought that this was a wonderful day! The world was pretty, and this young couple was doing things right. With a stick, I wrote the date and their names in the snow and encircled them with a heart, offering a prayer of thanks. Both had an alive Christian faith. Both had finished college and had jobs, and it sure didn't hurt that both were of Scandinavian stock!

From January through June, weekends were spent on planning the wedding. It would take place June 24th at Grandpa and Grandma Meland's church, Goodhue. I had planned my wedding; Karen should have the joy of planning hers. She estimated the cost, we wrote a check, and she could make her own budget. She could scrimp here and splurge there, as she pleased. I thought her dress would be a main item, but she said, "Well, Mom, you need a new dress, too." Funny, I hadn't even thought of that! I obliged.

Some days before the marriage, Thomas' family came from Canada: his mom, dad and two brothers. His Uncle Holger came from Denmark. Also, my cousin Annie and her husband, Jack, came from Canada. Steven was home from military duty in Germany. With tents and picnics, our yard became a campground. The reception would be in the newly built workshop on the farm. The planned menu had some favorite and very unique foods on the list, as this was a real smörgåsbord. The above mentioned work crew joined in preparing for homemade hospitality. This even included taking down the old windmill—improving the ambiance of our yard.

After the rehearsal at the church, we went to the Ramkota in Watertown. The groom's dinner was full of proper relaxing and mirth.

The next day at the church, pictures of the wedding party were taken ahead of the family photo. That helped me a lot. The pleasant and light-hearted photo opportunity sealed my sentimental Mother's mind so I could totally enjoy the ceremony. The bride was lovely! The groom was handsome!

One hundred and fifty well-wishers (exactly how many the church could hold) were in the pews! The knot was tied June 24, 1989. Even on a wedding day, people in dry South Dakota welcome a shower of rain. This happened while we were in the church. On the way out, via the parents' reception line, people gave congratulations, then reached for hats and umbrellas and commented on the welcome moisture. Lastly, Mr. and Mrs. Thomas Asfeldt came down the steps to a shower of birdseed.

The brothers had borrowed Harlan Hagen's old junky farm pickup to use for a limousine. It was complete with fencing equipment in the back. One door didn't shut right. There were rust holes in the floor, and the brakes were quite lacking. This was a real ice breaker! Thomas and Karen passed the adaptability test and were royally chauffeured to the decorated shop on the Meland farm. There, the Danish custom of guests giving little speeches and sharing funny anecdotes made it a very fun evening.

Steven returned to Army duties, but must have invested some time in romance. Over the years, he had introduced us to several American lady friends, but this time a Deutsch lass named Silke Hemmerich won his heart. We learned, on short notice, that the time and place of their union was to be January 13, 1990, at a cathedral in Frankfort, Germany. This was in the middle of our school year here, and his father thought it very impractical for us to try to be there. I sort of agreed, but felt very sad to not be a part of the occasion. There was pain on both sides of the Atlantic. He would have liked to have had us there. Receiving a picture and a letter was the extent of our participation. We held a reception for them in our new workshop when they came back to the United States.

Nathan never talked about getting married, but he noticed all the good qualities of Kathy Bierschbach—and liked the fact that she noticed and respected him. About Thanksgiving time of 1990, a diamond was placed on her finger, and before long a wedding date was set and announced for June 22, 1991, at Christ the King Church in Webster. We were invited to a Sunday dinner at Kathy's home, and that began the blending of two supportive families.

Being of modest and sensible stock, Kathy's plans were of good taste—not lavish, but certainly lovely. She surprised herself in the choice of a very adorned dress, however. With typical humor, she told us that she would be wearing a big name tag so people would know who she was. We were not in on the preparations. I wore the same dress I wore for Karen's wedding, but Norris bought a new suit. We hosted the groom's dinner—chicken at Bain's Cafe in Webster.

The wedding day weather was perfect. This time, the sacred ceremony was longer and in more detail than in protestant churches. We sat in the groom's section. Most of us were Lutherans, and when the Catholics stopped the Lord's Prayer after, "deliver us from evil," we just about kept going to the "forever and ever" part.

There was a coffee and cake reception at the parish hall. I was pleased to see on display the quilt that I had assembled. (For each of the three children, I contacted friends and relatives, requesting a square for a memory quilt. I sewed the pieces together and hired the stitching.) An evening supper and dance was held at the V.F.W. The main meal request was that the salad should have large pieces of strawberry in it. A game, with the couple seated back-to-back and predicting their spouse's answers to questions, provided good laughter. Before the night was very late, the bride and groom slipped away for a honeymoon in Duluth.

## Chapter Forty-Eight

# Our New House

By 1991, when Nathan and Kathy were planning their wedding, he was already quite established in farming as a full-time job. He knew that this was what he wanted to do, and he was proving to be good at it. Norris had thought of himself as a hobby farmer, even if he put in sixteen-hour Saturdays and summer days and a lot of other overtime. Work was always fun for him. I, on the other hand, loved living in the country, but was never a real farmer's wife.

Nathan had lived with us until this time. I will always admire the smooth change-over Norris initiated. We would build a house nearby; Nathan could buy our house site and the land quarter on which it stood. I'm sure these thoughts had been formed before, but they were verbalized on Thanksgiving Day. I had papered, painted, and varnished nearly every inch of the old house, and I was not certain I had the energy or will to start over again. I was also in love with my yard and garden where I was. Ever capable and confident, Norris said he would build our house and carry me across the threshold! Who could refuse such an offer?

My husband quickly put on another cap. He was now General Contractor! We each made a sketch of what we'd like in a new house. I had studied some features from women's magazines and a building catalog. These drawings were given to Barry Kjetland, a carpenter employed by United Building Center (UBC) in Watertown. Rafters and floor joists would come from Holmquist, South Dakota; the remainder of the lumber from UBC. The Wallace, South Dakota, Kellers would do backhoe basement work, electric wiring and plumbing. Enger of Watertown did the block foundation work.

On Easter Sunday, we walked around in what had always been a cattle pasture when I was a child. (When I was sent to bring milk cows home, I would hang onto the tail of one cow and almost fly as I was being pulled along.) A big decision was made. Four sticks were placed in a rectangle shape and we marked the spot for our new abode.

Right before wedding time, a truckload of lumber was delivered. Rain had made the newly formed clay driveway slippery so that the tractor had to pull the trailer to the construction site. Barry's father and four carpenter brothers came on the scene, and things began to happen fast. After school each day, we would stop to see how much our house had grown. Blueprint plans were carried out with just one glitch, which pertained to the stairway and landing. After a brief conference, Patriarch Kjetland declared, "All things work together for good to those who love God." So, there was no big problem. Gospel music from their cassette player filled the air as the walls went up and the roof came on. I enjoyed my old house, but knew that this would be a good one, also.

Autumn came, and moving time was coming closer. I looked out at my clothesline one morning and saw three goldfinches chirping. I hadn't seen them at our place ever before. It seemed like God sent them at just the right time to cheer me. Emotionally, I would detach from the old place, begin packing up and set to making the new house a warm and loving home.

Holidays were the time marks of the whole project, so the first time we slept south of the road was, naturally, at Halloween time, after the threshold ceremony. Kathy and Silke helped unwrap the glassware I had wrapped, even for such a short shift. Placement of furniture had been planned and tested on Karen's computer, even before building, so everything fit fine in its assigned spot. "New Home" cards and housewarming gifts arrived from various friends, my favorite being the ice cream cone dishes from Harley and Judy Gulbraa. I've kept them in my china cupboard ever since.

At first, a sense of magic pervaded. I felt like a queen in this mansion on the hill. Now, our homegrown trees provide shelter from the wind; my gardens are long established; finches visit daily; and life is good in this new house.

## Chapter Forty-Nine

# The Blessing of Grandchildren

We married later than average, so I was fifty-six before the grandchild era began. Major events in our lives seemed to flow in a beautiful cadence. Our children's births: 1961, 1963, 1966. College graduations: 1986, 1987, 1988. Marriages: 1989, 1990, 1991. And then, at just the right time, God's gift of babies began arriving. For myself, who never really even dreamed about marriage, I was now awestruck.

The first arrival was Lars, and it happened like this. The funeral for Agnes' brother, Randy, was on November 19, 1991. After nine months of "expecting," Steven and Silke's baby picked that day for his birthday. It was like a holy replacement: we said "goodbye" to a 94-year-old uncle and "hello" to a brand new beautiful grandson.

I was very pleasantly surprised when Steven told me his name would be Lars Arthur. Steven thought his own name was too common. Lars would have a name all his own. It was also my grandpa's name. The middle name, Arthur, comes from Norris' dad. Lars' German grandparents also were here, just in time for the excitement. Elmar, Silke's dad, was glad that the plumbing parts worked! Yes, the miracle of a healthy infant deserved thanks to our Heavenly Father who created the earth and allows us to help keep it populated.

Norris and I were still teaching at the time. Lars and his parents came over for a Saturday morning pancake breakfast a few times. I thought that was so nice, and wish we could have continued the pattern.

We flunked our first babysitting test. Steven and Silke went out for an evening, and Lars was keeping us company. At bedtime, we placed him on a quilt on the floor beside our bed. Neither of us woke until morning, and then our baby was gone! The Mom and Dad were sneaky—quiet kidnappers who had taken him home.

Lars' coming had been foretold to us the evening of Nathan and Kathy's wedding. We did not know that Luke would be born within a year, but it has been fun to watch the two, nine months apart, grow up together. Norris and I were planting the two apple trees by our new house when we saw Nathan and Kathy leave in the car, seemingly in a hurry. It was August 8, 1992, when Luke arrived. Kathy's mom, Harriet, hung a blue stork flag by her house in Webster. This child would be rooted at his parental home and in the Webster community, where Kathy had been raised. Luke is a wonderful old Biblical name. His middle name, Bierschbach, honors his mother's heritage. (So as not to lose Kathy's maiden name, all of their children were given "Bierschbach" for a middle name.) By now, we were sort of used to the titles, "Grandpa" and "Grandma." Early evening, we went to see the latest addition. The burnished red hair was a surprise, but I guess the genes for it were right on both sides of the family, and I liked the variety. Norris brought along the tiniest (two-inch long) wrench he could find and placed it in Luke's little hand: an omen that he would be as mechanical as Nathan, Norris and Lawrence had been.

In 1993, we were told that a sister had been ordered for Luke. By some divine design, Lars would also be granted a sister. Little blonde Jordan Bierschbach Meland made her debut on September 24th, a perfect sunny Webster Homecoming day. I remembered when her mother had been Homecoming Queen and Steven and Nathan had been part of the royalty. So, I thought this was fitting. We celebrated with the tradition of lemon pie and coffee at Harriet's home, and then we went to the hospital to see another bundle of blessing.

On the way home, we drove by Steve's place. He and Silke and Lars were out walking, down by the hay bales. The last weeks of pregnancy require a lot of patience. I remembered that. Fortunately, six days later, Tanya Anna made entrance to the outside world: another lovely, healthy, average-sized full-term baby. My mother and three of her cousins also wore the name "Anna;" "Tanya" came from Silke's grandmother. A boy and a girl for each of my sons! My heart was absolutely filled with praises to God who instituted the family as the basic unit of social structure.

On opening hunting day in October, the Meland clan traditionally gathers for a day of shooting pheasants. Hemmerich's were here to see Tanya. Jordan and her Grandma Harriet were here. Karen and my two Meland sisters-in-law, Joyce and Paulette were also here. While the men hunted, we girls all rocked, talked to, smiled on, and loved the two living dolls.

So far, Karen and Thomas were enjoying each other and getting careers established. Then, the baby bug bit them, too. Thanksgiving of 1993 we were told to expect one more arrow for the Meland quiver. We were seated at the kitchen table when Thomas stood by our dividing spindles and called his mom and dad. They were in Canada, and we in the United States, but we could all rejoice together.

Five months flew by. Karen and Thomas had moved back to South Dakota and were living on East 19th Street in Sioux Falls. I was at the women's convention of the Lutheran Church in Webster when Thomas called and had me paged. He and Karen had just gone to the hospital. I came back to the pew and spilled a few tears. The lady next to me asked what had happened. I said, "My baby is having a baby." She took my hand and whispered, "We'll pray about it." The day was April 23, 1994. We picked up Norris' mother and went to Sioux Falls to meet Kristian Thomas Asfeldt. Kristian is a Danish name, fit for kings. The hospital had a modern suite for Mom, Dad, and the baby. Again, the firstborn was a boy, another perfect specimen sent straight from the "little boy mold" in Heaven via Karen and Thomas to us.

Each year seemed to expand the family. Who would come in 1995? Well, on March 21st, Mark Bierschbach Meland, namesake of the second apostle, was born to Nathan and Kathy. Being born on spring's opening, he would always be our harbinger of that season. We were shortly on the scene at his birth, but unfortunately, due to wintering in the South, we have missed his birthday parties ever since. I hope he will forgive us. When we are too old to travel, we'll have to do a make-up bash for Mark.

One more beyond-what-I'd-hoped-for child was announced for 1996. Repeatedly in the Bible, the number seven stands for perfection. That's what I thought of when I saw Karen and Thomas' newborn, Hannah Karen. It was déjà vu all over again, a bonus. Like the words of the 1925 song, "Tea for Two:" *A boy for you and a girl for me. Oh, can't you see how happy we will be..."* Hannah's first name is Biblical and Scandinavian, while her middle name carries on our three-generation tradition of giving a daughter her mother's first name for her middle name.

At birthday and holiday times, our home was filled with seven very interesting and curious little people, aged one to six. Tanya and Jordan, at three months, dressed in dresses of red velvet with white lace for their first Christmas seemed absolutely like dolls. Meanwhile, their big brothers, Lars, two years, and Luke, 18 months, were standing on tiptoe snitching grapes off the kitchen counter, while the adults enjoyed conversation in the living room. The kids had more fun in the crumpled paper and sitting in the boxes than they did with their new toys!

Kristian spent a week entertaining Grandpa and Grandma while his mom and dad were on vacation in the Cayman Islands. At 18 months, he was in love with numbers. First, he counted aloud the coffee mugs on my lower shelf. Then,

*The family, including all seven of the grandchildren, gathered for a photo on November 21, 2000.*

the steps were numerated as he crawled from basement to main floor. I had a hard time believing what I was hearing.

Mark, in early life, would pick the toys out of the toy box and then sit himself into it. Then, he reached out to pick up and examine the toys. He soon learned to keep up with the "big kids" and always has done a good job of it. At four years, he was seeking to catch an untamed kitty. He went to the shop and found an old minnow bucket with a lid and a pair of his dad's gloves. Being well-prepared, cats would be captured in the pail, but he would not be scratched, he said.

Early on, Grandpa dubbed Hannah with a "Little Viking" title. They were a team. Her innate sense of humor and naïveté could provide good comeback to his teasing. Those melodic, early vocal solos she delivered during a shower or on stage always delighted me.

Some childhood gems from my grandchildren include the following:

- Lars had been with his dad when he got a haircut. I asked why Lars didn't get one. "Because I screamed," was the explanation.

- Luke, when two years old, asked for lefse at our house. We'd had some for Thanksgiving. I explained two times that we didn't have any. Luke replied, "I suppose Grandpa ate it all up!"
- One afternoon, Tanya had asked me about angels. I said that each of us has an angel to care for us. Knowing Norris loved to entertain, she quipped, "I bet Grandpa has a really funny angel!"
- In a call from Texas, Kristian was put on the phone. There was no response to my chatter, but when I hummed, "Skip to My Lou," he burst out with "Aboo," his nick-name for me (because I said "peek-aboo" when playing Hide and Seek with him).
- Jordan was watching me put on some makeup when she said, "I know why ladies do that." I responded, "Tell me." And she replied, "To fill up the cracks."
- Nathan and Kathy's three children were here for a weekend. Luke wanted to wear the same shorts and tank top day and night. When we jested about it, Mark, age 6, explained, "He's kind of a survivor."
- Hannah recently had a bad case of "I want a puppy" fever. She read newspaper ads. She managed to get something about a dog in every other conversational sentence. She made a phone call; and yes, the creative moves paid off. Toby came to live at her house.

Their early childhood passed very quickly. I am so grateful that I was retired in time to give priority to spending hours with them. One forenoon, all seven were with me. We had noon lunch. As I did the cleanup, Norris told another chapter of the Gray Wolf legend. This was something he excelled in at bedtime. They all reclined on the floor. As minutes passed, the tale spinner's voice was dwindling. I heard Luke say, "What happened next, Grandpa?" Grandpa was asleep, but the kids were all still awake.

Nathan and Kathy's three were with us for the night one time. All wanted to sleep in our bedroom on the floor. A couple hours down, and Luke woke up, crying. He was having a bad dream. We talked about it, said a prayer, and he continued his sleep. Then, Mark was awake, calling out, "Owie, I'm stuck!" Having rolled too close under our bed frame, he was getting jammed. Moving him to a spot farther away solved that problem. About then, Jordan, typically forthright, sat straight up, asking, "What's going on? It's so noisy, I can't sleep."

One by one, these young ones came of school age. Except for the four years Thomas and Karen lived in North Carolina, Norris and I have had the pleasure of attending Grandparents' Day, Homecoming parades, band and vocal concerts, wrestling matches, swim meets, baseball, basketball, football and volleyball games. When I count my blessings, having grandchildren, able and willing to be good at studies and extracurricular activities, is certainly near the top. I'm glad the three families are situated so we can still enjoy our children, their spouses, and this growing-up generation.

## Chapter Fifty

# Retirement
## — 1993 —

When staff contract time came in April of 1993, the Melands did not sign. Instead, we turned in letters of resignation.

On Awards Night, near the end of that school year, Superintendent Leighton presented me with a plaque for nineteen years' work in the Florence school system. Co-worker, Lisa Furher, headed a Sunday afternoon retirement open house in my honor. A program, lunch, cards and lots of guests made it a very special day. The Music teacher, Glenda Knuth, had asked each student in 1st through 12th Grades to complete this sentence: "I remember when Mrs. Meland..." They had all passed through 1st Grade, so I had put a brick in their foundation. These notes were compiled in a three-ring notebook and given to me. It was very meaningful.

Norris wound up his duties at Lake Area Multi-District vocational center in Watertown. A few days later, the staff he had worked with and their spouses all came out to our house, bringing a pot luck supper and a fun evening of conversation. The gift of an engraved watch, accented with Black Hills gold, was very much appreciated. It was also rewarding to receive numerous cards with meaningful expressions of appreciation and well-wishes for retirement.

Free time! What a feeling! We had always been grateful for our jobs, but the race had been long. Summer had always been summer, but when fall came, with no school responsibilities, we noticed the impact. Being able to spend an hour in Bible study and prayer before breakfast was an overwhelming luxury for me.

While in the U.S. Air Force (1952-1956) Norris was stationed in Texas, California and New Mexico. This proved he didn't miss winter at all. In the nine years in New Guinea, I didn't need winter, either. Financially, South Dakota Teachers Retirement had performed well. Nathan was purchasing the farm. We were both healthy. Being so blessed, we left the cold of January for a trip diagonally across the southeast of the United States, aiming for Florida.

In Tampa, a sign on the Kulow's lawn read, "Yupela stop hia" ("You must stop here" in Pidgin English). A week of sightseeing and fun in the sun followed. As we led off westward across Alligator Alley, we noted that these animals were also enjoying the sun. They were lazily stretched on the banks, peeking at us, as we drove on the highway through the swamp. Across Alabama, Mississippi and Tennessee, the foliage looked as lovely to me as it had in 1961. In Texas, we rendezvoused with Jack and Mary Laschkewitsch. With Jack's gift for words, wit, and drama, mixed with Norris' opportune comebacks, their home pealed with laughter for three days. The last evening we watched a movie. Our men were overtaken by sleep, but being more the nighthawks, Mary and I enjoyed the show to completion. I'm so glad for that visit because, within a few years, Mary died from a rare disease.

The following year we explored Arizona. The third winter of our retirement we tried out Texas, renting a motor home in Big Valley Trailer Park in Donna. When a park model trailer came for sale, we decided to purchase and have returned to enjoy the winters each year since.

Time and space are limited. Otherwise, as I spend my retirement writing, much more could be said about:

- Experiences with the children during their 4-H years
- My years with the Sweet Adeline's chorus
- Steven's successful completion of Army Ranger training.
- Many seasons of beautiful flowers—I'm sure I grew a hundred different kinds over the years.
- Our Gideon and Auxiliary participation since 1985
- Many other church-related activities all along
- Norris' Township Clerk experiences
- Norris' many surgeries and recoveries
- Our 40th wedding anniversary celebration and the tapestry-covered Creative Memories book which Karen made
- Being a Godparent five times, and taking it seriously
- Many treasured quotes from young school students in my classes

As years go by I trust my children and grandchildren will take some interest in reviewing the past and understanding their heritage.

I'm thankful that God allowed me a time for writing as a part of my life's song. The melody of my life has unfolded on a daily basis, and it was always comforting to know that God doesn't make mistakes. This has been a life of more than I could have imagined that He designed specifically for me. I feel I've had a happy, wonderful life. THANK YOU so much for sharing it with me via this book. For all who make time for this reading, may God guide and bless you richly!

The End

There is a time and season for every thing under heaven.

*a time to be born, and a time to die;*
*a time to plant, and a time to pluck up that which is planted;*
*a time to kill, and a time to heal;*
*a time to break down, and a time to build up;*
*a time to weep, and a time to laugh;*
*a time to mourn, and a time to dance;*
*a time to cast away stones, and a time to gather stones together;*
*a time to embrace, and a time to refrain from embracing;*
*a time to get, and a time to lose;*
*a time to keep, and a time to cast away;*
*a time to rend, and a time to sew;*
*a time to keep silence, and a time to speak;*
*a time to love, and a time to hate;*
*a time of war, and a time of peace.*

— Ecclesiastes 3:2-8 (KJ21)